DOUGLAS A. JACOBY

COMPELLING EVIDENCE FOR GOD AND THE BIBLE

HARVEST HOUSE PUBLISHERS

EUGENE, OREGON

Cover by Koechel Peterson & Associates, Inc., Minneapolis, Minnesota

Author photo by Gina Cellino Photography

Published in association with Whalin Literary Agency, LLC, 23623 N. Scottsdale Rd., Ste D-3 #481, Scottsdale, AZ 85255, www.whalinagency.com.

COMPELLING EVIDENCE FOR GOD AND THE BIBLE
Copyright © 2010 by Douglas A. Jacoby
Published by Harvest House Publishers
Eugene, Oregon 97402
www.harvesthousepublishers.com

Library of Congress Cataloging-in-Publication Data

Jacoby, Douglas A.
Compelling evidence for God and the Bible / Douglas A. Jacoby.
p. cm.
Includes bibliographical references (p.).
ISBN 978-0-7369-2708-6 (pbk.)
1. Apologetics. I. Title.
BT1103.J33 2010
239.'7—dc22

2009039175

13 14 15 16 17 18 / VP-NI / 10 9 8 7 6 5 4

To Vicki,

You have poured out your heart
for the ministry of the Word and for your husband.
As the recipient of your gracious love, patience, and forgiveness,
I am truly humbled.

As a wise man put it three thousand years ago,
"Many women do noble things, but you surpass them all."

Acknowledgments

Thanks are due to you who have supplied encouragement and direction for this project, which has been more than 20 years in the making:

Bob Hawkins, Terry Glaspey, and Gene Skinner, of Harvest House Publishers—for your vision, warmth, and leadership in publishing.

Toney Mulhollan and Tom and Sheila Jones, of IPI and DPI—for 30 years of friendship and support. I will always be grateful for your faith in the international teaching ministry.

Terry Whalin, of Intermedia Publishing Group—for sharing your considerable expertise and connections. Thanks for taking a chance on me.

Elizabeth Thompson, Jason Goble, Neale Martin, Steve Jacoby, and my dear wife, Vicki—for honest feedback, knack for expression, and eagle eyes. I am fully aware of my weaknesses as a writer without you. Thanks also to everyone else who gave input into this book.

Finally, I owe an enormous debt to my fellow international Bible teachers and also to the entire North River leadership team.

Contents

Introduction:
In Search of Something

AFTER COMPLETING AN HOUR OR TWO of yard work on a hot and humid summer day, I was drenched in sweat and covered head to toe with grass clippings. I picked up the newspaper lying on the driveway and walked into the house through the garage, glancing down at the front page. The headline arrested my attention: "Youth Killed in Boat Works Accident." Looking below the headline, I was startled to discover that the unfortunate boy was a friend of mine.

Adam was electrocuted when he fell off a dock with an electric sander in his hand. He was one of the first friends I had made when our family moved to New Jersey a decade earlier. I still had the pictures of us trick-or-treating in the third grade—I was a skeleton; Adam was a clown. This intimate tragedy was a direct challenge to my blossoming faith. How could God allow this to happen? I was asking lots of questions then, and my faith was growing, but I wasn't spiritually capable to fully process the accident.

The next shock to my faith came soon after I entered college. A late-night phone call woke me from a deep sleep. "We need to talk," the familiar voice said. I met my friend in the darkened dorm hallway.

"Joe's dead," he told me simply. Joe, my roommate when I was a freshman, had been crushed by a train.

Yet another tragedy was even more personal. My younger sister, a diabetic, was alone when she suffered a ketoacidosis attack. Though these attacks can be easily treated, no one was around when she went into shock and passed away.

Each of these events made me ask deep questions that had no easy answers. As the number of questions grew, they seemed to fuse into something more, a personal journey to understand how faith and life's ugly reality could coexist. The questions were merging into a quest.

Questions, Questions

I was born in the South. If you know the Southern culture, you know that plenty of folks down here are religious. Going to church is in our blood, along with eating corn bread, black-eyed peas, and grits. Most people go to church without questioning their faith.

When my father was transferred to New Jersey, I experienced culture shock. The kids at school taunted me for my Southern accent and crew cut. Churchgoing wasn't quite so common as in Florida. Most of my friends were thinkers, and the majority were Jewish or atheists (or both).[1] They made me think, and my questions and insights made them think.

When I left home for college, I had to fight for faith. Duke has thousands of students who are not content to accept facile answers to serious questions. Many of their questions were mine too (especially about science and history), and I was highly motivated to continue to study Christianity. After I received my bachelor's degree, I entered Harvard Divinity School—a very liberal institution. I remember one fellow from Germany who told me, "Douglas, I would like to believe the way you are able to believe, but I can't accept the authority of the Scriptures." I was not alone in my convictions, but I was greatly outnumbered, and my faith was questioned. I learned a lot about world religions, church history, and ancient languages. The quest continued.

I was devouring books on science, philosophy, and apologetics—the study of the reasonableness of faith. As I devoured a stack of books that offered evidence of the validity of Christianity, I noticed a change. My faith in God and in Jesus Christ was growing.

As it turned out, this was superb preparation for the next stage of my life. I lived in Europe for ten years. Despite America's much-publicized biblical illiteracy, most people in the States have at least heard of "book, chapter, and verse." Londoners were much less familiar with Christianity. When I entered the university environment, which was particularly secular, I found myself swimming against the current. I interacted with atheists, Muslims, and others who were skeptical of Christian claims. Confronted with more questions, I continued digging for answers.

From London (where I met my wife) we moved to Sweden, which makes Britain look like the Bible Belt. Church attendance in Britain is the exception, not the rule, but it is not particularly strange. In Scandinavia, people were either intrigued or amused—usually the latter—when they heard I was a Christian and especially when I told them I attended church. When I explained that I was working as a minister, the look of pity-cum-contempt in most eyes put me in my place. "What's wrong? Couldn't you find a real job?" (I don't mean to imply that Scandinavians are unreceptive. Many come to faith just like anyone else in the world.)

Mental Laziness

My life is consumed by an exhilarating quest as I've searched for answers to many of life's most important questions. Unfortunately, many people are not interested in considering the questions or looking for answers. Genuine soul-searching has to compete with television, video games, and the Internet. The media serves up bite-sized, simplistic answers to the colossal questions of life. But if we want to find God, we are going to have to exert ourselves.

The world has changed since I began my quest. Now everyone has an opinion about relationships, animal rights, the environment, aliens, sexuality, and religion. There are no absolutes, and we must all be careful lest we commit a politically incorrect faux pas.

Fifty years ago, when people asked why they should believe in God, they usually meant, what is the proof? How can we be confident God exists? But nowadays, the same question more likely means, why should we invest our energy in religion? What's in it for us? Does it work? Formerly the question of truth was, which answer corresponds to reality? Today the question is, why should one person opt for someone else's version of reality? Don't all faiths have a legitimate claim to truth? This is hardly a subtle distinction.

In this book we will approach evidences for Christianity from several angles. What is the evidence for God and the Bible? Can we prove Jesus Christ is who he claimed to be? Why should we limit ourselves to one option—specifically, the Christian one—when so many other faiths are out there? Are these questions even important?

Examine the Evidence!

If you are like me, you may have believed (or hoped) that God exists, but you may have had your doubts because you were unacquainted with the evidence. True faith is in the heart and not just in the head; we must be convinced there is a God. "Now without faith it is impossible to please God, for the one who draws near to him must believe that he exists and rewards those who seek him" (Hebrews 11:6 HCSB).

In contrast to the spirit of this Scripture, one of Mark Twain's characters quipped, "Faith is believing what you know ain't so."[2] New atheist Sam Harris shares this contempt: "Faith is what credulity becomes when it finally achieves escape velocity from the constraints of terrestrial discourse—constraints like reasonableness, internal coherence, civility and candor."[3] But is that faith? Thinking men and women, I am now convinced, must reject this notion. Coming to faith is not a leap into the dark (as Kierkegaard famously claimed), but a leap into the light.

The truth is, the Christian faith is reasonable, logical, and practical, as this book will demonstrate. *Faith* has two senses in the Bible:

(1) a rational response to the gospel message, and (2) obedient trust (even if *complete* evidence is not available). The first sense is a kind of seeing; the second, a kind of knowing without seeing.[4] No one who has seriously examined Christianity can walk away and say, "Nonsense!" Christianity is one of the most influential movements in history and has inspired artists, philosophers, doctors, scientists... No one who conscientiously examines Christianity and dismisses it as nonsense should be taken seriously.

Becoming a Christian is not something that happens by osmosis (no one is born into the faith or saved by virtue of being raised in a Christian household). Nor does it happen through an esoteric, mystical spiritual experience. It is a personal response to evidence. With this in mind, we must examine the evidence—which is much stronger than many people realize—and then make a decision. God is looking for a verdict. In order for us to come to a saving faith in Jesus Christ, we must...

- be convinced of the reality of God
- be convinced of the truth of the Word of God
- be convinced of the truth about the Son of God
- make an informed decision

A Catalyst for Faith

Compelling Evidence for God and the Bible will be helpful for you regardless of whether you have any Christian faith. More and more people who investigate Christianity have never opened a Bible, attended a church service, or had a friend who was personally committed to Christ. That is why this book investigates various kinds of evidence that support the Bible, from history to prophecy and beyond. Even if you already believe in God, you may still feel as if you're trying to complete the puzzle and can't find some of the pieces. Believing that God exists is essential, so part 1 of the book demonstrates that the existence of God is reasonable.

Becoming convinced that the Bible is God's Word (his message to us) requires more than a casual acquaintance with the material. We need to explore, to open our hearts and minds. Then we will see that God's message to man makes sense. Accordingly, part 2 covers several issues related to the trustworthiness of the Bible.

If Earth is, as J.B. Phillips called it, "the visited planet"—if God has come to us in the person of Jesus Christ—then we need to consider his claims seriously. With this in mind, read part 3 for the facts about the uniqueness, divinity, miracles, and resurrection of Jesus.

But is the truth that simple? Are other ways to God viable? What about the other world faiths (Islam, Hinduism, and so on)? Do the other major religions of the world rival Christianity? Is Jesus' narrow road a logical consequence of the biblical message, excluding these other options?[5]

This is no mere intellectual quest. We might say we are seeking God, but perhaps we could more accurately say God is seeking us. That is why part 4 urges you to appreciate God's initiative toward us in Jesus Christ, to weigh the evidence, and to make an informed decision.

I wrote *Compelling Evidence for God and the Bible* to catalyze your faith if you are seeking, or at least to point you in the right direction. If you already believe, I trust it will give you a push and a reason to live even more keenly as a disciple of Jesus Christ. Christian discipleship includes bringing others to faith—atheists, doubters, seekers, and believers with questions. We all need to be equipped to handle life's challenges, both internal and external. In many ways, this book reflects the quest I began that hot summer day so many years ago. The journey has been arduous but joyful.

Perhaps you too will find joy in considering the evidence for Christianity.

Douglas Jacoby
October 2009
Marietta, Georgia

PART 1

God

In the first four chapters of this book, we will examine the evidence for the existence of God. People have posed questions about him for millennia. In light of the evidence, is theism (the belief in a personal God) justified? Or are the criticisms of atheists, agnostics, and other skeptics valid?

As we will see, the objections to theism are not convincing, and the alternatives to believing in God are utterly bankrupt. We find ample proof of God's action in the world, though not necessarily direct empirical evidence. The final chapter in this section explores God's personality. If God does exist, what might he be like?

Clearing Away the Debris:
Arguments Against the Reality of God

God's plan made a hopeful beginning,
But man ruined his chances by sinning.
We trust that the story
Will end in God's glory;
But at present the other side's winning.

OLIVER WENDELL HOLMES

Is Faith in Trouble?

HAVE ATHEISTS PROVED THAT God doesn't exist? Has science shown that he is "an unnecessary hypothesis"? Are record numbers of people quitting organized religion, finding all the truth they need deep within themselves? Outspoken atheists like Richard Dawkins, Daniel Dennett, Sam Harris, and Christopher Hitchens have boldly proclaimed the death of God.[1] Was Holmes correct in asserting that "at present the other side's winning"?

The answer to all these questions is no. And yet our obsessive tendency to latch on to simplistic answers keeps us from finding the information we need. We live in a time when students don't read books;

they read CliffsNotes. When we want information, we don't always take the time to make careful inquiries. We Google the answer and may even forward it to others before confirming it. More and more people look up easy answers to life's difficult questions by surfing the Web, hoping to land on a pithy piece online—perhaps in a blog or at Wikipedia. But is the World Wide Web going to give us the direction we need in life? Is God just one more snazzy application for our iPhones?

Not at all. Not if God is more than just a projection of our own psyche, and not if he is really worth seeking. The impatient and on-demand approach forms a vicious cycle. However, those who are willing to stop and listen, to weigh and digest, will find answers. But first, we must refute the false answers. We must sweep the debris aside before we can restore order.

The Unreality of God

I have been blessed with opportunities to present the evidence for God's existence to hundreds of thousands of nonbelievers and atheists—sometimes to rather skeptical audiences. Men and women the world over have come to an intelligent faith. It is especially satisfying to engage in personal Bible studies with people who have genuine questions. I firmly believe that if the gospel is presented with love, patience, and careful instruction, anyone can be led to Jesus Christ—provided he or she is willing and truly searching.

The reasons for faith in God are abundant, but few unbelievers have seriously examined the evidence for God's existence. Most embrace atheism because they cannot relate to God as some people portray him. Maybe they had bad experiences with organized religion, or perhaps they were galled by the widespread hypocrisy of those who claim to know God. For others, accepting God's reality and his authority in their lives would be inconvenient, so they conclude he simply doesn't exist. Having decided there is no God, they think of reasons to justify their stance, working backward from their rash conclusion. In this chapter we will look at some of the reasons people have decided that there is no God. Because of all the confusion, misunderstandings, and specious arguments about the issue of God's existence, we need to clear away the debris before building up a convincing case that he is real.

Lack of Proof

Outspoken atheist Christopher Hitchens exclaims, "Religion has run out of justifications. Thanks to the telescope and the microscope, it no longer offers an explanation of anything important."[2] But has science truly explained reality from the submicroscopic level to the unfathomably vast universe? Hardly. Nearly 50 years before Hitchens, the Soviets put a man into space. One of the early cosmonauts later went on record saying, "Some say God is living there [in space]. I was looking around very attentively. But I did not see anyone there."[3] This well represents the Soviet propaganda of the time. However, the underlying concept of God inherent in this statement is erroneous. Demanding visible proof of God was wrongheaded. Perhaps the cosmonaut would have been pleased to observe a large metallic throne orbiting the earth directly over Jerusalem! But, as I will argue in a moment, anyone who had seen God or taken his photo would have been mistaken. No one can see God.[4]

When people allege there's no proof for the existence of God, they usually make the same mistake the Soviet cosmonaut did. They are seeking empirical proof, like footprints or a photograph. But they have misunderstood God's nature. He isn't a man, so he has no DNA and leaves no footprints. He isn't a physical being, so don't expect any photographs.

Many real, scientifically observable things cannot be detected with the eye, such as sound waves, protons, gravity, and magnetism. Even though we cannot see them, we can be sure they exist. We understand them by properties and effects. No one would deny that electricity is real, especially after an electric shock! The same is true with believing in God. Though he is invisible, he is real, and we can detect his presence through his influence on the world.

Admittedly, at first blush, belief in an invisible God smacks of gullibility. ("How convenient—God is your invisible friend. Only those who accept his existence believe in him. We all know he isn't really there.") But God's invisibility makes sense for one natural reason and two biblical reasons.

First, many things are real even though they cannot be measured empirically. There is no strictly scientific proof that they exist, but they do. Part of reality is physical, but the other part is spiritual. Trying to photograph God is just as inappropriate as attempting to mark out two miles of justice, or to weigh three pounds of love. Love does not come in pounds, but it is certainly real. I know my wife and children love me even though I don't have scientific proof. The fact that God is invisible in no way means he is unreal.

God is either physical or nonphysical—that is, immaterial. Jesus affirmed that he is spirit (nonphysical).[5] The Bible also affirms that God is omnipresent, that he "fills heaven and earth." He is everywhere.[6] Now, if he were material *and* omnipresent, we would be in big trouble. No other beings could exist in the cosmos—there would literally be no space for anything else. But we do exist, as do other physical entities. We occupy space, and given our materiality, it is no surprise that we are visible. But this is not the case with God.

We can therefore conclude that he is invisible not because he does not exist, but because he is not material. If he were visible, he would be only a smaller part of this world. Of course, this line of reasoning is not a proof of God's existence. It is an answer to the charge that God is invisible because he does not exist. The tables are turned: Assuming the universe is real, an omnipresent God would quite likely be invisible.[7]

Is there no clear evidence that God exists? Of course there is—abundant evidence. It is not direct or scientific, yet it is just as credible as if it were—if we are open to being convinced. A court of law does not throw out the testimony of a witness just for lack of photographic evidence. Various kinds of indirect evidence are perfectly acceptable.

The Bible is not a book of evidence, nor does it attempt to prove God's existence. It assumes it. We find the greatest visible evidence for God in the lives of those who are in authentic relationship with him. God reveals himself through his action in the world, through his Son, through his Word, and through the work of his life-changing Spirit in the hearts of men, women, and children around the globe. God's nature is the subject of chapter 4, and we will resume this discussion there.

The supposed lack of empirical evidence may not even be a logical reason to question God's existence in the first place. It's called an argument from silence. As others have said, "Absence of evidence is not evidence of absence." Atheism is really an antiposition. It does not affirm anything; it only denies it. No one has discovered other intelligent life in the universe, but that does not prove it does not exist.

Atheism is philosophically untenable because it inevitably affirms the very thing it denies. It claims that there is no all-knowing being in the universe. But how could we be sure? We would have to possess knowledge of all the cosmos in order to know this for certain. To substantiate atheism, the atheist would need to be omniscient. He would have to be the very being whose existence he denies.

Science Disproves God

Some go even further than claiming that a lack of evidence proves he doesn't exist. They claim to have scientific evidence that he doesn't. However, many of these critics are merely refuting some believers' unsound arguments for God's existence or for the truth of the Bible. For example, some religious people claim that the world is only 6000 years old or that Scripture contains a secret code. Such claims are rightly rejected because the evidence clearly refutes them. Various would-be religious experts have presented the public with a false choice: science or Scripture. Atheists proffer a similar false dichotomy. Says one historian of science, "The whole point of faith, in fact, is to believe regardless of the evidence, which is the very antithesis of science." This is unfair. Faith is, in part, a response to evidence, and there is no correlation between faith and ignorance. When considering faith and science, why make it either-or? Why not both-and?

In 1914, a well-known survey of scientists revealed that more than 40 percent believed in a personal God who answers prayer. The survey was repeated in 1997. Surprisingly, after more than eight decades of enormous strides in the sciences, the percentage of scientists who believe in God remained unchanged. Of course, if a broader definition of God had been used, such as "a supreme being" (without specifying his responsiveness to prayer), the figure would likely have been significantly higher.

Faith need not be unscientific. Science explores the *hows* of the cosmos: how gravity functions, how cells replicate, how stars are formed. But thinking faith (which is what theology is) probes the *whys,* the deeper issues that lie beyond the pale of science. Science and faith are complementary.

To illustrate, consider how music works. From the scientific angle, various instruments create sound waves in the air. These waves are collected by the outer ear and focused through the ear canal to the tympanic membrane, which they strike, setting off a vibration that transmits a signal into the brain. The brain decodes the signal, and the listener experiences it as a symphony, jazz, an opera, or whatever. This is beyond doubt. But does that really explain what music is?

My wife and I went to Puccini's *Turandot,* which never fails to evoke powerful emotions, particularly during the much-loved "Nessun Dorma." An overzealous acoustical physicist might claim, "There's no such thing as opera or even music. It's all an abstraction—it's in your head! Sound waves, acoustical physics…that's the ultimate reality. Everything else is simply perception." A music lover might respond, "Nonsense. It's beautiful music, and attempting to reduce it to simply sound waves denies human perception." But they would be talking past one another. Both the acoustical physicist and the music lover experience reality, and they need each other for a comprehensive understanding. Together their perspectives give a fuller picture of "Nessun Dorma" than either one on its own.

I often speak at universities and recently presented a series on science and faith. The first evening I explained how the Big Bang theory provides evidence of a Creator. The second evening I clarified that the evidence from biology also points beyond pure naturalism and to God. The third evening I addressed the implications of the complementarities of faith and science, and then I fielded questions from the audience. One young man who was about to receive his PhD in plasma physics was thrilled. Soon afterward he became a Christian. He later confided to me that the series had been very freeing for him. Deep down he had doubted whether the Bible could be reconciled with science. This man was liberated; he did not have to reject science or suppress his intellect.

This is as it should be. So much of the tension between science and religion is unnecessary, misguided, and harmful. False battles are fought, and men and women with great minds are turned off to faith. This tragedy is repeated on campuses across the world.

As Psalm 19 has it, "The heavens declare the glory of God; the skies proclaim the work of his hands...The law of the LORD is perfect, reviving the soul. The statutes of the LORD are trustworthy, making wise the simple."[8] The psalmist is saying that God speaks in two ways: through nature (the heavens) and Scripture (the law of the Lord). I also like the way Francis Bacon put it:

> Let no man upon a weak conceit of sobriety or an ill-applied moderation think or maintain, that a man can search too far, or be too well studied in the Book of God's Word, or in the Book of God's Works—Divinity or Philosophy. But rather, let men endeavour an endless progress or proficiency in both; only let men beware that they apply both to charity,

and not to swelling [pride]; to use and not to ostentation; and again that they do not unwisely mingle or confound those learnings together.[9]

Again, the "two books" are Scripture and nature. Science in no way disproves God. Scientific theories are hardly written in stone; they are subject to revision as new data come to light. Science, like theology, thrives when men and women are open to changing their minds. Besides, many of the world's leading scientists are believers and are amused by the idea that one must choose between faith and reason. I myself have had discussions with many scientists—biologists, geologists, chemists, astronomers—and can confidently say that the majority are not materialists. They are open to the spiritual world. Moreover, they see no contradiction between their scientific work and their personal faith.

Hypocrisy

An atheist may object, "There are so many hypocrites in the church. Why should I believe in God when so many of his supposed followers are no better than those who have nothing to do with organized religion?" But this argument amounts to something like this. "Since most who believe in God are hypocrites—they don't practice what they preach—what they believe in must not be true."

What are we to say to the charge of hypocrisy? A doctor may be overweight, but that does not prove he is incompetent as a physician. A salesman may be greedy and even dishonest, but that does not mean that his company's product is worthless; he is just a poor representative. In the same way, many who claim to be Christians may simply be poor representatives of a good religion.

In recent decades, thousands of lawsuits have been filed against members of the clergy who have been accused of molesting children. Child abuse is an incomprehensibly terrible evil, especially when the perpetrators claim to represent God. Is there any direct connection between the inexcusable behavior of trusted church workers and the truth of their creed? Not at all. (This is not to say that the policies and doctrines that have led to, and sustain, such vices do not deserve serious scrutiny.)

The Inquisition is often referred to as an indictment of the church. The Roman Catholic Church began the Inquisition in the thirteenth century to fight heresy, but in the sixteenth century the Spanish Inquisition tortured and executed thousands. For three centuries, a thousand people a year were executed as the Roman Catholic Church utilized torture to create uniformity in religious opinion. Another stumbling block is the Crusades, which occurred mainly during the eleventh to thirteenth centuries when European Christians fought Muslims who had captured Jerusalem. Their excesses included massacres of Jews and Muslims and forcibly baptizing throngs of "infidels," or unbelievers. Those responsible were certainly poor representatives of their religion, but the abuses of Christianity are just that—abuses. They are not in line with Christ's teachings. Politically motivated persons led the Crusades, and Jesus would not have approved of them: "Put your sword back in its place...for all who draw the sword will die by the sword" (Matthew 26:52).

The Crusaders who killed in the name of Jesus and the Inquisitors who tortured in the name of truth were seriously mistaken, but they are not an embarrassment to true Christians—only examples of human abuses operating under the guise of religion. Spreading the faith is good—if Christianity is true, one would surely want others to benefit—but not at sword point. Persuading others to have correct views is fine, but not through fire and the rack!

The thoughtful reader may wonder, *Why defend Christianity in this way but not atheism? Does the hypocrisy of Stalin, Mao, and others point to the virtue of atheism?* Not necessarily. An ideology—whether Christianity, atheism, or any other—cannot be confirmed or refuted based solely on the behavior (or mistakes or failures) of its adherents. But perhaps, as I suggest elsewhere in the book, we should examine the lives of the ideology's best representatives. Of course, a connection need not exist between ideologies and social virtues or vices. Yet that is precisely the point. Religious abuses are hardly consistent with morality. Whereas—as we will suggest later—morality, where there is not belief in transcendent spiritual reality, is inconsistent at best and absent at worst.

Millions have been killed in the name of religion, but that is only one part of the story. The suffering inflicted through atheism and atheistic ideologies outweighs anything perpetrated in the name of religion. In the twentieth century alone more than 100 million people were "eliminated" under Hitler, Stalin, and Mao! The consequences of atheism, politically and personally, have been severe.

In an unexpected way, hypocrisy actually points to virtue, just as the counterfeit suggests the authentic. Someone said, "Even the hypocrite admires righteousness. That is why he imitates it." Hypocrisy among nominal Christians does not discredit Christ's teachings. It only proves how lost the world is without them. And interestingly, even the most tragic forms of unbelief have often masqueraded as virtue in quasi-religious garb. (Consider the totalitarian pretensions of state socialism and Communism, particularly during the twentieth century.)

Skeptics usually use the issue of hypocrisy as a smoke screen. Hypocrisy is a sad reality, but it has nothing at all to do with the existence of God.

Suffering

Probably the most heartfelt objection to God's existence is the presence of suffering in the world.

I am writing this chapter from Kampala, Uganda. This East African nation came to the center stage of current events in the 1970s while suffering unspeakable horrors during the reign of military dictator Idi Amin. Hundreds of thousands were tortured and killed. To this day, children are kidnapped and made into killers. I have read the history books and spoken to the survivors, and contrary to my expectation, I have found strong men and women who are ready to move on. Many have kept their faith, refusing to retaliate or take up the sword. Their strong, buoyant, and forgiving spirit is astounding.

I have visited a number of African nations recovering from civil wars. I have met men and women who have witnessed executions, lost all their property, or even endured the killing of family members. They do not necessarily conclude that God has abandoned them or that he doesn't exist. They have another way of looking at the facts. In many of the countries where I have lectured—including Romania, Vietnam, Peru, Lebanon, and Ukraine—I've been overwhelmed by similar resiliency, faith, and willingness to process the past and move on.

I am not saying suffering improves people. This is rarely the case. The majority of human beings who suffer catastrophically become discouraged, defeated, or embittered. That is at least partly because of their choices. I recall an older man I spoke with on London's Underground, hoping he would accept an invitation from a total stranger to a Christian event.

"Don't believe in God," he replied curtly. I pressed him a little, and he replied, "Where was God during the War?"

This man had seen a lot of suffering during World War II. Like many in Europe, his responses to his experience of pain had allowed it to steal his faith. "Can't believe in God—no way." Suffering hardens many individuals while others grow stronger. Where faith meets a gracious spirit, a silver lining emerges.[10]

Christianity offers no facile answer to the problem of human suffering. It does, however, offer grace, comfort, and strength so that in the face of suffering we may live with dignity, poise, and purpose.

Yet many agnostics and atheists contend that suffering invalidates faith. Seeing so much suffering in the world, they reason that if God exists, either he is good (well-intentioned, perhaps) but not all-powerful, or he is all-powerful but not good (because he does not prevent suffering). If God exists, he is not the omnipotent and omnibenevolent being described by the monotheistic religions. However, this argument against the existence of God—or the existence of a good, all-powerful God—is not as strong as it may first appear.[11]

This is not a true dilemma. The word *dilemma* means "two branches." In this case there is a third branch. How does one know that it is possible to make a better world than the one in which we live? Perhaps conditions are already optimized for maximum good and minimum evil. No one is in a position to make such an assessment. And ironically, and rather inconsistently, many atheists reject the categories of *absolute* good and evil, so they have no moral ground upon which to stand as they make (any) ultimate moral demand.

Some unbelievers demand that if God exists, he ought to remove all pain and suffering from the world. Yet most suffering is inflicted by people (including war, drunk driving, stealing, lying, and the like), so to root out all suffering, God would have to destroy all evil in the world.

But consider for a minute what would happen if God did this. To completely root out evil, he would have to destroy us! As for evil actions, he would have to overrule our decisions, and we would become pre-programmed puppets. And how about evil thoughts? They, after all, are the source of human wrongdoing. God would have to reprogram us, reducing us to the level of automata. Our hard drives (brains) would have to be wiped clean. Would it really be better to live in a world without choice, without free will? Would we be willing to lose our personalities just so we would never feel pain?

Time has a way of putting suffering into perspective. Imagine living your full "threescore and ten years" in a state of perpetual medical agony, fighting arthritis, migraines, ulcers, cancer, or some other form of horrible suffering. Seventy years of pain. Then, what if the Bible is true? What if eternity awaits you after death? You would die, your suffering would end, and you would spend eternity with God. How much of your suffering on Earth do you think you would remember after 7 thousand years? After 7 million years? How strong do you think the memory would be after 7 quintillion years? No length of suffering on Earth will seem significant compared to the time we will spend with God afterward.[12]

The problem of suffering is not a match for God and not a solid reason for us to deny he exists. Besides, if we really want God to weed evil out of the world before the day of judgment, we would all be destroyed along with it.

Perhaps you are contemplating another option: God could have decided not to create the world in the first place. Why did he take a chance on beings as risky as humans and on a world that would become so devastated by greed, corruption, betrayal, war, broken families, pollution, violent crime, and the like—results of man's selfishness? If this is your question, let me ask you a question. Why decide to have children? Whether we procreate, foster, or adopt, can we be absolutely sure that our little ones will turn out perfectly or that they will not disappoint us or even become criminals? No—so why do we take the risk? For love. For relationship. It's about family.

The Christian Scriptures teach that God created man so he could love us. God desired children to love. Was he lonely? No, he is good and wants to share his love. Whether we choose to enjoy that love or to abuse the free will he has given us is our decision. Let's not blame God for human selfishness or for our mistakes.

Besides all this, suffering plays some positive roles in our lives— one in particular. On the physical level, pain is important medically. The neurologically impaired—those who cannot feel pain run the risk of grave injury. For decades doctors have known of a rare condition in which children are born without the ability to feel pain. Their parents wish they *did* feel pain because the children rarely live long enough to escape their self-inflicted injuries.

> The six children come from three families from northern Pakistan. The research team found the children after hearing about a boy who apparently felt no pain. The boy stood on burning coals and stabbed his arms with knives to earn

money. He died in a fall before the researchers could meet him. But the team was able to find members of the boy's extended family. They also seemed unable to feel pain. These children were six to fourteen years of age. They sometimes burned themselves with hot liquids or steam. They sat on hot heating devices. They cut their lips with their teeth, but felt no pain. Two of the children bit off one-third of their tongue. Yet they could feel pressure and tell differences between hot and cold… [All] had a gene with a mistake, or fault. Except for the genetic fault, the children had normal intelligence and health. The researchers found that each child received a faulty version of the gene from a parent. The gene is called SCN9A. It gives orders to a protein that serves as a passageway for the chemical sodium. All nerve cells have such passages. This is how pain signals from a wound or injury are communicated to the spinal cord and brain.[13]

Pain alerts the brain that tissue is wounded and needs protection. Pain also tells us when we have eaten too much. (With no discomfort, we could eat to the point of rupture.) Pain also teaches us to respect boundaries. Walls exist for a reason; we should hurt when we run into them. Similarly, we must respect social boundaries, or we will hurt others and ourselves.

Some suffering is caused not by human sin, but through contact with nature. We live in a dangerous world with plenty of storms, floods, fires, earthquakes, and more. Earth scientists assure us that these are all necessary for life to exist on our planet. Meteorological catastrophes are an inevitable part of existence. They are necessary concomitants of life on Earth. People often aggravate the discomfort and suffering caused by natural disasters by building in flood plains, erecting large structures that cannot withstand seismic tremors, or choosing to live on the side of a volcano. If we take risks like this, we should not blame God when injury or death ensues.

Some suffering is generated by genetic errors: cleft palate, clubfoot, spina bifida, various types of anemia, and countless others. God's plan for building life includes a complex yet elegant tool: DNA. This is a powerful engine for biological diversity and is the fundamental plan for all life forms on the planet, from bacteria to humans. During cell replication, copying errors in the genetic code sometimes lead to birth defects or even prenatal death. The overall plan is good, and it works well. We are "fearfully and wonderfully made," but that does not necessarily mean *perfectly* made.[14] (Which Adonis among us claims to have a perfect body?)

Suffering can lead to significant emotional development. As the apostle Paul reminds us, perseverance through suffering produces character.[15] Were it not for pain and suffering in our earthly lives, bravery, heroism, and even stamina would be meaningless. We would live in a soft, mushy realm without challenge or thrill. As others have said, "God promises a safe landing, not a calm voyage."

Pain and suffering, we see, are indispensable parts of life. Christianity does not promise freedom from pain. If it did, everyone would flock to it! No, Christianity promises the ability to endure and grow through pain with faith. Christian apologist C.S. Lewis (1898–1963) memorably summed up the value of pain: "God whispers to us in our pleasures, speaks to us in our conscience, but shouts in our pains: it is His megaphone to rouse a deaf world." The best answer to the problem of suffering is actually the cross of Christ.

><•••••<

A little girl whose parents had died lived with her grandmother and slept in an upstairs bedroom. One night there was a fire in the house, and the grandmother perished while trying to rescue the child. The fire spread quickly, and the first floor was soon engulfed in flames. Neighbors called the fire department and then stood helplessly by as word spread among the crowd that firefighters would be delayed a few minutes because they were all at another fire.

Suddenly a man appeared with a ladder, put it up against the side of the house, and disappeared inside. When he reappeared, he had the little girl in his arms. He delivered the child to the waiting arms below and then disappeared into the night.

An investigation revealed that the child had no living relatives, and weeks later a meeting was held in the town hall to determine who would take the child into their home and bring her up. A teacher said she would raise the child, pointing out that she could ensure her a good education. A farmer offered her an upbringing on his farm, mentioning that living on a farm was healthy and satisfying. Others spoke, giving their reasons why it was in the child's advantage to live with them. Finally, the town's richest resident arose and said, "I can give the child all the advantages that you have mentioned here, plus money and everything money can buy."

Throughout all this, the child remained silent, her eyes on the floor. "Does anyone else want to speak?" asked the meeting chairman.

A man came forward from the back of the hall. His gait was slow, and he seemed to be in pain. When he got to the front of the room, he stood directly before the little girl and held out his arms. The crowd gasped. His hands and arms were terribly scarred. The child cried out, "This is the man who rescued me!"

With a leap, she threw her arms around the man's neck, holding on for dear life, just as she had that fateful night. She buried her face on his shoulder and sobbed for a few moments. Then she looked up and smiled at him.

"This meeting is adjourned," said the chairman.[16]

>-◆-◆-◆-◆-◄

Jesus Christ entered our world, proving the full extent of God's love. Let it never be said that God does not understand suffering or is some kind of heavenly spectator, aloof to our pain. The definitive response to the problem of suffering is the cross.

Absurd Questions

The Scriptures warn us about trick questions and slick arguments. Around AD 60, Paul said to the Christians in Colosse (in what is now western Turkey), "I tell you this so that no one may deceive you by fine-sounding arguments."[17] Some people think they can dismiss the vital question of God's existence merely by posing clever questions. Let's consider two:

> If God created everything, who created God?
>
> Could God create a rock so big that he couldn't move it?

As for the first question, the reasoning is that either (a) God created himself, which is ridiculous (how can nothing create something?), or (b) some other being created God, in which case God is not really God. (For if he were really God, he wouldn't need someone to create him.) The question is misleading because it assumes that everything must have a creator. It could be rewritten like this:

> If God created everything, and everything has a creator, then who created God?

Of course, the idea that God exists would be ridiculous if he were created. In that case we would have to ask, who created the being who created God?

But why must everything have a creator? Why should the creator be part of the creation? Is the artist a part of his or her painting? Or the architect a part of the building he or she designed? Then why should God, who by definition is the (original) Creator, be part of the universe?

People who ask the question have made a huge assumption. It's somewhat like asking, have you stopped beating your wife yet? Unless you are guilty, a yes-or-no answer will not do. The question assumes you are guilty. In the same way, many questions about God are based on false assumptions. In fact, God is eternal, so attempts to describe him as limited by our world of space and time assume a false concept of him.[18] Maybe you were never beating your wife in the first place, and maybe God was not created, but has always existed.

The second question, about God creating a rock too large for him to move, is a similar sort of query, though the solution is more difficult. Apparently God does limit himself. If he did everything within his power, he could create and destroy each of us constantly, move galaxies and planets about at random...but what would be the point? God is a God of order.[19] But the question of God's ability to limit himself is not the real question here. Let's take another look at the original question:

> Could God create a rock so big that he couldn't move it?

The question is inappropriate. It is against reason to ask it, since it would be absolutely impossible for God to create a rock so big that he could not move it. Does that mean that God isn't God? No, but you must understand what I mean by *absolutely* impossible.

Some things are *absolutely* impossible, others are only *relatively* impossible. It is *relatively* impossible for a man to lift a car over his head—no man is strong enough. At least, I don't know anyone who could do this, though such a feat could be imagined. But what about the immovable rock? This is impossible logically, or absolutely. That is, even an all-powerful being could not do it because it would require a violation of logic and truth. God cannot be untrue to himself.

Here are some other things that are absolutely impossible: loud silence, boiling ice, a 19-ounce pint. These are impossible by definition, or absolutely (logically) impossible. They are as nonsensical as a conscious rock or the smell of the color of 11. Others are merely humorous, such as mud bath, new used cars, jumbo shrimp. But none of these impossibilities says anything about the existence of God.

Complicated, you may be thinking. Why don't we agree that the rock question is absurd? If you want a good short answer to the question, here it is:

> Maybe, but he could certainly build a bulldozer big
> enough to do the job.

But of course this is a silly answer to a silly (or illogical or childish) question.[20] At other times a more thoughtful response is warranted, and in such cases we need to be willing to push ourselves to think at a deeper level. No logical question has proved God doesn't exist. Moreover, most such questions fail to take into account God's true nature. Logic alone can neither prove nor disprove God's existence.

Religious Truth

When we were children, we learned to distinguish truth from falsehood, and in time, reality from imagination. Certain things were true, and others were false or make-believe. In our minds we put true and false ideas into separate boxes.

For example, many of us were taught to believe in Santa Claus or Father Christmas, Kwan Yin or Krishna, the tooth fairy or the Easter bunny. *The Lord of the Rings* and the Harry Potter series have offered substantial entertainment to millions. They feature legions of fictional characters. Do we really wonder, *Are there hobbits and orcs? Can witches fly on broomsticks?* No, because it is all make-believe. But many of these beings were real to us at one time, so we put them into the True box.

As we grew older and wiser, we quit believing in these make-believe beings, and our beliefs matured. We did not blame friends or parents for leading us astray—after all, there was no harm in make-believe, and believing in these beings was fun. We simply took these concepts or ideas out of the True box and put them into the False box. I remember Christmas Eve, 1966. I was seven and was wondering whether there really was a Santa. That night my father built a fire in the fireplace.

Asking him if we could talk, I led him to the kitchen and asked him to tell me whether there really was a Santa. He said, "No, but don't tell your brother." (Actually, my brother, who was five years old, had already figured it out.)

Many of us were also taught as children to believe in God. As we matured, our ideas about God and his reality were challenged as well. We learned that lots of nice people, including famous persons and eminent scientists, don't believe in God. So, just as we had reevaluated imaginary animals, ghosts, the boogeyman, and Santa Claus, it was time to reevaluate God.

But would it be right to put religious truths into the False box? That would be awkward because so many adults live their lives by their religious convictions (such is not the case with Santa Claus), and this might offend them. One thing, however, was certain: We could not leave God in the True box. So what could we do?

To solve this dilemma, we created a third box, one for religious truth. Items in this box were not exactly true (maybe true for you, but not necessarily true for me), and yet they were not false either (because so many people strongly believed them). Thus religious truth, somewhere between truth and falsehood, became the realm of God, the Supreme Being in the fairyland of religion.

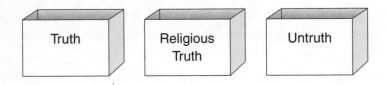

There is one problem with all of this. Exactly what is religious truth: true or false? Is there really a God or not? Believing in God is fine if you don't seriously care to answer the question, but what if you do want real answers? For modern man, religious truth is confused with religious ideas. We have undergone a subtle transition from tolerance of persons (who are all of equal value) to tolerance of behaviors and ideas (which do not have equal merit). Intolerance is unpopular, so we are willing to grant that all religious ideas are true—provided, of course, that they are not too extreme. But to say that we tolerate another fellow's religion scarcely means we agree with him. On the contrary. It implies that we disagree.[21]

I do not just tolerate spinach. It's my favorite vegetable. Ever since I was a little boy watching the old Popeye cartoons on television, I have loved the leafy green vegetable—raw or cooked, in a salad or in a can. On the other hand, I tolerate Brussels sprouts. Their acrid taste makes them difficult for me to swallow. When they are served, I always take one because I don't want to appear to be a picky eater. But as hard as I try, this is one taste I just can't seem to acquire! But is truth really only a matter of taste, as with vegetables? In fact, tolerance is not the opposite of faith; it is one of its components. In the modern world, tolerance is just apathy in disguise.

Interestingly, atheistic ideologies and regimes often exhibit near-zero tolerance for different opinions. Consider the lamentable religious persecutions in China, Cuba, Myanmar, and North Korea, just to name a few. As in Orwell's *1984,* atheist governments have generally shown themselves unable to tolerate open faith.

This is not to say that others are not entitled to their own religious beliefs, only that it is nonsense to say all ideas are equally true. (How can all ideas be equally true when they contradict each other?) This confused way of looking at truth, popular with the masses and promoted by some academics, theologians, and popular icons, must be wholly abandoned if we are to reach a sensible conclusion about God's existence. Is he real or not?

Modern man is confused about faith. He thinks that faith creates truth. That is, if you believe it, it is true (at least for you). If you believe in heaven and hell, fine. It may be real for you but not for me because I don't look at things that way. Whether heaven and hell exist may be debated, but ultimately either they exist or they don't. I have met men so deluded that they claimed to be Jesus Christ himself. Is that possible? Were they who they claimed to be? Of course not. But what if these men were truly sincere? Then they would be sincerely wrong—but wrong nevertheless.

No, faith does not create truth. Faith, however, can be completely mistaken about what is true, and we can place our faith in the wrong thing. For example, it would certainly be better to have a weak faith in a strong bridge than a strong faith in a weak bridge. Christians could be wrong about the strength of their bridge, but they do not pretend that the bridge exists only for those who believe it is there.

Your belief in God (or unbelief) has no bearing on his existence. If he exists, he exists, and no amount of disbelieving can change that fact. In the same way, if God is not really there, no amount of faith can change that fact. Strong belief does not give us the power to flap our arms and fly, nor does it allow us to conjure up a God who exists only in our hearts or imaginations.

Yes, the question of truth is a crucial one. Indeed, many of us are misinformed about faith because society regularly dodges the question of truth, speaking instead of religious truth. Truth—religious or otherwise—must still be true. Religious ideas must be able to stand the test of criticism—after all, they are either well grounded or ill founded, useful or useless, true or false. If they are so delicate that serious investigation topples them, they aren't true anyway.

This is also the position of the Bible.[22] In the late AD 50s, the apostle Paul attempted to communicate his faith to King Agrippa. Paul was interrupted by Governor Festus:

> Festus interrupted Paul's defense. "You are out of your mind, Paul!" he shouted. "Your great learning is driving you insane."
>
> "I am not insane, most excellent Festus," Paul replied. "What I am saying is true and reasonable. The king is familiar with these things, and I can speak freely to him. I am

convinced that none of this has escaped his notice, because it was not done in a corner. King Agrippa, do you believe the prophets? I know you do."

Then Agrippa said to Paul, "Do you think that in such a short time you can persuade me to be a Christian?"

Paul replied, "Short time or long—I pray God that not only you but all who are listening to me today may become what I am, except for these chains" (Act 26:24-29).

As the apostle Paul insisted to Governor Festus, those who believe the truth about Christ and tell others about it are not insane. The Christian faith is "true and reasonable." Few religions invite you to examine their claims as Christianity does.

Personal Distance

If we have difficulty believing in God, or if God seems unreal to us, part of the problem may be our own lifestyles. We fill our lives with so many things, we have no time for God, so he seems distant. (No wonder! My wife would seem a bit distant too if I talked to her only once a week or only when I was in trouble, felt lonely, or craved a good meal.) The old maxim is right: If God feels distant, guess who moved?

Moreover, for millions of people, believing in God would not be very convenient. It would necessitate changes in their values, schedules, friends, habits, and more. It might lead to stigma or even (in many nations) oppression. So they deny his existence and justify their position with some philosophical technicality, complaint about his justice, or alleged contradiction in the Bible. For many people, the real issue is likely to be that they simply do not want to change.

God will not force us to follow him; it's our decision. Does God exist? Absolutely. Does he seem distant, or unreal? Perhaps that's because we prefer it that way. When the apostle Paul shared this faith with Governor Felix, he challenged him on his personal life. Felix responded,

"That's enough for now! You may leave. When I find it convenient, I will send for you."[23] Many people echo Felix's response today.

Who's Winning?

No atheist has ever proved that God does not exist. As a rule, when most people decide there is no God, at least one of the underlying reasons for that decision is the inconvenience that would result if they decided that God really exists. God's existence does not depend on our decision. In fact, our existence depends on his permission.[24] He is there regardless of whether we choose to live for him.

Despite its loud protests to the contrary, atheism is now and has always been a minority position—not that truth is determined by consensus or majority rule. Most people in the world believe in a spiritual world, a moral code, and an afterlife. They always have. In the twenty-first century, more and more thinking persons are receptive to spiritual things and to the idea of a Creator. Are you?

Now that we have cleared away some of the debris—notions that cloud our understanding—we are in a better position to consider the evidence for the existence of God. But first, let's consider further why atheism is not only invalid, but even bankrupt—powerless to effect good in this world.

2

Why Atheism Fails:
The Bankruptcy of the Godless Worldview

The central neurosis of our time is emptiness.

CARL JUNG

If God is dead, then man is dead too.

FRANCIS SCHAEFFER

WHAT WOULD HAPPEN IN A STATE where God was entirely removed from society—where irreligion was institutionalized as the official ideology? Where religion was banned and godlessness was the order of the day?[1] This scenario has occurred in several nations in recent history. I would like to share about one.

In all my travels, I was hardest hit emotionally by my first visit to Cambodia. In the 1970s this nation of seven million lost two million citizens through execution, forced labor, and starvation during a misguided and devastating Maoist revolution. Khmer Rouge leaders, headed by former schoolteacher Pol Pot, followed the counsel of Chinese Communist advisers (whose ill-founded policies eventually led to the deaths of some 40 million in their own country!) and forced the populace into the fields. That is, unless they were educated. Nearly every educated person, including doctors, teachers, and academics, was killed by the most lethal regime of the twentieth century, worse than Stalin's Soviet administration. This was a political experiment gone terribly wrong.

As I spoke to the Cambodians about their enormous loss, I was stunned. Visiting the central torture center, seeing the implements of barbaric cruelty and the photographs of those executed, I could hardly restrain myself from thinking about the issue of divine justice. Walking around the killing fields, I saw multiple mass graves, where men, women, and children had been shot, knifed, or bludgeoned to death. Bones, teeth, and shreds of clothing lay in situ, vestiges of destroyed lives.

Of all the people I was able to speak with, the one who suffered the least was a 20-year-old woman who had lost her four grandparents. And yet she was joyful, not bitter. Her demeanor in light of what she had suffered was striking. I think what I saw was grace. She had made sense of the tragedy in the light of Christ.

My heart was filled with horror and a sense of pathos. Returning to the United States, I phoned up journalist Sydney Schanberg of *The Killing Fields* fame. The movie follows Schanberg, then a journalist for the *New York Times,* and Dith Pran, his Cambodian counterpart, who had been covering the Vietnam conflict from Phnom Penh and finally escaped the country. Schanberg told me that his thoughts of Cambodia are only of unspeakable sorrow.

I began to buy books about the Cambodian genocide. Then I started reading about other genocides—and there have been many.[2] One day my wife said, "Doug, I think this may be affecting you." (It was.) "You're getting kind of heavy." (She wasn't referring to my weight.) Yes, history affects you. There's much to learn, interesting stuff, but also so much that is dismal, even deplorable. I became more convinced than ever that there is a judgment day. In this life, good is often unrewarded and evil is rampant. Worse, even those who never practice violence are desensitized. We are taught to be tolerant, but does anything go? We are marinated in materialism, which numbs our hearts to the spiritual world. On top of all this, we are inured to violence because of the thousands of TV and movie images of violence we soak in.

Amoral

But what is wrong with genocide? Who is to say it is evil? A few years ago a man boasted to me that he had drowned a litter of kittens. He had told his wife, "We ain't gonna feed all them cats. You get rid of 'em, or I will." Coming home from work that evening, he carried out the deed. He felt no more compunction in telling his account than we would expect from someone who had swatted a fly.

According to the atheistic view, humans are just animals, without ultimate moral obligations to one another. Who's to say what is good or bad? Isn't it all mere smoke of opinion? I have talked with murderers and with Mother Teresa. Are *vicious* and *virtuous* vacuous words? Do they correspond to anything in reality? Not if German philosopher Friedrich Nietzsche (1844–1900) was right.

Nietzsche's famous dictum "God is dead" is an observation about a world without God. The death is functional, not biological. In a world without God, absolute morals simply do not exist, despite all rhetoric to the contrary. True absolute morals transcend social consensus. For example, if society agreed that premarital sex was not illicit, but useful, that would do nothing to change the rightness or wrongness of such behavior. Good and evil are not legislated by governments; these categories exist whether or not society acknowledges them.

Nietzsche correctly saw where the death of God was leading. Without God, "might makes right," as Plato's opponent Thrasymachus maintained.[3] Without God and a sense of transcendent morality to guide our actions, power—or "rightness"—may very well go to the most powerful—often the most greedy, ambitious, and ruthless. Few unbelievers are willing to be so audacious as to agree with this idea, but to our short list we can add the Marquis de Sade, with his determinism ("Whatever is, is right") and eponymous sadism, and of course, Machiavelli.[4] In this respect, the death of God is also the death of man. When God dies, morality dies with him; and without morality, we are doomed to a world where either brutality or majority rule will dictate social definitions of morality. Free thinking and free will, two essential qualities of humankind, could be shut down—resulting in the emotional and spiritual death of man, if not his literal self-annihilation.

As Malcolm Muggeridge trenchantly jibed, "If God is dead, somebody is going to have to take his place. It will be megalomania or erotomania, the drive for power or the drive for pleasure, the clenched fist or the phallus, Hitler or Hugh Hefner."[5] The killing fields of the Khmer Rouge are a natural and even predictable consequence of a world without God.

Instead of talking about morals, postmodern persons prefer to use the word *values,* itself a term laden with relativism. What one person values another may find worthless, such as industry, virginity, or integrity. Morals have been reduced to the level of individual preference.

About ten years ago, I gave a presentation called "Philosophers and Philosophy" at Michigan State University, followed by a lively session of questions and answers. One woman did not like my assertion that there are moral absolutes in this world. In order to expose the error and inconsistency of her position, I asked whether she thought it was wrong to kill and eat babies. If she answered yes, she would be implicitly admitting her belief in absolute morals.

Before she could reply, a Nietzschean philosophy student shouted out to her, "Don't say yes!" He knew where I was heading even though his fellow student did not. Needless to say, the Nietzschean did not score any points for atheism. As soon as the audience realized that he was rejecting the (absolute) evil of cannibalizing babies, they emotionally turned against him, making my position as a defender of absolute morals seem all the more reasonable.

I am not saying that the atheist cannot act morally, only that if he is moral, it is not because of his ideology, but in spite of it.[6] In the same way, a man may deny that our atmosphere consists of various gases because he has not *seen* them, but he still breathes the air just like the rest of us. Atheism is amoral, not immoral.

One wonders whether there might be a degree of wish fulfillment in the belief that there is no God. For example, some people say they would do the right thing regardless of whether they would be rewarded or punished. However, when the police are visible on the highway, drivers really do slow down. When they think "the law" is far away, they take significantly greater liberties. Denying the increase in immorality when the law is absent is as naive as discounting the connection between belief in a judgment day (and a Judge) and right living. I am reminded of a Web page that pictured a red, waxen cross. It was melting. This text was included:

> No God, no guilt.
> The belief in God awakens
> fanaticism and guilt.
> Live free and responsible.
> Debaptize yourself!

But can we really free ourselves from guilt by simply denying the law? Either we have violated the moral law of the universe or we have not. No amount of wishing can change the reality. If there is a God, we can do nothing to free ourselves from him. To do so would not be responsible or bring freedom. Atheists often accuse believers of projection, of creating spiritual reality for their own comfort. But I believe the opposite is true. The atheist imagines a world without ultimate accountability, where he is answerable to no authority beyond this life.

Meaningless

A world without God would be not only amoral but also meaningless. Life would have no objective purpose. In a world without ultimate meaning, all we can do is to pursue our own made-up purposes: career advancement, popularity, family, fitness, hobbies, and so forth. Yet nothing will last. We cannot take our hard-earned wealth with us, and in time no one will remember our achievements. Do you know anything about your great-grandparents or great, great-grandparents? Probably not. Generations come and generations go. As for popularity, those with whom we seek to ingratiate ourselves—if there is no infinite being—will disintegrate into nothingness just like us. Net gain: zero. If there is no God, our proudest accomplishments and most enviable awards and honors all will fade away into oblivion. Solomon described this attitude:

> "Absolute futility," says the Teacher. "Absolute futility. Everything is futile." What does a man gain for all his efforts he labors at under the sun? A generation goes and a generation comes… All things are wearisome; man is unable to speak. The eye is not satisfied by seeing or the ear filled with hearing… There is no memory of those who came before; and of those who will come after there will also be no memory among those who follow them (Ecclesiastes 1:2-11 HCSB).

Solomon is saying that without God in the picture, existence itself is empty, vain, futile. Later in the book, after recounting his own search for meaning apart from God, he urges us to "fear God and keep his commandments."[7] In view of the existence of a righteous God, and in view of the reality of a final judgment, we ought to prepare ourselves, beginning now to live in sync with spiritual reality and to follow God's Word.

Before the fall of the iron curtain, when my family lived in Sweden, a man from Moscow named Sergei occasionally visited our church. He was a quiet soul and seemingly devoid of passion and purpose. He was an atheist, but for some reason he kept coming to church. One day I asked him, "Why are you here? Are you beginning to believe the message? You say you're an atheist, but don't you see there is something more to life?" He would never tell what his profession was, but we knew.

One day my wife and I invited Sergei to lunch. He enjoyed his afternoon with us and our young children. We tried to get him to open up, and Sergei almost admitted he was a KGB agent, but he would not give his identity away. Still, he knew that we knew. As he spoke about his native Russia, his family, his life, and his idle hours, there was no enthusiasm, only ennui. He also knew that we knew his life was aimless.

After all, if there is no God—in accordance with the official Communist party line—what end was he serving? What would happen after his career was over? What would happen after his life came to an end? Nothing at all. It was as though something inside him had died. He could no longer respond. Life was meaningless, and no one could do anything about it. How tragic—that a man could go through decade after decade unaware of his true purpose in life. I am encouraged, however, by the myriads in the former USSR who have found God in the years following the collapse of Communism. (And equally encouraged by the myriads who kept their faith even in the midst of severe oppression.)

Another time I was speaking at Stockholm University. I was making what I thought was a fairly obvious point: Humans are the high point of creation. One of the students was offended and accused me of speciesism, an unwarranted bias in favor of my fellow *homines sapientes.* I sought an analogy.

"If terrorists burst into your home and threatened to kill either your grandmother or a mosquito, what would you say? Whose life is more important?" Surely the answer was obvious. But not to this particular student.

"Well, of course I would favor my grandmother—but that's only because I am a human. If I were a mosquito, I would feel differently. So I am not sure which is more important." Such is the confusion of the creature alienated from his Creator.

In the 1960s, existentialism was in vogue. Life is absurd, this philosophy holds, and so we must create our own meaning, even if it means taking our own life. Philosopher Jean-Paul Sartre taught that suicide can be an authentic action of the will in a godless world. But surely even this is meaningless.

The emptiness of life without God is so disheartening, so starkly futile, that people will do anything to avoid the implications. And so we attempt to escape through medication, education, indoctrination, recreation, vocation... Think about it. Truly Jung was right: Emptiness is the central neurosis of our time.

Incoherent

Existence without God is inherently amoral and meaningless, but the problems do not end there. Atheism is also incoherent. As an antiposition, it is not verifiable. Nobody has ever proven the nonexistence of God, nor is this possible. An antiposition is not necessarily incoherent, provided the implications are not pressed. But atheists do usually press their position at least partway toward its natural conclusions.

As we saw in the previous chapter, atheism as a philosophy is doomed to fail because it affirms the very thing it denies. That is, total knowledge of all of reality is required in order to prove there is no being with total knowledge.

Atheism self-destructs in at least two other ways. Theists accept absolute truth, which is itself anchored in the nature of deity, but atheists reject absolute truth. Yet if an atheist makes the statement "There is no absolute truth," it is self-refuting. For if nothing is absolutely true, then that must include the statement itself—which means that there *is* absolute truth.

Whether making physical or metaphysical measurements, some sort of external yardstick is needed. For example, I am 6 feet 4 inches tall and weigh 220 pounds (193 centimeters and 100 kilograms). Is this a fact? Says who? How do we measure? If someone from another world, whose meter was three Earth yards or whose kilo was an Earth ton, came to Earth and measured me, would my dimensions have changed? Without a fixed, external standard, dimensional pronouncements are empty.

Another example of incoherence involves the meaninglessness of existence. Consistent, rigorous atheism admits that meaning is in the mind of the thinker, not out there in reality. The world is wholly bereft of ultimate meaning. But think about it. The statement "Everything is meaningless" cannot be true because the statement itself would be included in the analysis—in which case it could not possibly be true. For if all statements are meaningless, there can be no exception. By the standards of sound thinking, atheism appears to be nonsense.[8]

Incomplete

Atheism is not only incoherent but also offers an incomplete view of reality. The real world comprises physical entities, with attributes of mass or energy, but also spiritual entities, which are incorporeal and not empirically verifiable. We believe in the existence of mountains and rivers, protons and neutrons, because we observe them directly or are able to measure them with instruments. We also believe in justice, mercy, and love, to name only a few nonphysical realities. Atheism explains away the spiritual phenomena as mere social consensus, functions of neurochemistry, or projections of the mind. Thus it fails to apprehend all of reality because reasonable people believe in love and justice and often appeal to their existence.

An opera (see chapter 1) might be rationalized by examination of the musical score. What would you say to someone who insisted, "The opera is nothing but black ellipses on paper, connected to vertical strokes, appearing on parallel lines in certain mathematical relationships to one another"? The analysis would not be entirely wrong—music does have its own calculus and can be put to paper—but it is incomplete. More to the point, atheism fails to answer the seven basic questions of human existence:

> *Origin*: Am I the result of blind forces, or am I created by God?
>
> *Destiny*: To what end is history moving? Are there grander purposes in play?

Identity: Who am I?

Relationship: How am I to relate to others?

Morality: What is right and what is wrong? What about the problem of evil?

Meaning: What is meaningful, valuable?

Purpose: What am I supposed to be doing with my life?

Clearly, atheism is not only amoral and incoherent but also incomplete.

Inconsistent

One final weakness of atheism is that its advocates cannot live consistently within its limits. They cannot even reason consistently within the constricting confines of unbelief. We will examine six areas where this is clearly the case.

First, although thoroughgoing atheism rejects absolute morality, atheists are unable to do so. On the one hand, they claim that absolute evil does not exist. Our thoughts about evil are, after all, only the product of evolution.[9] On the other hand, the atheist rejects God because of the problem of evil. With so much evil and suffering in the world, there cannot be a God. But which way will he have it? Is there no evil, or is there a superabundance of evil? Does it exist or not?

Second, atheism rejects a Designer, but it cannot break away from the language of design. As Darwin himself (an agnostic, not an atheist) wrote, "My theology is a simple muddle. I cannot look at the universe as the result of blind chance, yet I can see no evidence of beneficent design, or indeed of design of any kind."[10] Darwin also wrote, "There seems to be no more design in the variability of organic beings and in the action of natural selection, than in the course which the wind blows. Everything in nature is the result of fixed laws."[11]

Notice that the last sentence attributes everything in nature to "fixed laws." This sounds suspiciously like design. Again, we must ask, is there design or not? Why are these laws inviolable? I am typing these sentences in my laptop computer at a local library. There are walls and ceilings, columns and beams, acoustic tile, carpet, and lighting. Would you think I was sane if I claimed there was no evidence of "design"—and thus no designer—and that I could explain the library by the principles of engineering alone? For what is the difference between the two?

Third, atheism's adherents pretend to occupy higher philosophical ground than believers in God. But there is a fatal weakness in the area of epistemology. This term refers to the philosophy of knowledge, or how we know that we know what we think we know. Since most atheists believe that their organ of cognition (the brain) is the end product of a process that is driven by chance accidents, do they have a strong reason to trust their perceptions? The theist, on the other hand, expects that the brain (regardless of how it came to be) is adequate to apprehend reality (though not necessarily perfectly) because God's hand is in, or behind, the processes of biology. It is consistent with the theistic worldview that the organ of cognition functions in a more or less satisfactory manner. Thus theism is on more solid ground epistemologically than atheism.

A fourth area of inconsistency is language with theological overtones. Atheists often employ circumlocutions to avoid referring to God. They may speak of Mother Nature (a goddess in place of a god?), fate, or even creation. But such terms are redolent of theism. Some atheists go even further. While rejecting God, they venerate the earth (Gaia), which they conceive as a living being. Is neopaganism really an improvement on classical theism?

The fifth area is ecology. Unbelievers often emphasize our environmental responsibility. The crux of the problem is whether we humans are part of nature or above nature. Of course, there is no reason we might not be part of nature *and* above it. If, however, we are only on the level of the other animals, it is difficult to explain why caring for the environment is natural in the first place. Isn't it "natural" for humans to trash the environment? On the premise of atheism, why is "natural" right or wrong? Yet the Bible provides an authentic basis for ecological responsibility: "Be fruitful and multiply; fill the earth and subdue it; have dominion over the fish of the sea, over the birds of the air, and over every living thing that moves on the earth" (Genesis 1:28 NKJV). Of course, ecological concern is a good thing, but it is hardly justified on the premise of atheism. We will take this up further in the next chapter.

The sixth and final example of inconsistency—ironic in the extreme—has to do with judging. Unbelievers often denounce believers (and others) for their convictions, typically labeling them as intolerant. Interestingly, the Bible nowhere condemns all judging, only hypocritical, arrogant, or selfish kinds of judging. The unbeliever's accusation is deeply inconsistent. For if it is wrong to tell others they are wrong, then what right do atheists have to tell others they are misguided?

Perhaps a distinction ought to be made between judging (affirming that a proposition is incorrect or a behavior is immoral) and being judgmental (judging without grace or concern for the other). Being judgmental is never commended in Scripture.

We have seen six areas in which atheists speak and act inconsistently. In short, no one lives as a fully consistent atheist.

The Conclusion

Atheism is intrinsically amoral, meaningless, incoherent, incomplete, and inconsistent. It offers nothing save a false freedom. Oxford theologian Alister McGrath highlights the ineffectiveness of education alone:

> The great liberal dream was that education would radically change [the selfishness that characterizes humanity] and produce a generation of morally enlightened and responsible people, dedicated to the construction of a better world. Sadly, the history of the world lends little support to such a

utopian dream. All too often, education seems to turn out people who are merely informed and self-centered.[12]

Most of our political and intellectual leaders have rejected God—if not in thought or word, certainly in deed. Ours is a secular society. Given the failure of liberals' predictions of the better world to come, we should hardly be surprised that the new millennium has seen a resurgence of faith. This should be a time of hope, progress, and greater openness to truth and change.

And yet, as Christians at this pivotal time, we often find ourselves inhaling the stale air of prejudice. An atmosphere of hostility toward the Bible and biblical religion surrounds believers. Many governments (including Saudi Arabia, China, and Cuba) discourage or forbid Bible study and evangelism outright while others severely restrict the practice of religion in public.

The media mocks God and his Word, educational institutions deride absolute truth, and the younger generation craves what is cool. But this is shallow, an elusive goal. What is cool is the broad road, not the narrow path of God's commands. Christianity seems to be on trial, and the Bible especially is subjected to jests, gibes, and undeserved ridicule. The most notorious atheists' books have become bestsellers even though many of their arguments are specious, as we have seen in these first two chapters.

Has the alternative to faith proven its worth? We have already seen that its primary arguments are unpersuasive. Besides, atheism doesn't work. No one can follow its rationale to its logical ends. Atheism leaves us cold.

In the words of the epistle to the Ephesians, before we come to faith, we are "without hope and without God in the world."[13] Atheism cannot and will not have the last word.

3

Is Anyone at Home?
Compelling Evidence for the Reality of God

The cosmos is all there is,
or ever was, or ever will be.

CARL SAGAN

IN THE FIRST CHAPTER WE EXAMINED a number of reasons why people do not believe in God: lack of proof, religious hypocrisy, scientific questions, suffering in the world, absurd questions, confused notions of truth, and the personal inconvenience of surrendering their lives to God. In the second chapter we saw how hopeless the atheist worldview is. It leaves us in the cold. We needed to lay the atheistic objections to rest and spell out the implications of disbelief before moving on. But now that we have cleared away the debris, we are ready to examine some of the positive proof for God's existence.

So far all that we have established is that there *could* be a God. There are no cogent arguments against his existence. "The cosmos is all there is, or ever was, or ever will be" is a quasicreedal statement that puts the creation in the place of the Creator.[1] However, if anyone is at home in the universe, we should find some clues to his existence. What sort of pointers should we be looking for?

Traces

In our Atlanta-area neighborhood, we find a wide array of fauna. We have spotted many animals, including raccoons, opossums, rabbits, foxes, and even coyotes. But never deer. I told a guest the other week that if deer lived here, we would have surely seen them. A few days later I was walking our dog and came across telltale tracks in the mud only a quarter of a mile from our home. The lone mammal was not present, but the traces he had left were unmistakable. Could I have been wrong? Yes. I suppose a neighborhood prankster could have forged the tracks, or the rain could have eroded the mud into cervine patterns. Aliens could have done it. But the question is, what is the most logical explanation?

The evidence for God is suggestive. It is like forensic evidence, the kind of deduction and testimony that wins court cases in the absence of video footage and signed confessions. Probabilities are weighed. What are the chances there is a God (or a deer)? And what are the chances that we have entirely misinterpreted the evidence for a divine being (or *Odocoileus virginianus*)? More than one conclusion is possible, but what matters is which explanation is most reasonable.

This chapter explores the data pointing to God's existence.

Cosmology

When I was five, I became fascinated with astronomy—caught up, I suppose, in the fervor of the space race. My grandfather took me to Cape Canaveral (called Cape Kennedy at the time). I perused picture books, reading of faraway stars and galaxies. When I was eight, I learned in science class that light had a velocity. In a darkened hallway, I asked my brother to turn on my father's flashlight but not before my signal. I would try to race the beam of light from one end of the hallway to another. Of course, I failed, though not before accusing my brother of foul play. Little did I know that I was doomed; no one can run 300,000 kilometers per second!

Nor did I imagine that there were 10^{11} stars (100 billion) in each of 10^{11} galaxies, for a mind-numbing total of 10^{22} stars in the entire universe, which itself is 28 billion light-years across. That is, moving at the velocity of light, an object would require 28 billion years to traverse the cosmos. Where did it all come from?

The existence of the universe (cosmos) itself points to a God. The cosmological argument underscores the improbability of the universe coming into existence apart from a deity, given that nothing finite and contingent can cause itself. God is the First Cause.[2] I would like to modify the argument and ask three questions:

> Did the universe have a beginning or not?
>
> Is the universe caused or uncaused?
>
> Was this beginning personal or impersonal?

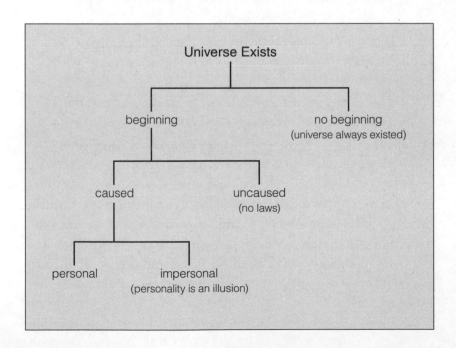

Has the Universe Always Existed?

An overwhelming majority of scientists now believe the universe had a definite beginning, but this was not always the prevailing viewpoint. The scientific community long believed that the universe had always existed. Then in the 1920s, astrophysicists observed that the universe was expanding. The discovery of redshift, as well as trigonometric analysis, proved this expansion. Rewinding the tape, so to speak, meant that in the past the cosmos was smaller—in fact, infinitesimally smaller. At this point, the *singularity,* the laws of physics break down. Before the singularity (though this is surely an inappropriate proposition), there was no matter or energy, space or time. Everything came into being at this point, which is the literal beginning, through a massive explosion. Yet the scientific community of the 1930s scoffed:

- "The notion of a beginning is repugnant to me…I simply do not believe that the present order of things started off with a bang…the expanding universe is preposterous" (Arthur Eddington, British astronomer).
- "To deny the infinite duration of time would be to betray the very foundations of science" (Walther Nernst, German chemist).
- "It's such a strange conclusion…it cannot really be true" (Allan Sandage, American astronomer).
- [The idea is] "annoying" (Albert Einstein, German physicist).[3]

What was annoying about the idea? Dispensing with "infinite time" (itself an impossibility) seemed to open the door to a creation, a specific point in time at which the cosmos came into existence. The Big Bang (the name was originally a pejorative) was novel, disturbing, and subversive of the prevalent wisdom that the universe was infinitely old.

When the long-sought cosmic background radiation was accidentally discovered in 1965 by Bell Labs engineers in Holmdel, New Jersey, the final nail was driven into the coffin of the idea of the eternal universe.[4] The logic was irresistible, and as a result, many scientists today, regardless of their faith or lack thereof, use the language of creation. What else are you going to call it?

The laws of physics state that everything that comes into being requires a cause. God never came into being because he is eternal, so he requires no cause. Thus the question of who created God is illogical because God by definition is uncreated. This is not the case, however, with the physical universe. Some agent outside the cosmos was necessary in order for it to come into existence.

If this is hard to wrap your head around, perhaps a summary will be helpful. The universe has been expanding as a result of a massive explosion approximately 14 billion years ago, according to the calculations of cosmologists and astrophysicists. Before the enormous explosion—which set the universe in motion and ultimately prepared a place for mankind—space, matter, and energy existed in one supercondensed mass. Thus, before this definite beginning point, there was no universe. This singularity emerges from nothing, or rather, it has no physical cause. But how about a spiritual cause?

The universe has not always existed. If it had, the universe would have wound down or "stopped ticking" long ago. Like any other machine, according to the second law of thermodynamics, the universe cannot run forever. It would need maintenance, new parts, and a qualified mechanic to keep it in working order. Without a mechanic, the whole system would run down in a matter of time (physicists call this "heat death"). Thus we see that the physical world could not possibly have always been. Science and the Bible are agreed that the world has existed for only a limited time.

Did Something Cause the Universe?

Next, we must ask whether the beginning was caused or uncaused. The evidence we see in our world points to physical law, order, and direction (or teleology). Everything fits into the overall system in a remarkable way. Scientists proceed on the assumption that there is order in the world, that the observations they have made at one time and place are useful for understanding other situations as well. If the physical world had no law and order, science would be meaningless.

Imagine the chaos in a world without consistent laws. One day, water boils at 212 degrees Fahrenheit, or 100 degrees centigrade. The next day, you look for a cool drink at the water fountain but are scalded by steam because water now boils at 50 degrees Fahrenheit, or 10 degrees centigrade! Or envision a world with fluctuating gravity. One day you stroll through the park; the next, unaware of a change, you push too hard with your left foot and accidentally propel yourself across town! Obviously, under such conditions, scientific measurements would be meaningless.

Everything we observe leads us to believe the world is orderly. The fact that it can be described by physical laws itself requires explanation. How could this order have just happened if before (or, strictly speaking, outside) the universe, there was no law or order? If order came from non-order or disorder, surely a force acted on the non-ordered material to bring the ordered world into existence. It's that simple. The universe was caused. Let's recount the possibilities:

- *The universe has existed forever.* Scientists are nearly unanimous in agreeing that this is impossible.[5]
- *The universe created itself.* It would have had to already exist in order to create itself, which is absurd.
- *It happened without cause,* for no reason at all.[6] In light of Big Bang cosmology, this seems highly improbable.
- *A powerful agent caused it* to come into existence.

So we see that the universe had a beginning and a cause. We can add one final element.

Does the Universe Have a Personality?

We have established that the world had a beginning and that this beginning was caused. But how do we account for the elements of personality that we see in the world today, such as love and hate, reason and reflection, music, art, worship, and philosophy? What could have caused impersonal matter to take on a personal nature? If there is no spiritual (nonphysical) part of the universe, where did personality—which we so clearly observe in human beings—come from? Some element of personality (or at least its potential) must have been present at the beginning.

Even if personality is an "emergent property" of matter, as skeptics Dennett and Shermer claim—an argument with some plausibility—we may, and should, still ask, why should such properties exist? Naming them *emergent* is hardly the same thing as explaining them. Another explanation is more reasonable. The Bible teaches that the personality was present at the beginning. "God is love"; personality is an attribute of God.[7]

Some may object that God could not be love without creatures toward whom he could direct his love. But Christian theology has a simple, elegant answer. God is triune, so relationships have existed forever among the persons of the Trinity. (For more on this, see appendix B.) The universe had a personal beginning.

God

We have reasoned that the universe had a personal, caused beginning. This cause had to be incredibly powerful, logical, and provident to account for what we observe today. Most people call this first cause God. Of course, this line of reasoning does not tell us whether there is one God or many, or exactly how powerful he is, or even whether he is good or evil. It is doubtful man on his own would have figured out that there is a benevolent God, at least not by looking at nature, which is "red in tooth and claw."[8] But I am certain that a look at nature greatly strengthens our belief in the existence of God once we accept that he is there.

The beginning, cause, and personality of the universe suggest the existence of God, and the biblical notion of God seems a strong contender for the first cause. "In the beginning, God..." (Genesis 1:1). Science cannot prove that the God of the Bible created the cosmos. It does strongly indicate, in terms of probability, that the cosmos was created by a spiritual (not physical) power external to the cosmos itself—a transcendent cause.

Something doesn't come from nothing, so theism appears to be on firmer ground than atheism. One thing is certain: The atheist, who claims that the world's origin and existence can be explained without any reference to God, is interpreting the evidence in a very constricted way. The truth is, as we understand more about the world, science and theology seem to converge, not diverge.

> For the scientist who has lived by his faith in the power of reason, the story ends like a bad dream. He has scaled the mountains of ignorance; he is about to conquer the highest peak; as he pulls himself over the final rock, he is greeted by a band of theologians who have been sitting there for centuries.[9]

The cosmos is not all there ever was because in the remote past there was not even a cosmos. Nor is the physical universe all there is; denying the spiritual world does not undo it or make it go away.

Teleology

The universe seems to be designed.[10] The argument from design, in its simplest form, is this: Design suggests a designer. If there is natural law in the world, there must be a lawgiver. If there is structure and consistency in the creation, there must be a creator.

Not long ago, my wife and I were at Hadrian's Wall, the second-century AD structure on what was the northwestern frontier of the Roman Empire. Today it divides Scotland from England. It certainly appears to be designed—caused with a specific purpose in mind. Could colliding glaciers have formed the wall? Theoretically, I suppose, but where is the evidence? And can glaciers explain not only the line of elevated stones but also the watchtowers and Roman forts? I am just as confident that Hadrian's Wall is man-made as I am that the Great Wall of China is man-made. I have seen other, more impressive structures, like the Sydney Opera House and the Taj Mahal. None of these edifices or walls is likely to have occurred by chance. They all bear the marks of design.

The most common illustration of the teleological argument involves a common wristwatch.[11] Suppose you are walking through a field and notice a wristwatch on the ground. You would certainly assume that someone had lost it and that the watch was crafted by a watchmaker.

If I suggested that there was no watchmaker, but that squirrels had made the timepiece, you would laugh, saying it was too complicated to be made by a creature so simple and unintelligent as a squirrel. If I claimed that the watch just happened over a very long period of time and through natural processes, you would think I was joking, arguing that a watch is much too complex to be the product of random forces. If I insisted that it was created by no one, but had always existed, you would correctly reply that if that were the case, it would have stopped ticking ages ago.

Now which is more complicated: the watch or the whole universe? The universe is incredibly more complicated than the watch, so we must assume that it has a maker.[12] Obviously, the "clockwork universe" is far too complex to have been created by a being of lower intelligence—like man. It appears to be too complicated to have come into existence by itself and is much too orderly to have always existed.

The most reasonable explanation is that the universe was created. If there is a universe, there must be a God who created it—it's that simple.

But there is even more evidence of teleology: the anthropic principle. Princeton physicist Freeman Dyson suggested that the universe, in some sense, "knew we were coming." Einstein noted, "The most incomprehensible thing about the world is that it is at all comprehensible."

Many have written about the incredible fine-tuning of the universe. Donald Page, of Princeton's Institute for Advanced Study, calculates that the odds against our universe randomly taking a form suitable for life as we know it are 1 in 10^{124}. How big is that number? Consider this: All of history has taken place in about 10^{18} seconds; there are 10^{22} stars; and the cosmos contains about 10^{80} atomic particles.

If the magnitude of the explosion (the Big Bang) were weaker by only a factor of 1 in 10^{60}, the universe would have collapsed back in on itself. If it were too strong by this same seemingly infinitesimal amount, the expansion would have proceeded too rapidly for star formation. If the strong nuclear force (which holds protons and neutrons together) were 5 percent different, life would be impossible. If the gravitational constant varied by as little as 1 in 10^{40}, life-sustaining stars would not have formed. If the ratio of the mass of a neutron to the mass of a proton were any different than it is (approximately 1.001 to 1.000), we would end up with a universe of all neutrons or all protons. And this is just to mention a few of the variables that give every appearance of being fine-tuned. Without fine-tuning, there would be no matter, no chemistry. It is not a question of having *our* type of world, or human life, but of there being any life at all.

A friend of mine proposed to his girlfriend in a very unusual way. During their Chinese dinner, she opened her fortune cookie. The message said, "The man sitting across from you is going to ask you to marry him." Was there any doubt that there was some serious teleology in that fortune cookie? Would anyone believe it was chance? Surely, there is a minute possibility that there was no collusion at all. But no one would take such a small chance seriously. We are seeking the *best* explanation, not the most imaginative one.

Like the paper slip in the fortune cookie, the genetic code, writ large in DNA, is information. Spirituality, contrary to the message popularized by pop religion, does not begin with feeling. It begins with truth, communicated in language. Interestingly, in John 1:1 we read, "In the beginning was the Word." The definitions of the Greek word *logos* include "word, reason, principle." (*Logos* also gives us the word *logic*.) The cosmos began, and life exists, because of information. Again, this suggests a personal source.

In the blinding light of teleology, some unbelievers, sensing the weakness of their position, seem to try to buy time. Maybe complex life didn't evolve on Earth; it could have been "seeded" from elsewhere. Francis Crick, codiscoverer (with James Watson, in 1953) of the structure of DNA, the double helix, admitted that self-replicating protein synthesis through spontaneous generation seemed unlikely, given its extreme complexity. Crick later opined that life was "seeded" throughout the universe, guided by alien intelligence. Thus the famous scientist advanced his notion of "directed panspermia."

Amazingly, in an interview with Ben Stein in the 2008 film *Expelled: No Intelligence Allowed,* atheist Richard Dawkins uttered something along the same lines. When Stein asked him how he thought life came to be, Dawkins replied that it may have been seeded from another world. I could scarcely believe my ears—Dawkins is normally a first-rate biologist—and surely others were embarrassed by this radical suggestion. The quaint notion of life being "seeded" in the universe ends up scoring a point in favor of the creationist position.[13]

Indeed, our universe shows signs of both design and intelligence. Are these likely to have come from amoral, impersonal matter? The best explanation is that there is a God.

Morality

In our discussion in chapter 2, we saw that atheism offers no ultimate basis for absolute morality or anything more reliable than situational ethics. The reality of good and evil is, not surprisingly, a potent pointer to the existence of God.

One day my wife and I were discussing whether there were any snakes in our yard. Unbelievably, at that very second a large black snake fell from a tree (40 feet up) and landed just six feet from me. The southern black racer had a baby squirrel in its mouth, which it had just nabbed from a squirrel nest. As he slowly swallowed the helpless mammal— squealing for its mother, who was protesting, but to no avail—I neared the reptile for a photo. It was effectively gagged with the squirrel, so it could not bite me, although the species is aggressive. Now, would anyone—even a sentimental squirrel lover—call the snake's behavior immoral? Of course not; moral law does not apply to the animals. We may be tempted to personify them, but snakes and squirrels are simply not human. The next example may elicit a different reaction.

My great aunt, who is a widow, was raped and robbed in her own home. To add to the indignity, she was 99 years old at the time; the rapist was 18. Was this unconscionable act wrong because society says so or because it really is immoral? Because it broke state law in her native Texas, or because it violated the law of God, whose character determines what is righteous and unrighteous? Only if there is a God is there an absolute basis for morality. According to some prominent ethicists, there was in fact nothing *absolutely* morally wrong with my aunt's rape.

"The notion that human life is sacred just because it is human life is medieval," says atheistic ethicist Peter Singer. "Since a speciesist bias, like a racist bias, is unjustifiable, an experiment [on an animal] cannot be justifiable unless the experiment is so important that the use of a brain-damaged human would also be justifiable." He has also written, "Killing a disabled infant is not morally equivalent to killing a person. Very often it is not wrong at all."[14]

Might we not go further? Who is the evil one, the surgeon or the cancer? Does the tumor have as much right to life as a human? In a perverse way, one might reply that it's all relative. It depends on whether you are a human being or another cancer cell. This is what happens when God and morality are taken out of the picture.

Another atheistic ethicist, Richard Taylor, follows the reasoning of atheism to its logical end: "The concept of moral obligation [is] unintelligible apart from the idea of God. The words remain but their meaning is gone." Later in the same work, he writes, "To say that something is wrong because…it is forbidden by God, is perfectly understandable to anyone who believes in a law-giving God. But to say that something is wrong…even though no God exists to forbid it, is *not* understandable."[15]

Thoroughgoing atheists admit that true morality depends on God. This is not to say that an unbeliever cannot act morally. Rather, morality is real only if there is an external moral standard. Before English spelling was standardized, Shakespeare's name could be spelled 20 different ways (including Shexpere, Shackspeare, and even Shakspe). Who's to say one spelling was right and another wrong in the absence of a consistent orthography? Isn't the value of paper arbitrary, unless it is tied to a (gold or silver) standard? Do not be confused. Before we speak meaningfully about morality, we need a reference point, a standard. Moreover, there are only two options: moral relativism and an absolute moral standard.[16]

Often I am asked, is something wrong because God says so, or does he forbid it because it is wrong? The answer is neither, for this is a false choice. The first clause implies that God's moral decrees are arbitrary, which is false. The second clause suggests that good and evil are external to God—that he is bound to follow the rules, just like the rest of us. (Whose rules would those be?) Morality is an expression of God's character. He did not create morality, nor is he judged by any external standard.

Furthermore, when we evaluate courses of action, deliberating between options, our conscience—even if we choose to ignore it— tells us to obey the moral law. This fact points to a standard external to ourselves. We also observe that vice is not always punished in this world, nor is virtue rewarded. This suggests a time of reckoning on the other side of the grave.

To sum up, the only reason right and wrong, good and evil can exist in our world is because there is a God. Reject God, and out goes morality, both ontologically and practically. An amoral world is entirely consistent with atheism but wholly inconsistent with the real world. Therefore it is most reasonable to assume that there is a God.

Experience

I have seen God move; I have experienced him—and I am not alone. Atheism would explain this all away. Can all spiritual experience be rationalized? Few unbelievers will be convinced by someone saying, "I believe in God, and it feels good, so you should believe too." After all, countless persons claim religious experience in every religion of the world. But if by *experience* we mean a willingness to put to the test the principles in Scripture (almost like experimentation), or if we are referring to personal familiarity with a system that makes sense and works, then experience can be one of the strongest and most conclusive arguments for the reality of God. The difference between the lives of those who are living for God and the lives of those who do not have this hope is often evident. Faith in God makes us better people when we live by the truth.

We currently see a false modesty among some critics of faith. For example, in a debate with me, historian of science Michael Shermer challenged me, "Is there a God? I don't know—and you don't know either!"

It would be one thing to say, "Maybe there's a God, and you may be on to something, but I remain a skeptic." But to claim ignorance for yourself *and* your opponent is not modest, for you haven't necessarily been exposed to the same experiences as he or she has. It is hardly irrational of me to believe Christianity is true if it makes sense of my experience. It would be irrational, for instance, to think I was a Martian with X-ray vision and an invisible ray gun. Or if I denied the existence of love, justice, or anything else that isn't empirically measurable. But to believe in a religion that is rooted in history, offers credible explanations for some of life's greatest riddles, and urges me to think—this is highly rational.

I embrace and promote a healthy skepticism.[17] My religion urges me to carefully scrutinize everything. It warns me of so-called miracles that can lead to compromising positions. It urges me to test every-thing, filtering out error and holding to what is true. It commends honest seekers after truth, those who are willing to investigate the message before accepting it.[18] This is not blind unbelief, but a bold willingness to search the Scriptures and experience how practical and realistic they really are.

If atheism isn't true, one might counter, why do so many edu-cated people embrace it? Probably for the same reasons that so many uneducated people embrace it. It is convenient and in many circles even fashionable.

I am not saying that millions of people can't be mistaken, for the mind can mislead us, and besides, truth is not determined by major-ity. But I am rejecting the notion that belief is irrational. Faith is not a flight from reason but a response to evidence.

A Better Worldview

Is anyone at home? Yes, God is at home in the universe. He is still there, and he has not left us without evidence of his existence. The evidence of cosmology, teleology, morality, and spiritual experience all imply the existence of God.

A good few atheists have abandoned their unbelief, most famously Anthony Flew, Lee Strobel, and C.S. Lewis. In 2004, Flew, an Oxford philosopher and popular lecturer and debater, left his unbelief for some form of theism. For Flew, the evidence from biology was especially compelling. With classic British understatement, the distinguished scholar pronounced, "The argument to intelligent design is stronger than when I first met it."[19]

We cannot *prove* in an empirically irrefutable way that God exists, but we can make an inference to the best explanation. As a deer left hoofprints that traced its path through our neighborhood, so the Lord has left traces of his presence in this cosmos. The detractors' arguments are inadequate. Theism is a better worldview than atheism for its vastly superior explanatory value. In answer to the question, why believe in God? several answers are appropriate: (1) because of the evidence, (2) because the alternative is unacceptable, and (3) because it's true.

The testimony of Scripture and the entrance of Jesus Christ into history provide proof even more convincing than the reasons we have studied in this chapter. We will soon explore what is meant by *Word of God* and *Son of God* (starting in chapters 5 and 8, respectively). Before we do that, however, we need to sharpen our picture of God himself.

4

❖❖❖❖❖❖❖❖❖❖❖❖❖❖❖❖❖❖❖❖❖❖❖❖❖

God: Sleeping, Retired, or Dead?
The Nature of God

❖❖❖❖❖❖❖❖❖❖❖❖❖❖❖❖❖❖❖❖❖❖❖❖❖

*At noon Elijah began to taunt them. "Shout
louder!" he said. "Surely [Baal] is a god! Perhaps
he is deep in thought, or busy, or traveling. Maybe
he is sleeping and must be awakened."*

1 KINGS 18:27

WE HAVE SEEN THAT GOD'S EXISTENCE is reasonable. Now it is time
to clarify who God is. Elijah, a prophet of God in the ninth century
BC, playfully challenged the worshippers of Baal about their concept
of God. Theirs was a very human conception of God: He slept, traveled, and had a limited ability to concentrate. Sometimes we make the
same mistake by assuming that God is limited like us. As we will see,
the most reasonable concept of God is quite different from this one.

Without an accurate understanding of God, productive discussion
is difficult. Let's not just assume everyone knows what is meant by the
word *God*. In fact, atheists don't have a clear picture of who God is.
Atheists' concepts of God vary considerably from the truth. They usually envision God as petty, petulant, arbitrary, or worse. If you are a

Christian, you may have noticed that sometimes simply agreeing that we don't believe in that sort of being opens doors—and hearts.

In this chapter we will examine a number of inadequate conceptions of God and then demonstrate that the biblical description of God makes sense.

Popular Concepts

The Human God

A lot of people speak of God as if he were human, no more than an upgraded version of ourselves. People indicate this concept of God when they ask, "How old is God? Is he male or female? What color is his skin?" God is often portrayed as an old man in the sky with a long, flowing robe and a great white beard. He is lonely up there in heaven but can be cheered up if we will take some time to remember him or say a prayer to him—which salves his sadness and insecurity. In the old days, he used to get out more, visit the earth and perform miracles. But these days, as his health declines, he doesn't get out as much. This is the sort of God most of us were led to visualize, perhaps by well-meaning parents, through simplistic Sunday school lessons, or by artists' representations. This is what I call *the human God*.

In school I studied the ancient Greek and Roman gods: They were violent, drunk, lustful, inept, and immoral, playing tricks on mortals and each other. Maybe people would behave that way if we were all-powerful—like the petty dictators of so many failed nation-states—but that doesn't mean God shares our weaknesses. Similarly, the Norse and Celtic gods (ancient northern Europe) were human in their antics. Even today, the gods of Hinduism (India), Buddhism and Taoism (China), and the many African tribal religions have cruel tendencies, sexual desires, and other human weaknesses. Nearly all religions, both past and present, picture God as somehow human, and the impression of God as an old man in the sky is still amazingly common today.

Such a concept of God was made even more popular by Friedrich

Nietzsche. It assumes that God is not the Creator; man created God, and now that he doesn't need God anymore, he has discarded him. Nietzsche is famous for saying, "God is dead." At seminary I once saw this graffito scribbled on a wall:

God is dead.
Nietzsche

Nietzsche is dead.
God

But Nietzsche has been grossly misunderstood, as we discussed in chapter 2. He was not proclaiming that God had expired after a shelf-life limited to prehistoric man and his classical and medieval heirs. Nietzsche meant that *functionally* God was dead, and without him, who is to distinguish between right and wrong, sanity and insanity? No, God did not expire.

Maybe your god is like the ancient Roman gods, or maybe he is more of a gentleman. Perhaps he is absent, absentminded, or even dead. Either way, chances are that the God we heard about from childhood is more human than divine. The concept is inadequate and must be discarded.

I Am God

Many men and women who have been influenced by Eastern religions claim that God is everywhere (which is true) and everything (which is false). All is one. Their God is identical with the universe, and everything in it is God, so they too are God. This view is called *pantheism*. If this is true, then obviously whatever humans think must (somehow) be true because each is God. But what about the countless logical contradictions among the various philosophies and religions on the planet? Furthermore, if we are divine, did we create the universe, and do we dictate natural laws? Does this make any sense to you? Ultimately, this is an impersonal worldview because in the final analysis there is no independent *you;* all is one. Nor is there right or wrong, God or non-God, being or non-being. All such distinctions are false. This view reminds me of an old joke:

> Did you hear about the Hindu who ordered a hot dog?
>
> "Make me one with everything," said the swami, handing a twenty-dollar bill to the vendor.
>
> After waiting for some time, he asked, "What about my change?"
>
> The vendor quipped back, "True change comes from within."

Why the levity? Because, despite their appearance of wisdom, the Eastern religions promote lightweight worldviews. They crumble under examination. Yet they have become not only popular but also widespread through the influence of the New Age movement and its numerous prophets and prophetesses, including James Redfield (*The Celestine Prophecy*), actress Shirley MacLaine, Eckhart Tolle (*A New Earth*), Rhonda Byrne (*The Secret*), and others.[1] To be explicit, Byrne's secret consists of three words: *I am God.*

The Force

Influenced by the popular science-fiction Star Wars films, many people, though unwilling to agree that there is a God, do acknowledge some sort of force in the universe. Star Wars popularized the supreme power known as the Force, an omnipotent, omnipresent, and impersonal spiritual energy source with both a good and a bad (dark) side.

At first, believing in God as the Force may sound more scientifically respectable than believing in an overly human God, but when we really think about it, the Force seems even less likely. And to be honest, the Force wasn't always helpful to the Star Wars characters who tried to harness its power. In the movies, the Force was never proactive; it influenced lives only when tapped into by good or evil men (or creatures). It was not inherently good or evil. In fact, when it came into contact with men, evil desires and actions often ensued. Most of those who sought to know this substitute for God intimately found that it could be a corrupting influence.

Similarly, one of Dan Brown's characters expresses her view: "God is not some omnipotent authority looking down from above, threatening to throw us into a pit of fire if we disobey. God is the energy that flows through the synapses of our nervous system and the chambers of our hearts! God is in all things!"[2] But equating deity with one's life force is no explanation at all, despite its popularity.

Now back to the real world. Forces like electricity, flowing water, magnetism, or gravity are useful if controlled, but they certainly do not create new life forms, increase complexity, or underpin natural laws. Any uncontrolled force of nature—like lightning, a flood, or a tornado—is frighteningly unpredictable and can cause electrocution, drowning, and destruction. Random forces are certainly not the creators of law, order, and personality.

The Force theory explains nothing but instead makes the origin of the world and the explanation of spiritual ideas even more of a mystery. Another derisible idea goes to the scrap heap.

A Nice Warm Feeling

I have heard some people say something like this: "I can't define God, but I feel him. When I feel at peace and happy and have that nice warm feeling in my tummy—that's God." These people confuse their feelings with truth. Yes, we may feel something special when we are convinced there is a God—but we may also feel something special after a delicious dinner. Or perhaps we just have indigestion. Any idea of God that reduces him to a level of a hot meal or a warm shower certainly misses the point. Are people equating their circumstances (immediate reality) with God (ultimate reality)? That sort of notion explains nothing and answers none of the important questions about God and the universe. Another proposal to the rubbish heap of illogical views about deity.

Idolatry

Billions of people in the world worship idols—statues or images of gods that they believe are somehow linked with the gods themselves. Idolatry is widespread, even in traditional Christian circles. One weakness of idolatry is that it breeds a physical conception of God instead of a spiritual understanding. Another is that it encourages mankind to manipulate God. The worshipper presents offerings to the statue or picture, and the god is somehow obligated to answer his prayer. Or perhaps he offers the idol some special food, paper, money, incense, or even a prayer, and he thinks he will be blessed. Instead of God controlling man, man controls God. This is the fundamental error of idolatry. The early Christian leader Paul gave this explanation to the idolatrous residents of Athens:

> The God who made the world and everything in it is the Lord of heaven and earth and does not live in temples built by hands. And he is not served by human hands, as if he needed anything, because he himself gives all men life and breath and everything else (Acts 17:24-25).

Modern Idolatry

Many in the Western world do not worship religious idols, but they make their own idols of countless other things: other people, fine cars, electronic gadgets, money, sex, leisure, education...the list goes on and on. On top of all this, their concept of God is also idolatrous because they try to control him.

In modern society, we may try to control God through becoming more religious during times of trouble. Years ago I was struck by a car and nearly killed—I quickly became "spiritual." I saw life in a more sober light, and I lived accordingly—for a whole two weeks! Another time I nearly drowned in a rip current. Of course, I began to think a lot about God, life, and death. But this too passed. Sometimes we feel a special need for God when we are sick, struggling financially, uncertain about the future, or mourning the death of a friend. We use God as a crutch, and when the trouble has passed, we abandon him. Our mind-set is that he is there whenever we need him. But in the Bible we learn that we are also to be there whenever he wants us. We must abandon modern forms of idolatry if we are to understand God and find a personal relationship with him.

Ask No Questions!

Asking honest questions is almost always helpful. Children are naturally curious, receptive to reason, and open to truth. Unfortunately, they do not always get good answers, especially about religious paradoxes. When I was a young boy, a group of us were making noise in church. We were told, "Hush! This is the house of God." I looked up: The ceiling of the cavernous sanctuary threatened to swallow me up. I glanced around, wondering whether God was home at the moment, but saw nothing—or rather, no one. All I learned that day was the rule of church behavior: no talking and no noise! In my mind, God remained abstract, remote, a blurry conception. Over time, I saw that questions, like noise, were discouraged in church.

Many adults—perhaps because of childhood experiences like mine—exemplify a simplistic, one-dimensional attitude toward religion. They ask no questions, and they are uncomfortable answering other people's questions about their faith. They are happy for others to believe or disbelieve in God, and they don't care whether another's concept of God agrees with theirs. "After all," they reason, "it's all the same God, whatever you call it. What does it really matter?" Theirs is the ultimate flexible God. He is whatever you want him to be. As long as the name *God* is used, everyone is happy, and no one asks any questions. But whether intentional or not, this mind-set is a clear attempt to avoid learning the truth about God.

As a whole, mankind has been unwilling to respond to God in a reasonable way. God created us in his image, but we have re-created God in our image.

A Reasonable Concept

Beyond Space and Time

Attempts to limit God to a particular location or time are bound to fail because God is beyond space and time. Physicists, following the mathematical insights of Einstein and others, know that space and time form a continuum. You do not have to be an Einstein to realize the implications: Anything or anyone outside our universe must be outside time—or at least experience transition in a different way than humans do. God is outside our universe, so he is not limited by time in the same way we are. He has all eternity to listen to the split-second prayer of the pilot of a plane going down in flames. He views our lives from beginning to end, spread out before him like a sheet of paper, and he can easily work all things together to answer our prayers. He is not limited by space, so he can be in all places at the same time and at work in the life of every human being in the world simultaneously. These passages support this perspective:

- "God is spirit" (John 4:24).
- "For in him we live and move and have our being" (Acts 17:28).
- "Before a word is on my tongue you know it completely, O Lord" (Psalm 139:4).
- "Even from eternity I am He; and there is none who can deliver out of My hand; I act and who can reverse it?" (Isaiah 43:13 nasb).

What does this mean?

- God is spiritual, not physical. He is not part of the physical world. Though he is omnipresent and near to every one of us (immanent), he is also utterly beyond the cosmos (transcendent).
- With complete knowledge of the future, he is in some sense timeless.[3]

Flatland, a brilliant and imaginative book written in the late nineteenth century by an Oxford mathematician, describes the adventures of a square (a man in Flatland, a two-dimensional world) as he tries to understand the three-dimensional world and such beings as cubes and spheres. Although the book is a mathematical adventure and is not overtly religious, it yields valuable spiritual applications.

One day, a sphere passes through Flatland. At first the square sees only a point and then a circle, but soon the circle grows larger and larger. This is extremely frustrating to the square because natural laws appear to be being broken. *Nothing* is becoming *something!* Then the circle starts to shrink and eventually vanishes completely. What a mystery!

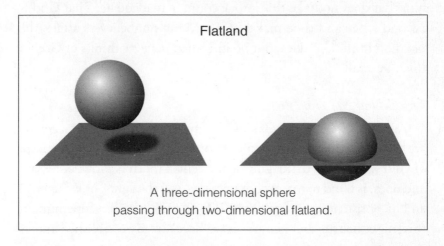

Flatland

A three-dimensional sphere
passing through two-dimensional flatland.

The sphere tries to communicate with the square, to help him to understand his nature. But the square cannot comprehend a three-dimensional circle, only a two-dimensional circle. Only when the bewildered square travels to a three-dimensional world is he even willing to believe that three-dimensional circles might exist. Finally the square believes and returns to Flatland, but he is unable to convince his family and fellow citizens of what he has learned, so they decide he is crazy and have him imprisoned.

God exists in a different dimension from our own, so we have only the faintest inkling of his nature. Understanding him fully would be as difficult for us as it was for the square to comprehend the sphere. We may see various facets or cross sections of him as he acts in the world, and we can certainly see the effects of his activity, but we cannot have complete knowledge of him. Similarly, the Bible teaches that God's ways are far above our ways: "'For my thoughts are not your thoughts, neither are your ways my ways,' declares the LORD. 'As the heavens are higher than the earth, so are my ways higher than your ways and my thoughts than your thoughts'" (Isaiah 55:8-9).

As the Bible teaches and science requires, God is outside our world of space and time. This is one reason why he is God. Any concept of him that does not take this into account is inadequate. That God is beyond space and time makes sense. Many nonbelievers attack the "old man in the sky" idea, but no informed believer thinks of God in this way at all.

Personal but Not Human

As long as we insist on making God human (in our own image), we are bound to project our weaknesses onto God. A humanistic concept of God will lead us to imagine he has selfish motives for what he says and does, is blind to many of our actions and thoughts, or is forgetful and inconsistent in his standards. If God were merely a superhuman, this might be true, but he isn't, as we have already established and as the Scriptures teach:

- "God is not a man, that he should lie" (Numbers 23:19).
- "God is love" (1 John 4:8).
- "[His] eyes are too pure to look on evil; [he] cannot tolerate wrong" (Habakkuk 1:13).

Consider what these verses teach us:

- God is not human, so he has no human weaknesses, such as fatigue, selfishness, subjectivity, lust, and envy.

- God is good; his love is constant. The purpose he has for our lives is good as well, and we should seek to discover it and live by it.

- He is sinless and cannot compromise his character by tolerating evil.

Once again we see that the biblical concept of God is both true and reasonable. We all need to adjust our conception of God to match the biblical description. He loves us, and all our good qualities come from him, but he does not share our weaknesses.

One comment is in order on the personality of God. If God is loving and is in fact love, what is the source of such love? How could God love if he has always existed, even when there was no one else to love? Was God lonely? Is that why he created man? No, for although he created man in order to love him, God was already loving.

Christians believe that the one God is composed of three persons—the Trinity. As you can see from the diagram below, God is Father, Son, and Spirit, but all three are God. This teaching is difficult to understand, but it explains beautifully how love has existed in God eternally.

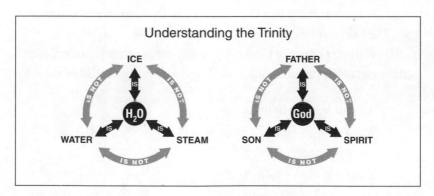

The water analogy introduces the subject, yet it has serious limitations. The Father is not a hardened version of the Son, nor is the Spirit a more ethereal version of either. A better illustration, based in human nature, would be the relation between our mind, our ideas, and our words. These three have obvious unity without complete identity. In this sense, they illustrate the Trinity. The second-century Christian apologist Tertullian suggested these analogies: root, tree, and fruit; sun, sunbeam, and sunlight; and source, river, and current.

No single analogy captures the divine mystery, and different analogies emphasize different aspects and will be helpful to different people. Of course, we cannot capture God in an illustration; his nature will always be somewhat of a mystery. See appendix B for a fuller explanation of the Trinity.

Spiritual, Not Physical

The Bible's teaching that God created man in his own image has been misconstrued.[4] God did not create man in his physical image. (He doesn't even have a physical image.) Rather, God created man in his spiritual image. We love, reflect, have free will and spiritual values, contemplate the universe and eternity... These are part of what it means to be created in God's image.

We may share 98 to 99 percent of the genetic material of chimpanzees and great apes—and occasionally resemble them in our antics—but the gulf between man and the other animals is apparently unbridgeable. They do not bear the image of God.

An accurate picture of God must take into account that he is a spiritual being, not a physical one. Look again at what the Bible says:

- "God is spirit" (John 4:24).
- "Where can I go from your Spirit? Where can I flee from your presence?" (Psalm 139:7).
- "God is light" (1 John 1:5).
- "The heavens, even the highest heaven, cannot contain you. How much less this temple that I have built!" (1 Kings 8:27).

And what do these verses mean?

- God is a spiritual being. This does not mean he is unreal or make-believe but rather that he is nonphysical.

- Because God is spirit, he can exist in all places at all times.

- God brings spiritual light into our hearts and helps us to see spiritually.

- God is not a vapor that can be trapped and forced into a box (remember *Ghostbusters?*).

- As others have said, if God is small enough for us to understand, he isn't big enough for us to worship!

This concept of God makes sense; it's reasonable. It is found nowhere outside of the Bible. It is taught by no other world religion, and yet it squares perfectly with physical and metaphysical reality.

A God We Can Believe In

The God of the Bible is one in whom we can believe, the only one who fills the God-shaped hole in our heart. The ancient psalmists expressed the restless longings of the human heart:

- "As the deer pants for streams of water, so my soul pants for you, O God. My soul thirsts for God, for the living God. When can I go and meet with God?" (42:1-2).

- "From the ends of the earth I call to you, I call as my heart grows faint; lead me to the rock that is higher than I" (61:2).

- "O God, you are my God, earnestly I seek you; my soul thirsts for you, my body longs for you, in a dry and weary land where there is no water" (63:1).

All over the world people are discovering the reason why we were created: to exist in a relationship with God. For example, in 1991, as the Soviet Union was disintegrating, I had the opportunity to speak in Moscow on the subject "Does God Exist?" I was staggered by the keenness the Muscovites showed for the subject, although I suppose such enthusiasm is understandable where religion had been suppressed for the greater part of a century. I have preached in underground churches in mainland China and in other nations where freedom of religion is either restricted or nonexistent, where singing a hymn can lead to arrest and severe penalties.

But is such zeal and fascination only for people deprived of religious choice? What about nations with religious freedom? I have encountered tremendous curiosity about reasons to believe in God's existence in places as far-flung as Australia, Hong Kong, and Brazil. Why would believers be so enthusiastic about a matter they have presumably already settled for themselves? I was taken aback when my friend Moufid invited me to fly to Lebanon to speak on the existence of God. This is a nation where almost everyone is either Muslim or Christian; surely an argument for God's existence was unnecessary. The meeting, held in Beirut, was advertised through radio, television, e-mail, and personal invitations, and the turnout was terrific. Arab television picked up the event.

We easily underestimate the importance of asking (and answering) the question of God's existence, even in societies where faith and freedom of worship are taken for granted. People may be religious, but mere religion does not satisfy. They want to know God. Everyone needs assurance, and the study of apologetics often helps the believer as much as the nonbeliever.

Sleeping, Retired, or Dead?

God is not sleeping, retired, or dead. He is awake, active, and very much alive. But we must have some idea of what we are looking for if we are to recognize him. Unfortunately, many of us have had a distorted view of who God is and have failed to recognize him because of our misconceptions. Fortunately, we can understand much about God, and what we can understand makes sense. His communication to us in the Bible is the subject of part 2. Moreover, his nature is revealed perfectly in the character of Jesus Christ, as we will see in part 3.[5]

The Word of God

❖❖❖ ❖❖❖❖❖❖❖ ❖❖❖❖❖❖❖❖❖❖❖❖❖❖❖❖❖❖❖❖❖❖❖❖❖

In part 1 we discussed some good reasons to believe God exists. Yet many people grant that God may exist but scoff at the idea that he would involve himself with people. They think of him as the silent God, one who never speaks. Many picture God as a heavenly clockmaker who wound up the universe eons ago and left it to run. Now he has lost contact with his creation, and all the claims about his speaking to men and women are merely wishful thinking on our part.

But is this reasonable? If God exists, could he not speak? Yes, of course he could. And if he could speak, would he not communicate to the people he created? Naturally. Indeed, why would God go to all the trouble of creating the world and mankind, only to break off contact?

The insight of Ambrose (AD 340–397) captures the connection between God and Scripture. "As in Paradise, God walks in Scripture, seeking man."

◆◆◆◆◆◆◆◆◆◆◆◆◆◆◆◆◆◆◆◆◆◆◆◆◆◆

The Bible:
Word of Man or Word of God?

◆◆◆◆◆◆◆◆◆◆◆◆◆◆◆◆◆◆◆◆◆◆◆◆◆◆

What is truth?

Pontius Pilate

Does the Almighty deign to speak to his creatures? Some think not. They believe that like an absentee landlord, God cares little for his creation—he set it in motion and then abandoned it in favor of more interesting pursuits. This view is called Deism, the religion of many leading European intellectuals in the 1700s and 1800s as well as most of the founding fathers of the United States.

Others take a more mystical approach. They believe God speaks but not in any objective, verifiable way. What do we say to those who claim that God does speak to us but only through nature or our feelings? It is debatable how much we can learn about God from nature— including human nature. (Not that they do not give us an inkling of his majesty.[1]) Once we accept sunsets, breezes, shivers, and feelings of joy as messages from God, anything goes. Your guess is as good as mine; who is to say what the truth is? We need an objective standard.

If God is real and truth exists, then it makes perfect sense that God himself is the one who tells us what truth is. Believing in the evidence for God leads us to search for what is true—truth from God.

Truth

Truth is a sensitive subject these days, one which can easily offend. This is especially the case in politics, religion, and ethics—all areas that affect us personally. Some topics are less likely to stir the emotions, like mathematics. What is 12 x 12? One man may say 132, another 144, and yet another 122. But should those who said 122 and 132 be offended when we show them their mistakes? Of course not. Or consider the field of chemistry: Doctors and dentists use nitrous oxide (N_2O), or laughing gas, as a mild anesthetic. Nitric oxide (NO), on the other hand, is deadly. Or is it the other way around? The answer to the question definitely matters, and scientists and other users would do well to find a safe way to determine which one is harmless and which one is poison!

Why are some people affronted by others who express their religious views? Just as in mathematics and chemistry, there are right and wrong answers to the basic questions of life: Is there a God? Why do I exist? Does God care about me? What is my purpose in life? Is there life after death?

Many people believe religion is a private thing. They hide behind slogans, such as "Religion is a personal matter," and are in effect unwilling to open their lives to the possibility of faith and truth. They refuse to investigate, scrutinize, and debate. Yet surely we need to be open to truth, learning from whomever we can.

Now, it will hardly do to tell modern men and women, "Don't question the authority of the Holy Bible; just believe." In fact, asking someone not to think, as though faith were antithetical to reason, would not be right. However, some well-intentioned believers open their Bibles to 2 Timothy 3:16, which says, "All Scripture is God-breathed," and urge their friends, "See—the Bible says it's inspired, so it must be true. You should believe it too!"

But this is circular reasoning. True faith does in fact come from understanding the biblical message, but this is no catch-22.[2] Faith results when people understand the message, when it strikes a chord in their heart. It also results when they feel the presence and love of God.

"What is truth?" Pontius Pilate asked (John 18:38). Pilate, the Roman governor who authorized the crucifixion of the Son of God in AD 30, was not alone—the entire world of his day was confused about truth. Our world is also hopelessly confused. Many in our day ask, "What is truth?" Few have an answer.

Subjective or Objective?

Unfortunately, most people base their decisions about truth on their feelings. But feelings are an extremely unreliable means of discerning the truth. They change like the weather. Some days we feel more spiritual, sacrificial, or selfless than others. What does not feel right one day may feel fine the next. Feelings are simply too subjective. We cannot know the truth through feelings (emotions, intuition, conscience, and so forth) alone.

There are many subjective ways to try to understand spiritual reality. They may convince the one having the experience, but they do not normally convince others. Nor are most of these methods sound. For example, interpreting one's own dreams, paying a palm reader, or breathing methodically while praying for insight into the one—such approaches to truth are neither verifiable nor apologetically valid.

We need an objective standard—something that is consistent and based on facts, not on changing human emotions. Three possibilities emerge.

The first is to die. Surely, if there is something beyond the grave, death is one way to find it. But dead people do not generally return to life to tell others about their experience.[3] The second is an empirical epiphany—God's personal disclosure to an individual. One obvious problem is that our minds can play tricks on us and either create an illusion that we interpret as real or rationalize away a real experience that we interpret as an illusion. Besides, God is not at our beck and call, subject to the whims of his creatures. The third possibility is that God himself would take the initiative, revealing his will to us in words. After all, we think in words—or more precisely, in sentences. Propositional revelation would still require mental processing, but the message would not be private, so a community of thinkers could weigh each other's interpretations.

Some Subjective and Objective Pathways to Truth	
Subjective	Objective
coincidences	death
intuition	empirical epiphany
feelings and sensations	written message
astrology and horoscopes	
dreams and trances	
extrasensory perception	
meditation	

God's Message to Man

Once we have come to grips with the fact that God can and in all probability does communicate with mankind, we are ready to consider what sort of message God would provide. We would expect it to meet seven basic criteria.

Intelligible

To begin with, God's message must be capable of being understood, not mysterious, like hieroglyphics, or vague, like a horoscope. (What sort of God would he be if he were unable to express himself clearly?) We think in language, so his message would likely be verbal. Furthermore, it must be intelligible to all mankind, not only to the educated or one particular culture. Imagine if the Scriptures were written like this:

> Eschatologically and soteriologically, all accountable members of species homo sapiens eventually translocate into

metaphysically salvific, or else punitive (if not pyrotechnic), juxtaposition with the immanent presence of the sublime omnipotence of the First Cause and upholding principle of the cosmos.[4]

(Translation: At the end of time, we will be saved or punished— perhaps with fire—when we see God, the Creator and Sustainer of the world.) Such convoluted verbiage would make the Bible inaccessible to most people.

Fortunately, the Bible is intelligible. (By way of contrast, the Qur'an, the holy book of the Muslims, is highly confusing. Even according to Islamic scholars, a good portion of the Qur'an is obscure.) The Bible certainly has its difficult passages, but the overall message is clear, and believers around the world and in every culture understand it.

Another component of intelligibility is brevity. For example, there are millions of units of scientific material on cosmology and the origin of life. Yet this topic of origins is addressed, for the most part, in the first 31 verses of the Bible. Or consider this: Jesus lived for approximately 13,000 days, and he ministered publicly for about 1300 days. Yet the Gospels record only 34 of those days. Throughout the Bible, many significant events are abbreviated or told with an impressive economy of words, such as Joseph's reunion with his brothers, Moses' early years, and even Jesus' baptism and resurrection. The Bible packs an amazing amount of information into relatively few pages.

Biblical Christianity fits all its teaching within the pages of the Bible. In life, we trust a concise speaker more readily than a rambling one. We will listen to people who make their point without confusing us, trying to impress us, or clouding the issues.

Consistent

Second, we would expect a message from heaven to be consistent. The message from God should not be confused, nor should it contradict the facts of history and geography, because the biblical story takes place in time and space. It must pass the test of congruence (and the Bible passes beautifully). Numerous persons in the Bible are confirmed in extrabiblical sources. The Bible mentions a number of kings and queens, and archaeologists have recovered likenesses of many of these individuals, confirming their historical existence. The existence of 80 persons named in the Bible has been confirmed by extrabiblical sources, and likenesses of nearly 20 have survived.

Nearly 30 people named in the New Testament are known from other records. Further, Luke, the author of Luke and Acts (a quarter of the New Testament) was an exact and careful writer.[5] He has a concern for history and uses the correct terminology for a number of political figures. His geographical accuracy is equally amazing. He mentions 32 countries, 54 cities, and 9 islands—a total of 95 place names. He commits no errors. These are all real persons, real places. The characteristic vagueness of legend and fairy tale is wholly absent. ("Once upon a time, in a land far away, lived a very good king...")

Moreover, archaeologists have unearthed hundreds of artifacts that illuminate biblical life and times, a number of which have refuted skeptical critics. These finds confirm or illustrate both the Old Testament and the New Testament.[6] I have personally seen abundant evidence in situ in various excavations in Israel, Lebanon, Jordan, Turkey, Greece, Egypt, and Italy, and I have seen artifacts relocated to European and North American cities. On the other hand, hoaxes abound (like the "missing day" of Joshua), and when believers uncritically accept them as factual, skeptics cannot help but smile.[7]

Another aspect of consistency is internal coherence. The Bible has scores of authors from many national, ethnic, and linguistic backgrounds, all writing over the period of many centuries. Remarkably, one consistent picture of God and mankind emerges, a single storyline, and a comprehensible and reasonable view of the meaning of history. Though there is development of thought within the Scriptures, there are no fundamental contradictions. (See appendix C for information regarding the alleged contradictions.)

Some of the Bible Writers	
king's aide (Nehemiah)	priest (Ezra)
fisherman (Peter)	prime minister (Daniel)
general (Joshua)	prophets (Amos)
king (Solomon)	rabbi (Paul)
musician (Asaph)	shepherd (Amos)
physician (Luke)	tax collector (Matthew)
political leader (Moses)	

One additional mark of consistency would be this: A message from God would not change with time. When we read a passage from the Scriptures, we should ask, "What was the intent of the biblical writer?" A fundamental axiom of interpretation is that a passage cannot mean (now) what it never meant (when it was originally written). The number of applications may increase, but not the underlying principle.[8]

Uncorrupted

A message would benefit us today only if it was transmitted accurately through the centuries. If it was corrupted in the copying process, its initial accuracy or truth content would be a moot point. As we will see in the next two chapters, no ancient document comes close to the remarkable accuracy of the textual transmission of the Bible.

Authoritative

The fourth criterion is that the message must be authoritative. The Bible presents itself over and over as the ultimate message from God to every nation of the world. Writers and speakers in the Bible do not apologize for their bold statements of truth. They expect their readers and hearers to accept the message and change their lives accordingly. Such statements as "Thus says the Lord" are important for imparting security and confidence. Like a reliable map, the Scriptures direct us through life. Imagine if the Bible were written like this:

- "Excuse me, could you please possibly change a little if it's not inconvenient?" (Luke 29:5).

- "For me it feels as though this is true, but maybe it isn't for you. Anyway, I think God could be saying something to me" (2 Corinthians 22:4).

- "I just feel we should all try to be nicer people" (1 Peter 6:1).

Actually, none of these passages is in the Bible. God does not offer tentative suggestions; he speaks to us definitively. If these concocted sayings sound familiar, perhaps they remind us of the way many religious people tend to speak. (If you want to get a feel for how the Scriptures really read, take a look at Luke 13. Jesus was hardly in the business of coaxing people to do what is right.)

The Bible repeatedly and unapologetically identifies itself as the Word of God.

Honest

We would expect spokesmen for God to identify themselves authoritatively, but we would also expect to see some signs of their humanity. That is, the lives of the principal men and women in Scriptures ought not to be whitewashed. This is exactly what we see in the Bible. Abraham and Sarah lie, David commits adultery, Esther hesitates, and the apostles are fearful.

If the Bible were the word of man, prophets would be portrayed as perfect—as the Muslims have done in the Qur'an. The Bible does not dress up its characters; they are routinely presented "warts and all." This enhances the credibility of the biblical documents. Only one man is presented as sinless, and he is also the one who was most scrutinized by his enemies' watchful eyes. Though they accused him of being in league with the devil and cast ethnic and other slurs on him, they could not convict him of any moral blemish.[9]

Supernatural

A message from above would be expected to show some signs of its supernatural origin. There are many astonishing facts about the Bible. As already mentioned, the unity of its message, though mediated by at least 60 different authors, is stunning. The Bible has been translated into thousands of languages. It is the world's bestseller and was the first religious book sent into outer space. But none of these facts is inherently supernatural.

What do we mean by *supernatural*? The natural world is the province of science and includes all empirically observable or verifiable phenomena. The supernatural world is the world of the spirit and the proper province of theology and philosophy. Neither is more real than the other.

As evidence of the supernatural, consider the fulfilled prophecies. Some accurately predict the rise and fall of nations; others announce the coming of the Messiah (the Christ, or anointed one). For example, Micah 5, Isaiah 53, and other passages foretell the birth or saving death of Jesus in remarkable detail—hundreds of years before the events! Or consider the miracles. A message from heaven would naturally contain some element of the miraculous.

Some skeptics say, in so many words, "Well, if the Bible didn't have all those miracles, and if Jesus wasn't born of a virgin and didn't rise from the dead, maybe I would believe it." To which we might reply, "Then what sort of a book would it be?" One thing is sure: It would not be the Bible. In other words, if Jesus is God incarnate, the *lack* of the miraculous would give us cause for suspicion! We will focus more closely on the miracles and resurrection of Jesus Christ in chapters 9 and 10.

The Bible accurately describes two levels or stories of reality. Our existence includes both natural and supernatural elements—an "upstairs" (spiritual reality) and a "downstairs" (empirical reality). When we first moved into our home in the Atlanta area, we had trouble sleeping. We heard noises in the ceiling and in the walls. We could not easily prove this to our friends because the scrabbling sounds were audible only in the middle of the night. Sitting downstairs discussing the problem revealed no answers. Perhaps we had a poltergeist, or a fugitive from the law was hiding in the space above our bedroom. What was going on? After actually going upstairs to explore the attic, the problem became clear: Flying squirrels had taken up residence. Closing the construction gap in the roof solved the problem.

The Bible opens up both stories for us, spiritually speaking. To maintain that the upstairs is empty and not worth exploring is not only unimaginative; such a stance runs counter to the facts. Moreover, in the Bible, neither "story" of reality is minimized to the detriment of the other.

Undeniably, the Bible has the marks of a supernatural book.

Practical

Surely a message from heaven would contain valuable and practical information. The Bible more than fulfills this qualification. Indeed, it enables us to live gracious, productive lives in this world and prepare for the next as we enjoy a dynamic relationship with God.

The Bible equips us in multiple areas: dealing with anxiety, stress, and pressure; building healthy family relationships and strong marriages; growing in confidence and security; counseling others through the challenging situations of life; making and keeping friendships; protecting our health; maintaining personal integrity and living morally; managing money; exercising personal discipline and working for social justice; and finding a meaningful, rewarding life.

No wonder the Bible has often been compared to an owner's manual. Yes, it does work! Throughout history, millions of men and women the world over have been living proof of the fact.

This is what Christians mean when they speak of the Bible as the Word of God. It is God's message to us. No other religious writings in the world even come close to substantiating such a claim or meeting the seven criteria we have discussed. One popular acronym for *Bible* is Basic Instructions Before Leaving Earth. (With this in view, the entire second section of this book has been devoted to demonstrating the uniqueness of the Bible.)

This claim, if true, has serious and far-reaching consequences. Have you read the Bible or only glanced through parts of it? Have you seriously examined it? If God has spoken to man, it would be a tragedy not to hear his voice.

The Answer

Back to Pilate's question: "What is truth?" To answer his question—and it *can* be answered, as we have seen—we must do two essential things: start reading God's Word, the Bible, and be willing to obey it. Jesus said, in his prayer to God on the night before his execution, "Your word is truth."[10] Jesus knew that we must turn to God to find the truth and that the truth is the Word of God. This is why we must read the Bible.

He also said, "If you hold to my teaching, you are really my disciples. Then you will know the truth, and the truth will set you free."[11] Jesus is saying that we cannot truly understand the truth unless we are willing to follow the truth wherever it leads. And again, "If anyone chooses to do God's will, he will find out whether my teaching comes from God."[12] This is why we must be willing to do God's will. If we are unwilling, then even when we stare the truth in the face, we will be unable to recognize it. As G.K. Chesterton perceptively noted, "The Christian ideal has not been tried and found wanting; it has been found difficult and left untried."

We have seen that it is completely reasonable that there is a God and that he speaks. He speaks to us not in a subjective way (through our feelings or opinions) but in an objective way. Christians recognize that this objective communication from God to man is found in the Bible, a book unique among all religious writings. But the Bible is not a "good book." It is the Word of God. There is a world of difference between the two. As the apostle Paul wrote to the Thessalonians, "We also thank God continually because, when you received the word of God, which you heard from us, you accepted it not as the word of men, but as it actually is, the word of God, which is at work in you who believe."[13]

Dialog with a Critic: How Honest Discussion Facilitates Faith

If Christianity is untrue, then no honest man will want to believe it, however helpful it might be: if it is true, every honest man will want to believe it, even if it gives him no help at all.

C.S. LEWIS (1898–1963)

As WE HAVE ESTABLISHED, the Bible fits the criteria for a message from God (intelligible, consistent, uncorrupted, authoritative, honest, supernatural, and practical). Despite this fact, critics often confidently assert that the Bible is not the Word of God, but only the word of man. It has been accused of mistranslation, sloppy transmission, and outright manipulation. Critics deny that we have any reason to trust the Bible, that what Jesus and other biblical characters originally said and meant has long been lost to history. For example, self-styled "Christian atheist" Robert Price, whom I debated at Houston Baptist University in 2009, said, "There might have been an historical Jesus, but unless someone discovers his diary or his skeleton, we'll never know."[1]

Of course, criticism is not bad. Exercising our critical faculties—using the brain the Lord gave us—is a positive thing. Moreover, if Christianity is really true, it should be able to stand the test of criticism. Nor should Christians be hypersensitive when challenged.[2] After all, if our assertions are not true, they are outrageous. But if they are true, the startling claims of the Bible deserve careful scrutiny.

The evidence points to the Bible being the Word of God, faithfully preserved through the millennia, as we will see in this chapter and the next. To frame some of the more popular objections, let's listen in on my dialogue with an imaginary skeptic, Mr. Hans Kritic.

❧❧❧❧❧

HK: Jacoby, my friend, I find it interesting that one as educated as you would believe the Bible is the Word of God, when it is probably just another work of men. Are you so out of touch? It has some very good things in it, as I recall, but I can't imagine myself as a Bible believer. Most likely what Jesus originally said is irrecoverable anyway.

DJ: Mr. Kritic, if you will just give me a few minutes of your time, I would like to show you why I believe the Bible is the Word of God. There are also good reasons we can trust that it has been accurately preserved over the last 2000 years.

HK: I'm up for a good discussion. But I warn you, I think of religion as a crutch. It gives people comfort. The world is a rough place, and people are looking for meaning. You are no exception.

DJ: So you're the realist, and we believers are living in a fantasy? You say that faith provides comfort in the face of the meaninglessness in the world. I imagine you think that when I pray, I am only calling out into the void—that no one is there. My beliefs are a projection of my own desires, as Feuerbach and Freud taught.

HK: Yes, something like that.

DJ: Well, the psychological explanation of religion may be an old one, but it is far from conclusive. What if I said that *your* worldview, including your lack of faith, gives you comfort for rejecting God, and that's why you believe what you do? What would you say to that?

HK: Interesting, the way you turn it around on me. But even if you were right, surely there would be a sociological explanation. You Christians have been indoctrinated, growing up in a Western culture.

DJ: I would say that you yourself have been indoctrinated—in secular humanism. Atheists and agnostics have been desensitized to spiritual things, and their lack of faith is reinforced through fellow nonbelievers in the circles in which they tend to move.[3]

HK: Look, I know you were born in the South. Everyone believes in the Bible down there. So how do you know your faith isn't just environmental? Besides, you were raised in a Christian nation—that's why you accept Christianity.

DJ: Well, the United States is hardly a Christian nation. And to tell the truth, I was the first practicing Christian in my family. When I was growing up, no one I knew read the Bible, though there were six copies on the living room bookshelf, some going back to the 1800s. But you are committing the genetic fallacy. Attributing the genesis of someone's beliefs to ambient culture or social conditioning ignores the truth content of those beliefs. Their truth or falsity is independent of their origin. A Jordanian is more likely to believe in God than someone from Japan, but being able to predict a person's religion is not the same as verifying or falsifying the religion itself.

HK: I see. That's a good point.

DJ: If you dismiss my faith because I am born in the United States, then by the same token I could dismiss your worldview because you were brought up in a secular society and a non-Christian family. Anyway, that's what I mean by the genetic fallacy. But you're right: Many folks casually refer to the Bible as the Good Book. The cliché doesn't mean the Bible is their favorite book to read or that they mean to put it into practice. They may respect the conviction of those who do, but instead of genuine openness to the Word, they offer a compliment. It's like those who talk about the good Lord. They are the ones who seldom pray to him.

HK: I agree. I have met many Christian people who are full of bluster. But I don't believe them for a moment.

DJ: Okay, Hans. But why don't we try to focus on *what* is right instead of *who* is right. The world may be full of hypocrites, but that doesn't change what is really true. Either the Bible is God's book to man or it is not. If it isn't, it should be exposed as a fraud because its writers claimed to speak for God. But if it is God's Word, the weak tribute to it as good literature or the Good Book simply will not do. If the Bible is God's message, it isn't just a good book, but in one sense the only (completely) good book!

HK: But, Jacoby, loyal fellow that you are, you must admit that there is so much confusion about the Bible.

DJ: Yes, and much of it is caused by persons with strong opinions about the Scriptures, who in most cases have read little of it! I've heard it said that the three most referred-to books in history are Marx's *Das Kapital,* Darwin's *The Origin of Species,* and the Bible—and that these are also the three least-read books in history. Maybe that's an exaggeration, but you get the point.

HK: No, I think you are near the mark on that one.

DJ: Another thing: I am of the opinion that critics with certain impressive credentials cause a great deal of misunderstanding and are given way too much credence by a public that is increasingly unfamiliar with the basic facts of Christianity, not to mention history. Some of the clergy publicly deny one of the central Christian teachings—that Jesus rose from the dead. Many people are responsible for the confusion today about God's Word. Yet there is a group of people who I believe do even more harm. They are those who say, "I believe in the Bible."

HK: I wouldn't have expected that from you, Jacoby. What on earth do you mean?

DJ: Of course, I'm not saying that we shouldn't believe in God's Word. But these days many who say, "I believe in the Bible" are confused. You ask them, "Do you accept what Jesus said about sex before marriage?" And they say, "Well, not that part. The Bible was written so long ago, and this is the twenty-first century." Or you ask them about church, and they say, "I just don't have time for all that. I have such a busy life." But if you reply, "Then you mean that you *don't* believe in the Bible?" they say, "No, I *do*—I believe in most all of it, except..." And I add, "Except the parts you find inconvenient?" So many people cite the Bible when they think it justifies their position, or when it makes them feel good. But they have rejected the biblical message as a whole. Their inconsistency belies their faith. Does such a person *really* believe in the Bible? No, he believes in himself, and the Bible happens to support his opinions now and again. But whenever God's Word conflicts with his opinion, he stops believing in the Bible. So who's the real authority: himself or God?

HK: Point taken. But Jacoby, the original documents in the Bible were written several thousand years ago. How can we be certain that modern Bibles are reliable copies of the original books?

DJ: I agree, Hans, that this question is extremely important because significant changes to the Bible manuscripts over the years would have caused God's message to be lost or distorted. How could God entrust such a vital task to humans, especially in the days before photocopiers? Perhaps you have played the telephone game. A message is whispered into the ear of the first person, who turns and whispers it to the next, and so on around the room. The end result can be surprisingly different from the original message. It may be much longer, and nearly always the content of the message is drastically altered. Many people think of the modern Bible in the same way. They view their English version as a translation of another language translated from another language from yet another language...which may very well have been miscopied from the original manuscripts. This notion is extremely widespread and equally misleading. In fact, our modern English versions are translated from the copies of the Hebrew, Aramaic, and Greek texts.

HK: But Jacoby, you surely know that all of the manuscripts of the Bible are not identical. Have you ever noticed those little notes at the bottom of the pages in your own Bible?

DJ: That's right, Hans, there are differences in the manuscripts. There are nearly 1200 chapters in the Bible, and although copyists took pains to avoid slips of the pen, there are still thousands of variants. Nearly all are spelling mistakes, minor differences in word order (such as *Christ Jesus* instead of *Jesus Christ*), or instances of a copyist missing a word or line (like "Jesus sat down began to teach"). When a manuscript has a variant, it is compared to other older manuscripts, and a decision is made about which reading is original. In more than 98 percent of these cases, agreement among scholars is total.[4] When it isn't, these trivial variants are indicated in the footnotes, as you pointed out.

HK: That sounds good, but wouldn't a single mistake contaminate the entire manuscript pool?

DJ: That's not the way it works. Soon after the originals were written, multiple copies were produced. Demand increased as more and more Christian communities wanted the Gospels, letters, and so on. Many of these copies were in turn duplicated, which led to what textual critics call *families* of manuscripts. Copying errors were confined to its descendants unless corrected by one of the scribes. The point is that idiosyncrasies are easily detected. To change the analogy, the wiring was in parallel, not series. A minor failure in one place did not break the circuit; the message still got through.

HK: So you admit the originals have been lost?

DJ: Well, not in the sense that someone misplaced them. But because of the high regard the early church had for the scrolls and parchments, they studied them incessantly, and in time they wore out. Besides, parchment and papyrus have a limited lifetime, especially in humid locations. It's amazing that so many copies have survived. Do you have a Bible in your home?

HK: Yes. It's an heirloom from my maternal grandmother. It hasn't been opened in years.

DJ: Well, that explains why it hasn't worn out. What I mean is, it might sound more respectful to handle a Bible with care, opening it only rarely, but I actually think this might show disrespect to God. If this is his message to us, we ought to be diligently studying it.

HK: I see.

DJ: Another thing occurs to me. The originals of nearly every work from ancient history have been lost. But copies were made, for the most part by careful copyists. Whenever there's a difference between one copy and another, historians do their best to reconstruct the original version accurately. I'd like to show you a chart, Hans. As you can see, ancient manuscripts usually don't survive; the oldest extant copies tend to be much later than the original.

Transmission of Various Ancient Manuscripts				
Author	Date	Oldest Copy	Interval	Copies
Aristophanes	400 BC	AD 900	1300 years	45
Aristotle	340 BC	AD 1100	1440 years	5
Demosthenes	300 BC	AD 1100	1400 years	200
Julius Caesar	50 BC	AD 900	950 years	10
Herodotus	435 BC	AD 900	1335 years	8
Homer	800 BC	AD 100	900 years	643
Plato	360 BC	AD 800	1160 years	15
Sophocles	415 BC	AD 1000	1415 years	7
Thucydides	410 BC	AD 900	1310 years	8

HK: I recognize these writers. The oldest surviving copies really are a lot later than the originals. But what if small errors crept in during the transmission process? Even if the error rate were small, over so many centuries it would really add up.

DJ: Manuscripts of the Old Testament survive from well before the time of Christ. And New Testament manuscripts have survived from as early as the second and third centuries AD.

HK: So the earlier manuscripts are weighted more heavily than the later ones.

DJ: That's right. There is a whole science called textual criticism. I can tell you more about it if you like.

HK: No, that's okay. You seem to have more answers than I have questions. But there is one more thing that's bugging me. Herodotus and Thucydides made some mistakes. What if the biblical writers committed some errors?

DJ: Well, other ancient writers are generally trusted, despite occasional slip-ups. No one says, "If Caesar named the wrong river, then everything he says must be discarded." Although I trust the Bible, it would not necessarily have to be accurate in every detail in order for the basic message to be true. Rather than getting bogged down in the minutiae, I think it is more productive to strive for the big picture. Not all details are equally important. As your understanding of the Bible grows, you'll be able to sort out any difficulties.

HK: That sounds reasonable. I noticed that your chart didn't include biblical manuscripts. Do you have data on the biblical manuscripts?

DJ: Sure. Overall the New Testament is supported by more manuscripts than the Old Testament, but both are extremely well attested. But let's begin with the Old. The record indicates that the Hebrew copyists were meticulous, showing special reverence toward the text. The Dead Sea Scrolls were discovered in 1947 and confirm the excellent transmission of the Old Testament. They predate Jesus and are more than a thousand years earlier than the medieval manuscripts from which our English Old Testaments were translated.

[More on this in chapter 7.] The New Testament was written in the five decades from AD 45 to 95, though the earliest papyrus fragment dates from AD 120. Manuscripts of entire books of the New Testament date from before AD 200, and the oldest copy of the complete New Testament dates from AD 325—a gap of only 250 years—compared with gaps of four or five times as long (1000 years or so) for most works by classical authors. The gap for most Old Testament books, by way of comparison, is as little as 200 to 400 years. The Greek New Testament is preserved in more than 5000 copies alone, though if we include ancient copies in other languages (especially Latin), there are more than 25,000 complete and partial manuscripts! In addition, there are tens of thousands of quotations found in the writings of ancient early Christian writers, most of which date earlier than the oldest surviving New Testament manuscripts. So even if all manuscript copies were lost, it would not be difficult to reconstruct most of the New Testament from these references. It's as though the Christian message were written in indelible ink. Putting together all the evidence, the Bible is by far the best-attested book from ancient times. No other classical work even comes close.

HK: Impressive!

DJ: The facts are impressive indeed. As we have seen, there is no reason to doubt the reliability of the biblical text as it has been passed down. So, Hans, would you agree that if he chose to an infinitely powerful God could communicate his Word to people?

HK: I'll admit the whole idea still sounds rather strange to me, but I suppose I would have to agree that an infinitely powerful God could do whatever he chose to do.

DJ: Exactly, and there is no reason on earth why he couldn't elect to give us his Word in a book.

HK: But, Jacoby, you Christians aren't the only ones who have scriptures. There are many other religions in the world that have their own and are just as devoted to them.

DJ: Hans, in many religions, the scriptures are seldom read by anyone but experts. On top of this, there are some vast differences between the Bible and the scriptures of other world religions. They don't even worship the same God, and the ultimate goals of the various faiths are radically different. For example, in Christianity the goal is knowing God (now and in eternity); in Islam, being rewarded by God in a paradise of wine, women, and song; in Hinduism, absorption into the One and loss of personal identity; in Rastafarianism, a paradise where blacks are served by whites; in Buddhism, loss of desire, once we realize that there is no God and no self; in other religions, discovering that you were God all along!

HK: I guess those are pretty big differences.

DJ: There is something else you might find interesting. Siddhartha Gautama (the Buddha) taught about five centuries before Christ, yet the Buddhist scriptures were not written down until around the time of the New Testament. A few years ago I was in Nara, the old capital of Japan. I saw what I believe are the oldest surviving Buddhist texts. They are from the eighth century AD! Similarly, the Vedas of Hinduism, dating back to 1500–1200 BC, were not written down until about 500 BC, yet the earliest extant manuscript dates to about AD 1300. Of course, Islam is a much more modern religion. The oldest Qur'an—there is no single, official Arabic version—dates to the eighth century. But Muhammad died in 632. Given the gaps between the

original texts and the oldest surviving copies, the degree
of distortion is potentially quite great in the other faiths
of the world. [See chapter 11 for more on world religions
as possible alternative paths to God.]

HK: But there are so many cultures. Do you really think the
Christian message would be of interest to everyone in the
world? Can the Bible be *that* relevant?

DJ: It not only *would* be of interest; it *is*. Many Albanians
were fascinated by the film *The Da Vinci Code* and wanted
to know what the Bible had to say. I flew to Tirana and
engaged the many believers, seekers, and Muslims in the
crowd, and my presentation even led to a television interview. In the West African nation of Sierra Leone, I was
asked to lecture on the Holy Spirit. Nearly all the audience
members were Muslims and former Muslims, and they
took a tremendous interest in the topic. In Thailand I have
spoken to people with a Buddhist background; in Canada,
to men and women from a more secular background; in
Brazil, to audiences immersed in their own versions of
Catholicism and animism. I can personally attest that in
mainland China the interest in real Christianity is huge,
even though much of it is underground. The Czech Republic has many highly educated seekers, eager to understand
how faith and knowledge fit together. The diverse popula-
tion of Malaysia (I lived there for a short time in the early
1980s) is also interested in biblical Christianity. Last year I
flew to Iceland to give a lecture titled "Why We Can Trust
the Bible." There were only six hours of sunlight that day,
but the light of the gospel attracted many. The small group
of Christians who hosted the event were greatly encouraged when they were completely outnumbered by guests
who poured into the meeting, drawn by newspaper ads,
posters, and especially by personal invitations. These are

just a few of the global locations where I have spoken. I have witnessed keen interest in the Bible that transcends cultural, economic, and language barriers. The message is undeniably appealing and relevant the world over.

HK: When you say "relevant," you sound like you really think people need this message.

DJ: Yes, I do. If you read with an open mind, the Scriptures will come to life. But it's not just about information. It's about transformation. I'd like to introduce you to friends of mine who have taken the Bible's message seriously so you can see the impact it has had on their lives. Their energy, drive, virtue, generosity, joy, faith, and stamina during hard times flow from their faith. Their marriages and families are noticeably above par. Something has happened in their lives, and it could happen in yours too, Hans. I appreciate your questions, but why not begin seriously reading the Bible today with a willingness to change anything you need to in order to find not just the Word of God, but God himself?

HK: Jacoby, I must admit that you have caused me to rethink some things. What time did you say that Bible study group meets at your house?

So Loved and Yet So Hated

Not all persons are as reasonable as our Hans. Armchair criticism prevails over sincere seeking. But why? Why is the Bible loved by so few and scorned (or worse, ignored) by so many? The reason must have to do with the fact that no other book is so challenging to the hearts of men and women:

This is the verdict: Light has come into the world, but men loved darkness instead of light because their deeds were evil.

> Everyone who does evil hates the light, and will not come into the light for fear that his deeds will be exposed. But whoever lives by the truth comes into the light, so that it may be seen plainly that what he has done has been done through God (John 3:19-21).

Those who accept the challenge stand in awe of God's Word because of the astounding way it touches every aspect of their lives. That is because the Bible, which stands head and shoulders above all writings ever penned by man, is from God.

In the next chapter we will see just how carefully the biblical manuscripts were preserved through the millennia.

7

Before Xerox:
Confidence in the Biblical Manuscripts

Gold?

Muhammad ed-Dib
Qumran Cave 1

Harvard Yard was covered with snow on an icy February evening. I made my way to the Science Center, the venue for my PowerPoint lecture on the reliability of the Bible. My angle was the careful copying of the ancient manuscripts, including the Dead Sea Scrolls. Everyone has heard of the scrolls, but not many can tell the story. As it turns out, they constitute convincing evidence for the accuracy of the Scriptures.

Nearly 30 years earlier, when I was a graduate student at Harvard Divinity School, just a short walk from the Science Center, I was part of a group Bible study. We considered ourselves fortunate if a dozen students attended on an evening. But this cold night in 2009 was different: 450 students and professors, including 200 guests from nearby universities, attended the lecture.

How 30 years can change things! As a poor graduate student in

1981, I had pushed a vacuum cleaner in the same Science Center, and now in 2009 I was returning to that same building to speak to an intelligent and motivated audience. For me, the 2009 visit closed a loop; it made the years I'd spent there all seem worth it. Moreover, the follow-up reports I received indicated that a number of people in the audience came to faith that night.

How could the facts about such a dry topic as ancient biblical manuscripts possibly help young men and women come to faith? This somewhat technical chapter establishes the confidence we should have in the historical transmission of the biblical manuscripts. As we will see, the case for the reliable transmission of the Bible is solid.

The Manuscript Record

Greek, Anyone?

What were your favorite subjects in school? I have always loved languages, both modern and ancient. The Old Testament was originally written in Hebrew, with a few chapters in Aramaic. This interesting language, revived in the modern state of Israel, is written right to left. Although I studied two years of Hebrew in my master's program and still have a working knowledge of it, I haven't really mastered it. My expertise lies rather in Latin and Greek.

The New Testament was originally written in Greek. The concise, somewhat lyrical Greek language is a joy to study.[1] So imagine my excitement when, in 1995, I had the chance to see the oldest New Testament manuscript in the world.

Many of the ancient New Testament manuscripts were written on papyrus, which was one of many available writing materials. There are nearly a hundred surviving New Testament papyri. One of them is p[1], a manuscript of Matthew 1, stored in the archives of the University of Pennsylvania. The letter p means "papyrus," and the number 1 indicates the number of the manuscript. The manuscript dates from about AD 200 and includes much of Matthew 1. Not surprisingly, p[1] is available for inspection by special appointment only. My colleagues and I have guided many groups of people deep into the protective bowels of the museum of the University of Pennsylvania to see this unique document. Many of these people had never seen an ancient manuscript of any kind. The university Egyptologist (our escort) speaks first, and then we explain the biblical import. A profound sense of awe lingers over our students even after we reemerge into the daylight.

Another papyrus find from Egypt, 80 years older than p¹, resides in the John Rylands Library of the University of Manchester in England. This manuscript, known as p⁵², is recognized by nearly all New Testament scholars and paleographers (experts in ancient handwriting) to be the oldest surviving New Testament document and the closest to an original. It contains part of John 18. Most believe John was written somewhere around AD 90 or 95, so p⁵², which dates to about 120, is only one generation younger than the original! In 1995, my friend Malcolm Cox made an appointment for us to see the papyrus, and the two of us eagerly ascended the stone steps into the library.

I had one of my Greek New Testaments in hand and two things on my mind. First, I wanted to make sure this was the genuine article. I imagined the curator handing me the ancient text, spinning some yarn, and then laughing as he confessed that the fragment was really a medieval comedy excerpt. (He turned out to be far too serious a person to jest.) I carefully compared p⁵² with the corresponding section in my Greek New Testament of John's Gospel. It was a perfect match.

Second, I wanted to be careful. This priceless fragment lay between two panes of glass inside a frame. Carelessness on my part would have made tomorrow's headlines in every English newspaper in the world: "Oldest Biblical Manuscript Destroyed by Bumbling American"! I was permitted to hold p⁵² in my hands, turning it around and examining it closely. Malcolm and I took our time; we realized the amazing historical significance of this papyrus.

I was elated. I had seen the celebrated John Rylands fragment with my own eyes! With abundant evidence like p⁵² in the world's museums and libraries, protests that the Bible has been changed over time just don't make sense.

The Record

These two papyri, p^1 and p^{52}, are by no means the only ancient manuscripts of the New Testament that have survived from antiquity. We have more than 5000 Greek manuscripts as well as 20,000 more in other languages, such as Syriac, Ethiopic, Georgian, Armenian, Slavonic, and Arabic. About half are in Latin.

One of the more interesting manuscripts, housed in Uppsala, Sweden, is the Codex Argenteus, or the Silver Codex. The original letters were written in silver and gold paint on vellum (calfskin), but they have long since oxidized to black. I had the chance to see this amazing manuscript first in 1980 on a visit to Uppsala to trace my ancestors and again about ten years later, when Stockholm was our home.

This marvelous Gothic manuscript dates to the fifth century and is the principal source for our knowledge of the ancient Gothic tongue. (Gothic was the language of the warlike Goths, the famed barbarians who sacked Rome.) Curiously, the translator deliberately omitted 1 and 2 Kings from his Bible because he was afraid these books would encourage bloodshed!

The wealth of manuscript evidence compares extremely favorably with the preservation of ancient writings in general. Take the works of Plato, for example. No more than 15 copies of any single work of Plato have survived, not to mention the fact that the gap between the time he wrote (about 360 BC) and the date of the surviving copies is much more than 1000 years. The most copied ancient work is Homer's *Iliad*, which bears some 600 copies. Once again, the gap between the time the copies were made and the date of Homer is enormous. In the case of the Bible, the gap is not many centuries, but just a few short generations—and many more manuscripts exist.

Two very important codices (a codex is a manuscript in book form) are Codex Sinaiticus (‭א‬) and Codex Alexandrinus (A), which are housed in special facilities in London. Sinaiticus dates from around AD 325 and is the oldest complete New Testament in the original Greek.[2] When I have conducted manuscript tours of the British Library in London, Sinaiticus has always been my favorite stop along the way.

In the Neighborhood?

Biblical manuscripts—ancient witnesses to the integrity of the Bible— may be found all over the world. For example, in Washington DC lies Codex W, housed in the Freer Gallery of the Smithsonian. It is a fourth-century copy of the four Gospels. (Interestingly, Mark comes before Matthew—but that's another story.) It is kept behind three security doors, and visitors may see it only by appointment (or by knowing the curator). But there it is: proof positive that the Bible has been transmitted faithfully. The only changes worth mentioning are minor: spelling variations, the occasional slip of the pen, writing *Christ Jesus* instead of *Jesus Christ,* and so forth—nothing that affects a single biblical doctrine.

Besides a few ancient Hebrew copies of the Bible, I have been privileged to see numerous ancient Greek New Testament manuscripts, including these:

- p[64] at Magdalen College, Oxford, dated to the early 100s.

- p[26] at Southern Methodist University, Dallas, dating to the 500s.

- Codex Purpureus (the Purple Codex) at the Isle of Patmos, also dating to the 500s. Some of the leaves of this codex are in St. Petersburg, Russia.

- p[46] and many more manuscripts at the University of Michigan, Ann Arbor, which houses the largest collection of papyri in the Western Hemisphere. (The Chester Beatty collection in Dublin houses complementary manuscripts.) This collection includes the oldest surviving copies of Paul's letters, from about AD 200.[3]

- X, or Codex Monacensis, at the Munich University Library. (X is the Greek letter *chi*.)

This last manuscript, Codex X, dates to the ninth or tenth century, so it is a little later than the others. It contains the Gospels only, in the order Matthew, John, Luke, Mark. But I spent more time with it than with most manuscripts and was even allowed to handle it without gloves. For the sake of comparison, my explorations in the Rare Book, Manuscript, and Special Collections Library of Duke University were permitted only under supervision in climate-controlled rooms while wearing white gloves.[4] So to leaf through Codex X was an unexpected privilege. And according to the ledger, I was only the fifth person to inspect the codex in nearly 40 years! Even better, the curator clearly shared my enthusiasm (though he did not read Greek).

Would you like to see some of this evidence? Do you live in the neighborhood of an ancient biblical manuscript? Here is a short list of some rather interesting viewing opportunities. Most of these manuscripts were copied in the first few centuries of Christianity. Remember, *p* means papyrus; the other notations designate codices. Some codices are divided between different libraries or museums. All are Greek New Testament manuscripts.

Locations of Ancient Manuscripts	
Allentown, Pennsylvania	p^{21}
Ann Arbor, Michigan	p^{38}, p^{46}, p^{53}
Athos, Greece	H, Ψ, Ω
Barcelona, Spain	p^{8}
Basel, Switzerland	E
Berkeley, California	p^{28}
Berlin, Germany	p^{8}, p^{25}, p^{63}, p^{79}
Cairo, Egypt	p^{15}, p^{16}
Cambridge, England	p^{17}, p^{27}, D
Cambridge, Massachusetts	p^{9}, p^{10}

Cologne, Germany	p^{86}, p^{87}
Cologny, Switzerland	p^{66}, p^{72}, p^{73}, p^{74}, p^{75}
Dallas, Texas	p^{26}
Dublin, Ireland	p^{45}, p^{46}, p^{47}, Z
Florence, Italy	p^{2}, p^{35}, p^{36}, p^{48}, p^{65}
Gent, Belgium	p^{30}
Glasgow, Scotland	p^{22}
Hamburg, Germany	H
Heidelberg, Germany	p^{40}
Kiev, Ukraine	p^{7}
London, England	p^{5}, p^{13}, p^{18}, p^{43}, ℵ, A, G, R, Ξ
Louvain, Belgium	p^{83}, p^{84}
Manchester, England	p^{31}, p^{32}, p^{52}
Milan, Italy	p^{88}
Modena, Italy	H
Moscow, Russia	K, V
Munich, Germany	X
New Haven, Connecticut	p^{49}, p^{50}
New York, New York	p^{12}, p^{44}, p^{59}, p^{60}, p^{61}
Newton Centre, Massachusetts	p^{24}
Oslo, Norway	p^{62}
Oxford, England	p^{19}, p^{29}, p^{51}, p^{64}, p^{69}, p^{70}, p^{71}, p^{77}, p^{78}, E, G, L
Paris, France	p^{4}, C, D, K, L, M, O
Philadelphia, Pennsylvania	p^{1}
Princeton, New Jersey	p^{20}, p^{54}
Rochester, New York	p^{39}
Rome, Italy	B, L, S, T
Rossano, Italy	Σ
Sinai, Egypt	p^{14}
St. Galen, Switzerland	Δ
St. Petersburg, Russia	p^{11}, p^{68}, N, P, Π
Strasbourg, France	p^{6}, p^{82}, p^{85}
Tblisi, Georgia	Θ
Tirana, Albania	Φ

Trieste, Italy	p⁸¹
Urbana, Illinois	p²³
Utrecht, Holland	F
Venice, Italy	U
Vienna, Austria	p³, p³³, p³⁴, p⁴¹, p⁴², p⁵⁵, p⁵⁶, p⁵⁷, p⁷⁶
Washington DC	I, W
Wolfenbüttel, Germany	P, Q

The evidence is truly abundant! God has seen fit to preserve his message for all generations.[5]

Reconstruction

No other book has been as widely copied, read, and cherished (or hated!) as the Bible. The evidence for its accurate transmission is overwhelming. In fact even if all the surviving papyri and codices were collected and burned, most of the Scriptures could be reconstructed through quotations from early Christian writings, the majority of which were written in the 200s and 300s. For example, we find some 86,000 verse quotations from the New Testament in the early Christian writers (the Patristic authors). This should give us enormous confidence that our Bible corresponds with the original manuscripts.

The Allegation of Alteration

Some allege that the Bible has been hopelessly corrupted, changed nearly beyond recognition. For example, Muslim apologists commonly claim that the Bible has been changed and that the transmission process caused myriads of errors. How can the believer in Jesus Christ respond to Islam's accusations?

Interestingly, the Qur'an (or Koran, the scriptures of the Muslims) never once insinuates that the Christian Bible has been corrupted. In fact the Qur'an, written in the seventh century AD, positively encourages Christians to obey the teaching of the gospel (*Injil* in Arabic). "The people of the Injil [the Christians] shall rule in accordance with

God's revelations therein. Anyone who does not rule in accordance with God's revelations—these are the wicked!" Similarly, believers are urged to follow the Old Testament as well.[6] Which revelations and which gospel exactly was Muhammad exhorting "the people of the book" to follow, if not the well-known and widely disseminated Scriptures of the Bible?

Nowhere did Muhammad allege that the Bible had been corrupted, though he often stated emphatically that the people (Christians and Jews) had been corrupted. So where and when did the allegation first pop up? Apparently, not until the twelfth century—in polemical debate with the Christians of the day. For 500 years, most Muslims cast no aspersions on the Bible. Then came the allegation that the Bible itself was untrustworthy. Muhammad himself, however, made no such claim.

Myriad Variants?

Muslim apologists often claim that the Bible contains hundreds of thousands of errors and that their Qur'an has remained unchanged since Allah dictated it.[7] Here is where that claim originates: As we have already learned, we have thousands of manuscripts of the biblical books. These apologists count one minor alteration appearing in 1000 manuscripts as 1000 errors!

Each manuscript was copied by hand, so errors in spelling, word omission, and the like were bound to occur. Through the science of textual criticism, we have near unanimous agreement on the original text of the New Testament. The exceptions are John 7:53–8:11, which sometimes appears in other places in John or Luke, and Mark 16:9-20, which supports several differing (though not contradictory) endings.

If we count all the minor differences in spelling, word order, and so forth as errors, it is not hard to generate a long list of mistakes from the thousands of Greek New Testament manuscripts and tens of thousands of New Testament manuscripts in other languages. But is this fair? Hardly.

Spelling differences and the like do not constitute true errors. What doctrine has been affected, corrupted, or introduced through such errors? Not a one. Such shadowboxing will never discredit the Scriptures in the eyes of one who is truly open-minded.

The Dead Sea Scrolls

Cache

In 1947, Muhammad ed-Dib, a 16-year-old goatherd, was looking for a lost goat. He threw a stone into the mouth of a cave—precisely the sort of thing many of us did as children. The sound that came back was not the normal report or an echo, but the *clink* of the stone striking a clay jar. *Gold?* Hoping he may have found precious metal, Muhammad returned the following day to the cave with his cousin. Inside, he found some old pieces of leather with writing in a script and language he could not read. Thinking he might be able to repair his shoes with the leather, he took it to a cobbler.

The cobbler told him to show his find to a local antiquities dealer. Through Muhammad ed-Dib these documents—found in what would later be called Cave 1 at Qumran—came into the hands of Kando (Khalil Eskander Shahin), and Kando introduced them to the academic world.[8] These were the first Dead Sea Scrolls, so named because the monastic community that had secreted them from the Roman armies during the First Jewish War (about AD 68) lived on the northwest shore of the Dead Sea, not too far from Jerusalem.

The scrolls contain many religious writings, including partial or complete biblical texts from every book of the Old Testament dating back to the third century BC.[9] Before this incredible discovery, the oldest surviving manuscripts were from a thousand years later.[10] Their significance for establishing the accuracy of the biblical text cannot be overestimated.

I have seen the scrolls many times, both in Jerusalem (at the Shrine of the Book, a subterranean and climate-controlled adjunct of the Israel

Museum) and in other cities as the scrolls were on tour in Europe and North America. Twice I have even gone up to Cave 6. The majority of the manuscripts were found, however, in the nearly inaccessible Cave 4.

The most famous scroll is 1QIsa[a]. This shorthand means Scroll *A* of Isaiah, found in Cave 1. This nearly flawless copy of the book of Isaiah is on display in the Israel Museum and, like the other manuscripts and manuscript fragments, is published for all to see. In my annual Biblical Study Tour in 2008, I took 150 people to the Shrine of the Book to see the world-renowned 1QIsa[a].

Conspiracy?

The Dead Sea Scrolls took more than 40 years to translate. Was there a grand conspiracy, perpetrated by those who would hide the truth from believers? Not at all. Various factors conspired to hinder the rapid publication of the DSS, including the death of several of the translators and project heads, many of whom were advanced in age when they began the work. Personal motives and some possessiveness have sometimes characterized the reconstruction, translation, and publication of the scrolls, but today this corpus is available to all who are interested.[11] Perhaps you will decide to learn more about this remarkable discovery.[12]

Summary

Impressive as they are, the Dead Sea Scrolls are not the oldest surviving biblical manuscripts. In 1979, other scrolls were discovered in Jerusalem's Hinnom Valley by Gabriel Barkay. The miniature scrolls contain Numbers 6:24-26 and predate Judah's exile to Babylon (early sixth century BC). And other ancient manuscripts from the area (which is arid enough to aid in the preservation of perishable materials) continue to turn up.

Back to my presentation in Cambridge, 2009. After sharing much of the material contained in this chapter, I concluded my lecture with these five summary statements:

1. The biblical manuscripts, though not copied perfectly, were copied adequately. Their truth content is unaffected by scribal error.

2. The transmission of the texts compares extremely favorably with the transmission of other ancient documents.

3. Early Christians therefore could not have fabricated prophecies of Christ by doctoring the texts of the Hebrew Bible.

4. Skepticism is understandable but unwarranted.

5. The preservation of the biblical texts is remarkable.

As both the prophet Isaiah and the apostle Peter said, "The word of the Lord stands forever."[13] The message has been preserved throughout history, and it is just as relevant now as it was thousands of years ago. We can have full confidence in God, and we can absolutely take him at his word. All this can be summed up in a single truth: We have no reason to doubt the text of the Bible and every reason to trust it.

Into the Word!

When our own confidence in the Bible is firmly established, what do we do with this information? How do we use it to help skeptics?

The best way to help anyone who is suspicious about the integrity of the Bible, including our Muslim friends, is to get them into the Word. As they read and apply the penetrating truths to their lives, faith will be born. Bring them to church so they can see Christian love in action.[14] Challenge them to study the Bible with an open heart.

When I ask Muslims if they have read the Bible—or just the entire New Testament—the answer is almost invariably no. When I tell them that I have read the entire Qur'an several times through and ask why they don't show more respect for their own scriptures, mouths drop, heads hang, and the pure of heart reconsider their priorities. Incidentally, I have met many Muslims, but none as far as I know have read the entire Bible. (Sadly, most Christians are no better off. Few of them have read the entire Bible either.)

By the way, reading the Qur'an does not take long. It is approximately four-fifths the length of the New Testament. Read with a highlighter. You will find many true passages and many contradictions to the biblical record. Above all, you will find a religion of works. Note this: All world religions (including errant variations of Christianity) tend to have man reaching up to God. Real Christianity, on the other hand, is God reaching down to man. No religion of works (such as Islam, with its doctrines of earning salvation, fate, and brutality toward infidels) accurately represents God himself, who is infinite in love, grace, and holiness.

When people start looking into God's nature, his Word, his people, and his plan, they soon come face-to-face with the truth and must make a decision.[15] As others have said, "When an honest seeker finds the truth, he must either act on it or stop being honest." Take God at his word; he is powerful enough to change any heart.

Part 3

The Son of God

In the previous section we examined the remarkable evidence that the Bible is God's Word to mankind.

The third part of this book addresses questions about the Son of God, Jesus Christ. He was a polarizing figure in his own day, and the fascination, adulation, and controversy surrounding him have increased over the years. He has been called an itinerant rabbi, a peasant do-gooder, a charlatan, a lunatic, and the Messiah. Who was Jesus, and what did he really do? Can a thinking person in the twenty-first century worship Jesus, believe in his miracles and resurrection, and maintain intellectual integrity? This section will address these all-important questions, for if Jesus is not who the Bible says he is, and if he did not do what the Bible says he did, Christians are wasting their time. As Paul put it, "If only for this life we have hope in Christ, we are to be pitied more than all men" (1 Corinthians 15:19).

Jesus' identity could be explained by one of four possibilities, and in chapter 8 we will weigh them all. In chapter 9 we will look at the evidence that he actually performed miracles, and in chapter 10 we will examine the reasons to believe Christ rose from the dead. After the incarnation itself, the resurrection is history's most significant miracle.

The Luminous Figure:
Legend, Liar, Lunatic, or Lord?

I am a Jew, but I am enthralled by the luminous figure
of the Nazarene… No one can read the Gospels without
feeling the actual presence of Jesus. His personality pulsates
in every word. No myth is filled with such life.

ALBERT EINSTEIN

IMMEDIATELY AFTER LANDING IN A DISTANT NATION, I was ordered to report to the police. I stood stiffly before the intelligence officer who had summoned me. The man in charge sat behind a large desk, sneering faintly as he questioned me, ordering me not to cast aspersions on other religions during my Christian presentation. I was not to state or imply that Jesus is the only way or that other religions might be misguided. Various firearms hung on the wall above the desk. Additional guards, stationed just inside the door, sported submachine guns. As I stood there, I couldn't help but wonder what the drama was all about. Did they think I was a terrorist? What were they afraid of?

Most people believe in a God (or gods). Many even accept the Bible or other writings as inspired Scripture. Most cultures tolerate believers, provided they do not believe too firmly. Yet when someone claims that Jesus is the unique way to God, many feel threatened or even take offense. Still, if we are to accept the claims of Jesus, we must believe he is the only way to God. This inevitably brings Christianity into conflict with the values and views of the world.

A Shallow Grave and Hungry Dogs

In Jesus' own day, people held many opinions about his identity and reacted to him in widely divergent ways. They regarded him as a resurrected prophet, a maniac, and even a demoniac.[1] Modern viewpoints are equally diverse. The Jesus Seminar has concluded that only 18 percent of the words attributed to Jesus in the New Testament are authentic. Jesus Seminar fellow John Dominic Crossan views him as an itinerant peasant whose social vision challenged contemporary political structures. For his rebellion he was crucified—and later buried in a shallow grave and eaten by dogs.[2] Another Fellow of the Jesus Seminar objects that Crossan has not gone far enough—that in truth "the historical Jesus has shrunk to the vanishing point."[3]

One of the bestselling novels of all time, *The Da Vinci Code,* posits that Jesus married Mary Magdalene and that the Council of Nicaea labeled him the Son of God in AD 325.[4] These assertions fly in the face of all the biblical and historical evidence. In a 2006 poll, 13 percent of Americans—approximately 40 million persons—said they believe that Jesus' death was faked and that he married and had a family—central ideas in *The Da Vinci Code.* Bart Ehrman, a former evangelical and presently a "happy agnostic," claims in his 2005 bestseller *Misquoting Jesus* that the absence of the original New Testament manuscripts and the "error-ridden copies...centuries removed from the originals" undermine any possibility of knowing what Jesus really said and did.[5] In 2007, the Discovery Channel aired a program that claimed the burial place of Jesus and his family had been found outside Jerusalem. This sensational suggestion was allegedly proven by statistical, historical, archaeological, and DNA evidence. This is just a sampling of the wild claims made about Jesus—others have gone even further!

What is the truth? Who was this luminous, if not numinous, figure? What did Jesus claim about himself? How can we evaluate those claims? And what was so disturbing about them that anyone would have bothered to crucify him?

The Radical Claims of Christ

Though fully human, Jesus was also aware of his heavenly origin, frequently implying his divinity. For example, he forgave people their sins—the prerogative of God. He set himself above the law, exercising an independent approach. He underlined his dual nature, his humanity and his lordship. His choosing of the 12 apostles symbolically replaced the leadership of the 12 tribes, with Jesus himself as their leader. (Who else but God was the leader of Israel?) Jesus said he would return on the clouds of heaven. (In the Old Testament, only God rode the skies.)[6] Why else would monotheistic Jews—the majority of the first generation of Christians—begin to worship a man as God?

Consider two dozen of the incredible claims that Jesus Christ made about himself. (I have reworded them slightly, putting them all into the first person. If you check the references, you will see that the phrasing is fair.)

I have always existed . . . . John 8:58; 17:5

I hold the keys to death . . . . Revelation 1:18

I have never sinned . . . . John 8:46

I have all authority on heaven and earth . . . . Matthew 28:18

I and the Father are one. . . . . John 10:30

I must be placed above your family . . . . Matthew 10:37

I have authority to forgive sins. . . . . Mark 2:5-12

I am the light of the world. John 8:12

I am prophesied about in the Scriptures . . . . . . .Luke 24:25-27

I am from heaven. . . . . John 8:23

I will be resurrected . . . . Mark 8:31

I am the bread of life . . . . John 6:35

I will send the Spirit of God Almighty . . . . .John 16:7

I am coming again to the earth . . . . .Revelation 22:20

I am a king . . . . .John 18:37

I give spiritual life . . . . John 5:24

I am the one through whom you must pray . . . . .John 16:23-24

I raise the dead and heal diseases. . . .John 11:38-44; Luke 13:32

I will judge the world on Judgment Day . . . . .John 5:22-30

I am the Son of God .Matthew 16:16-17

I will raise the dead at the end of time. . . . . .John 5:28-29

I am the only way to God . . . . John 14:6

My words will never pass away . . . . Matthew 24:35

If you reject me, you reject God himself . . . . Luke 10:16

The Possibilities

These are startling claims—so stupendous, in fact, that even if only some of them are authentic, they would require explanation. The New Testament is the proper starting place for any evaluation because it is the most ancient and plentiful source depicting what Jesus said and did.

Some say Jesus was just a good moral teacher. In so doing, they ignore his radical claims and offer a weak compliment in exchange. This is like saying Albert Einstein was a good physicist. Einstein was most certainly not merely a good physicist—he was *great,* as everyone admits. Similarly, if Jesus' claims are true, he was not just a good moral teacher; he is God and truth itself. Only by ignoring the Scriptures can one view Jesus as only a good moral teacher, so this view is hardly worth refuting. This leaves us with only four serious possibilities.[7]

- *Legend.* Some deny that Jesus ever existed or made the claims the Gospels record.

- *Liar.* If he was not merely a legend—if the Jesus of the Bible really existed—only two options remain: Either he spoke the truth or he did not. If he knowingly did not speak the truth, he was a liar.

- *Lunatic.* If, on the other hand, Jesus thought he was speaking the truth but wasn't, his incredible claims would lead us to believe he was insane, a lunatic.

- *Lord.* If the above three possibilities can be ruled out, only one option remains—that he spoke the truth.

Legend

The Legend view is represented by last century's noted atheist Bertrand Russell, who once said in a lecture, "Historically it is quite doubtful whether Christ ever existed at all, and if he did we do not know anything about him."[8] One of Russell's modern counterparts is G.A. Wells, professor emeritus of the University of London. Others do not go so far as to doubt Jesus' existence, but they do ascribe most of his words and deeds to the creative agenda of early Christianity. Nevertheless, problems with the Legend hypothesis are rife.

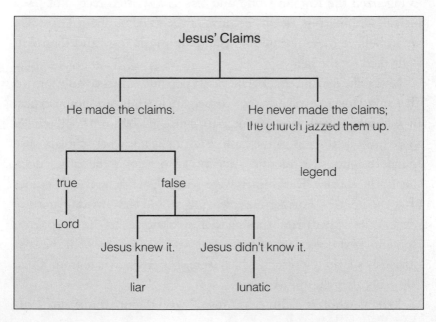

To begin with, Jesus' contemporaries who were skeptics and opponents admitted his existence. There is strong historical witness to Jesus and his movement. Nine non-Christian sources mention him in the first 150 years after his death, in addition to 33 more Christian sources.[9] In comparison, Tiberius, the Roman emperor when Jesus was crucified, appears in only ten sources all together, including the Gospel of Luke. If we don't have enough evidence for Jesus' existence, what do we do with Tiberius? To be consistent, we would have to relegate much of antiquity to the mists of uncertainty.

Next, as literature, the Gospels are not mythological documents. They utilize symbolism and occasionally adapt ancient myths and motifs, but the legend genre is absent. Differences between the Gospel accounts and the myths in other religions are enormous. Moreover, the divergence between the biblical narratives and later fables is considerable. These later stories were circulated through the false gospels, acts, letters, and apocalypses of the second to fourth centuries. (See the discussion in chapter 9.) In addition, most of the apostles who evangelized the Roman world and left us a written record of Jesus' life suffered martyrs' deaths because of their claims about Jesus. Are we to believe they invented an elaborate mythology and then willingly died for the lie?

Much like the universe, legends don't pop into existence fully formed. They take time to evolve. If the Gospels are legends, we should expect increasingly exalted claims about Jesus, a progression from good teacher to divine sage to God in the flesh. But this is not what scholars have found. In contrast, extraordinary claims are present in the earliest documents, the epistles. The Gospels were generally written several decades after the epistles. Furthermore, legends would have made heroes of the apostles rather than exposing their weaknesses, as the Gospels do. Romanticized depictions of the apostles do not appear until the later, obviously spurious writings, which were written anywhere from 100 to 300 years after the apostles died.

Liberal scholars claim that Gospel writers put words into Jesus' mouth in order to address the issues of their day. But if this were so, why does Jesus—in the Gospels, at least—say nothing about circumcision, the role of women, church offices, spiritual gifts, or whether Christians are permitted to eat idol meat? All of these were hot issues in the first-century church. The dearth of dominical directives legitimizing later dogma attests to the honesty of the disciples and the Gospel writers.

Some critics cite alleged parallels to the Gospels that undermine Jesus' uniqueness, words, and deeds. But the sources they cite are unconvincing. Three examples will suffice. The first is the legend of Apollonius of Tyana, a first-century Neopythagorean philosopher and wonder-worker. One of his wonders was intervening in the life of a friend who was about to marry a vampire! The supposed miracles are fanciful, and the document on which the stories are based was written for political purposes 150 years after the alleged events themselves.[10] The parallel also fails because the Neopythagoreans taught that deity is not influenced by prayer. Jesus, on the other hand, encouraged a personal relationship with God.

Some have suggested that Jesus was, like Diogenes, an itinerant Cynic. The Cynics traveled with their telltale staff, pouch, and cloak, spreading their message. But there the superficial similarities end. We find no evidence of Cynics in first-century Galilee, and their lifestyles and philosophies were at odds with most of what Jesus did and said. Jesus taught people to call God their Father; the Cynics taught that the gods are indifferent. Moreover, Cynics engaged in gross and insensitive practices, such as urinating, defecating, and copulating in public. Diogenes, like Jesus, called himself a light—but in a very different way: When Diogenes entered a brothel, he compared himself to the sun, whose light shines into a latrine without being polluted.[11]

Another popular alleged parallel is Honi the Circle Drawer, who lived in the first century BC.[12] This ancient Jew drew a circle around himself and petulantly told God he would not leave it until it rained. This behavior was no miracle at all, nor did Honi have any prophetic ministry, bring any new teachings, or make messianic claims. These supposed parallels do not convince.

Jesus' death on the cross is another strike against the Legend hypothesis. If the seemingly unheroic ending were not true, why would anyone have made it up? The death of the Messiah was not what first-century Jews were expecting; in fact, it was unthinkable. In a three-way debate I had with an imam and a rabbi, both my opponents insisted that if Jesus was killed, he failed. Such a degrading death would have made him a false prophet (according to Islam) and a false Messiah (according to Judaism). For some, the cross is foolishness and a stumbling block to faith.[13]

The Legend hypothesis ignores the integrity of the early Christians, who, along with their Master, were generally acknowledged to be persons of integrity. Early Christian leaders knew the difference between real life and legend. Many died for their faith in Jesus Christ. And if the early Christians were in the habit of making up miracle stories about their heroes, why does the Bible say that John the Baptist, an influential and powerful figure, never performed a miracle?[14]

Last, would a legend have such a tremendous positive impact on our planet as Jesus has had? His character and teachings were reproduced in his followers' lives. The exploits of legendary figures may make entertaining reading, but do they inspire men and women to die for them? Do they open hearts, release the addicted, heal marriages, sensitize people's social consciences, and create dynamic communities of disciples? No. No other person in history has had an impact on the world that compares to Jesus'. The Legend suggestion explains nothing and ignores the evidence. Jesus existed and made extraordinary claims. We must move on to consider the three remaining possibilities.

Liar

Jesus Christ was accused of deception in his lifetime.[15] For a moment, let's assume that he did lie. If Jesus knew that he was misrepresenting the truth, he was a liar. Is it really conceivable that Jesus, whom even unbelievers generally conceded to be a man of integrity, was a liar? Is it likely that a man known for his emphasis on truthfulness would himself be a deceiver? Or that he would send his followers to their deaths as they preached a message about him that he knew was a sheer fabrication? Is it even remotely probable that a man whose life was consumed with exposing religious hypocrisy would be the greatest hypocrite of all, a master deceiver? No, it is not. Many of his followers have failed, but this is because they were disregarding their Lord, not imitating him.

What would the motive be for this deceit? Money? Jesus, who taught that "it is more blessed to give than to receive," died penniless.[16] Hatred for humanity? Then why would he die for the sins of the world, including his enemies? Jesus had no reason to lie. Common sense tells us that it is more likely that he never existed at all than that he was a liar. Not surprisingly, few opponents of Christianity charge Christ with dishonesty.

Lunatic

If we continue with the assumption that what Jesus said was untrue, but now withdraw the charge of deceit, it follows that he must have been a lunatic.

Ego is one thing, lunacy another. If I claimed to be the most handsome man in Georgia (a claim manifestly untrue), you would not necessarily conclude I was mentally unstable—just the victim of a vicious ego. If I claimed to be the most gifted and eloquent communicator in all of North America (also patently false), you might feel irritated, perhaps even sorry for me; but again, you would not need to take my self-description seriously. But if I claimed to be "Doug Almighty, God incarnate, all-powerful and all-wise," how would you feel about me being your kids' Sunday school teacher? Would you tolerate that? I hope not.

No mere man could have made the extraordinary claims Jesus made and believed them if he were not insane. Yet when we look at the character of Jesus, what do we see? The unbalanced personality of a madman? No, we see perfect balance.

Jesus was tender and loving but not sentimental, zealous and fearless but wise and cautious, unworldly but not antisocial, confident but not arrogant, self-sacrificing yet still joyful, urgent and responsible but peaceful and unhurried, often under attack but always composed and never rattled, strong and uncompromising but not harsh, a man of dignity and authority but still humble, a powerful leader and yet a man of prayer and a servant of servants. Was Jesus unstable? Hardly!

In short, Jesus' personality shows none of the instability, obsession, irrational fears, paranoia, anxiety, mood swings, or introversion that we might expect in a lunatic. Jesus is so perfectly balanced, in fact, that he is the standard for sanity. He was no lunatic. The notion that he lived a lie, moving in a fantasy world of his own making, is not persuasive.

Lord

The ancient world was awash in myth, but the story of Jesus Christ is no legend. The parallels sometimes adduced simply do not work. Jesus really did live, and he made extraordinary claims. If the claims were false, he would be either a liar or a lunatic. But as we have seen, neither possibility is logical. Jesus spoke the truth, and his claims are true.

This leaves us with only one remaining option: Jesus is Lord, as his followers believe and teach. What he said was true, and he knew it was true. This would adequately explain the emergence of Christianity as well as its power to touch the human heart at the deepest level.

But the proof of Jesus' identity does not rest only on the mere process of elimination. There is more. The Old Testament prophecies confirm, with surprising detail, the identity of Jesus Christ as the Messiah.[17] Many extant manuscripts are older than the Christian era, which means the prophecies were not phony—not added later by believers bent on proving Jesus' messiahship—but authentic. They were not written after the fact, but centuries before. (See chapter 7 for a more thorough discussion of this topic.)

Jesus' lordship is verified not only by the transformative power of his words but also by his miracles, fulfillment of prophecy, and resurrection from the dead. We will explore the validity of his miracles in chapter 9 and his resurrection in chapter 10. It is reasonable to conclude that Jesus Christ was a real person, not a legend. The "luminous figure" we encounter in the Gospels is none other than the Messiah, the Lord of all.

Light of the World

God speaks not only in Scripture but also in another, highly personal way—through the incarnation. *Incarnation* refers to the physical embodiment of something that was nonphysical. God became man in Jesus Christ, the Son of God. The incarnation puts a human face on God, making the abstract concrete and the unknowable relatable. If the incarnation is true, Jesus' claims make sense.

Some people object that it is illogical to speak of Jesus being both man and God—like a square circle. A square circle cannot exist because both squares and circles are examples of shapes, and a single shape cannot have two irreconcilable forms. But whereas a square circle is impossible by definition, nothing in the definition of *human* rules out the possibility that a person could also be God. The *Oxford English Dictionary* defines a *human* as "a human being, a man." God and man are not both examples of the same thing; by definition they occupy no common ground. As a finite being, I cannot be in both England and the United States at the same time (not that I wouldn't like to, as our family lives on both sides of the Atlantic). But I *can* be in England and underwater at the same time, as there is no necessary contradiction. So it is with Jesus Christ, the God-man. He was fully human and fully divine.

God is light. Jesus claimed to be the light of the world.[18] The light of God is what makes Jesus the most luminous character in all of history.

> The Word was God…The Word became flesh and made
> his dwelling among us. We have seen his glory, the glory
> of the One and Only, who came from the Father, full of

grace and truth…No one has ever seen God, but God the One and Only, who is at the Father's side, has made him known (John 1:1,14,18).

God Threw the Switch

Why would the Lord of the universe concern himself with Earth, the lost planet, spinning its way to destruction? This is an excellent question. Fortunately for us, God is a God of love, and through the incarnation of Jesus we can personally know his love. Jesus chose to come to Earth, to share in all the blood, toil, tears, and sweat of human existence. He came not only to inform us but also to give us a personal knowledge of God, dying for our sins so that we could draw near to the holy God. This is the perspective necessary for understanding Jesus and his claims.

The story is told of a little boy playing on the railroad tracks, unknown to his father. By the time the father noticed him it was too late: He looked with horror as he saw the two passenger trains speeding toward each other from different directions; they were on a collision course! The only way to prevent the collision was to redirect one of the trains off onto another track, exactly where his son was playing. The father had to act fast—it was only seconds before the collision—but he loved his son! What would he do? He threw the switch and saved the passengers, but in doing so sacrificed his little boy's life. The passengers never knew.

God threw the switch for us. It was the only way. He watched his Son die for our sins. Most of the world, however, carries on along its selfish course, unaware and unappreciative of the sacrifice God made for us.

The case has been made, and the verdict is inescapable: Jesus Christ is Lord. And if he is Lord, we are called to be his humble servants.[19] The crux of the matter is that Jesus Christ, the Son of God, died on the cross for our sins.

That's Impossible!
The Miracles of Jesus

*Jesus of Nazareth was a man accredited by God to
you by miracles, wonders and signs, which God did
among you through him, as you yourselves know.*

ACTS 2:22

I SWAM IN THE ATLANTIC OCEAN TODAY on the Georgia coast. Looking up—I was not wearing my glasses—I saw people and dogs walking on water. After my double take, I realized they were actually strolling on a sandbar, the image refracted through the moist ocean air. Could Jesus' disciples have been similarly mistaken when they thought their master was walking on the Sea of Galilee? Could the miracles of Jesus simply be distortions or exaggerations of normal events?

Without a doubt, the human mind is capable of being misled, and there is no shortage of people willing to mislead. Skepticism therefore makes sense. But must skepticism necessarily result in incredulity? Not necessarily. In fact, as we shall soon see, without Jesus' miracles, we would have reason to doubt his identity.

A Priori

Of course, a skeptic may conclude a priori that miracles are impossible on this basis:

1. Miracles violate the laws of nature.

2. The laws of nature cannot be broken.

3. Therefore miracles are impossible.

Let's evaluate this line of reasoning. The first assumption is true if we define a miracle as an act that breaks the laws of nature, speeds them up, or in some other way violates the scientific order. Moreover, the third assumption follows logically from the other two. The argument seems valid. But we have not shown that the second assumption is true—and in fact we cannot do so. How could one substantiate such a premise?

But we need not think of the laws as being broken at all. Would not the Master Scientist be free to intervene in his creation any way he wanted to? He might accelerate natural processes or even work within the inherent randomness of physics at the quantum level. If Jesus Christ healed a blind man, would he not be more likely to work through normal physiological channels than to completely circumvent the laws of nature?

Let's say you invite your guests to a party at seven but later tell them that the time has been changed to eight. Have you broken an inviolable decree? Is not a time change within your prerogatives? You have simply made a slight shift without any compromise of integrity.

An infinitely powerful God unconfined by space and time could just as easily create a world, inspire a book, or raise a man from the dead as you can breathe or tie your shoe. We have already explored convincing evidence that God exists and that he has entered our world in Jesus Christ. We can therefore reasonably conclude that miracles can occur as well. There are no a priori reasons to preclude them.

Purpose and Prudence

By definition, a miracle is unusual and extraordinary, "a marvelous event due to some supposed supernatural agency."[1] If there were no God, *miracle* would be a meaningless term, applicable to anything we did not understand. And if supernatural wonders happened all the time, they would not be miracles. The Bible describes a number of such events, though they are rare. These events tend to be clustered around three epochs of revelation:

1. The Hebrews' reception of the Torah more than three millennia ago,

2. the rise of prophecy with Elijah and Elisha several centuries later, and

3. the advent of the gospel nearly two millennia ago. Jesus and his apostles performed the signs of this third epoch.

Very few people living in Bible times ever saw a miracle—even people living in Israel.

As we have seen, prudence does not require us to reject all miracles as false. Biblical miracles are different from the alleged miracles with which most of us are familiar. For example, biblical miracles were undeniable and were accepted even by enemies of the faith. Ancient extrabiblical sources do not contest the miracles. In fact, they confirm them. Jewish sources like the Talmud attest to Jesus' existence, miracles, and execution.

The Bible's miracles were performed publicly by men of known integrity. They never appealed for money, as modern miracle-workers commonly do. The purpose was not to stun or thrill, but to reinforce crucial spiritual truths.[2] Even though Jesus' own brothers advised him to use miracles to build up his reputation and stir up excitement, Jesus would have nothing to do with their sensationalism. He would not play to the crowds.

If the Almighty God, Creator of the heavens and the earth, visited our world in Christ, we would expect some unusual events. If nothing out of the ordinary were reported—*that* would be cause for skepticism. Would not God prove his deity in part by demonstrating his power over the natural world and its laws? Miracles are consistent with God's action and communication in Christ.[3]

Messianic Miracles

First-century Judaism expected the Messiah to work miracles. Even John the Baptist, who initially identified "the lamb of God, who takes away the sin of the world," later wondered if Jesus was really the Messiah. He sent messengers to ask Jesus, "Are you the one who was to come, or should we expect someone else?" Jesus replied, "Go back and report to John what you hear and see: The blind receive sight, the lame walk, those who have leprosy are cured, the deaf hear, the dead are raised, and the good news is preached to the poor."[4] A passage from Dead Sea Scroll manuscript 4Q521 sheds light on Christ's reply:

> [The hea]vens and the earth will listen to His Messiah [and
> all w]hich shall not turn away from the commandments
> of the holy ones...setting prisoners free, opening the eyes
> of the blind, raising up those who are bo[wed down]...For
> He shall heal the critically wounded, He shall revive the
> dead, He shall send good news to the afflicted.[5]

This ancient passage brings together the signs predicted in Isaiah 29:18-19; 35:5-6; and 61:1-2, with a possible allusion to 26:19. Jesus' reply to John could be paraphrased, "My miracles prove I'm the Messiah." As Peter preached—in a message that inaugurated the church of Christ in AD 30—miracles served a central function: they accredited Christ's ministry.

Jesus did not perform miracles at every turn. But when he did, they accomplished a specific purpose and sent a clear message to those who witnessed them (and now to those who read about them). Christ performed miracles that showed his power over sickness, nature, demons, and death. He displayed supernatural knowledge and prophesied. When Jesus calmed the storm, he displayed his divinity; such ability is attributed to God alone. When he raised Lazarus and others from the dead, he worked wonders that only God can perform.[6]

Real Mythology

Specious sources that date from the second to fourth centuries attribute apocryphal and fanciful wonders to Jesus, including these from his youth:

- The ox and the donkey worship the baby Jesus. When Mary is hungry, her infant son commands the palm tree to bow down and offer her dates.

- A colt descended from Balaam's donkey salutes Thomas as Christ's twin brother.

- Jesus forms pigeons out of clay on the Sabbath. To avoid suspicion of breaking the Sabbath, he transforms the inanimate figures into real birds, which fly away, thereby eliminating the evidence.

- Jesus strikes dead a boy for accidentally bumping into him. He curses another child: "You insolent, godless dunderhead…now you also shall wither like a tree."

Similarly, various wonders are ascribed to his apostles:

- In an apocryphal showdown in Rome, Peter commands a dog to lecture Simon Magus on the hellfire awaiting him. The dog delivers the message and then dies.

- Peter repairs a broken statue simply by sprinkling holy water on it.

- Peter also makes a piece of smoked fish come back to life, whereupon it swims away.

- Paul baptizes a lion.[7]

This is real mythology, next to which the miracles of Christ seem sober and their narration restrained. The later spurious works differ enormously from the authentic first-century documents of the New Testament. But today, many people try to explain away Jesus' miracles as legend, grouping them with the fictive accounts. But those who do so have not carefully read the Gospels and the apocryphal writings and then compared the two. Jesus' miracles recorded in the New Testament are neither out of character for him nor sensationalistic. They are recorded for a reason, as John explains: "Jesus did many other miraculous signs in the presence of his disciples, which are not recorded in this book. But these are written that you may believe that Jesus is the Christ, the Son of God, and that by believing you may have life in his name."[8]

Jesus Discouraged Sign-Seeking

Jesus could have been as generous with his miracles as he was with his teaching and personal sacrifice. But he did not always acquiesce to the sign-seeking mentality of his generation. He resisted the crowds' pressure to become a traveling sideshow.

> This is a wicked generation. It asks for a miraculous sign, but none will be given it except the sign of Jonah. For as Jonah was a sign to the Ninevites, so also will the Son of Man be to this generation. The Queen of the South will rise at the judgment with the men of this generation and condemn them; for she came from the ends of the earth to listen to Solomon's wisdom, and now one greater than Solomon is here. The men of Nineveh will stand up at the judgment with this generation and condemn it; for they repented at the preaching of Jonah, and now one greater than Jonah is here (Luke 11:29-32).

The comparisons in this passage deserve exploration: The Ninevites repented because Jonah preached the Word to them—without any supernatural signs to assist them in coming to faith. In fact, as far as we know, the prophet never mentioned his maritime adventure after the long overland journey from the Mediterranean to the Assyrian metropolis.[9] A bona fide miracle could have strengthened Jonah's case. After all, Jonah was not an Assyrian, he was all alone in his appeal, he was (presumably) unknown to the Ninevites, and his religion was different from theirs. Jonah performed no miracle, and yet the entire city repented.

More than a century before Jonah, the Queen of the South—probably from Yemen—had traveled 1500 miles to meet Solomon. She responded favorably to him and to his faith even though the king performed no miracles at all for her. She listened to his wisdom and was moved to praise the God of Israel.

In both cases, the response was not effected through or conditioned by miracles. Neither the people of Nineveh nor the Queen of Sheba received a sign—and yet they were moved by God's Word. Jesus' generation had little excuse compared with these believing foreigners.[10]

Again and again we see Jesus calling people to reason, even shying away from working wonders. Performing miracles on demand would have been the easy but temporary way out. People might have followed him from wrong motives, whereas Jesus wants us to base our faith on reason and conviction. And if Jesus had granted every request for a sign, his followers would have learned to insist on a sign whenever faced with an important decision. They would have become weak-minded, unable or unwilling to think for themselves or to take full responsibility for their own actions. Jesus seems to reason with others more than appeal to miraculous signs.[11] In the story of the Rich Man and Lazarus—not to be confused with the raising of another Lazarus in John 11—Abraham insists that no miracle can possibly convince us if we're unwilling to be convinced. In the end, we will do what we want to do—with or without a miracle to back our decision. As for believers (or would-be believers) like you and me, who read about the wonders of the Bible but didn't actually see them, Jesus knew that conviction can grow in the heart just as easily through reading the account of a miracle as by actually witnessing one.

That brings us to the most important wonder of all: the sign of Jonah. In this Jesus alludes to his resurrection—a central miracle, the crux on which all of Christianity hangs.[12] Does Jesus rise from the dead every time a seeker reaches the appropriate stage in his or her search for God? Will you or I ever have the opportunity to witness the resurrection in living color? No—the resurrection was a one-time event, and yet we can still have every confidence in its truthfulness, for the facts about the resurrection become real when we open our hearts to them. Like everyone else, we experience the power of the resurrection—and all of God's wonders—when we seek God.

As we will see in the next chapter, we have just as much reason to believe in Jesus because of the resurrection today as believers had 2000 years ago—no more, no less. The resurrection is the miracle on which our faith depends. If it is a hoax, so is Christ himself; if it really happened, the rest of the Bible, miracles and all, is validated emphatically, gloriously. But what else would you expect from an all-powerful God?

—————————————————————

Many Convincing Proofs:
The Resurrection

—————————————————————

Against the dark background of modern man's
despair, the Christian proclamation of the
resurrection is a bright light of hope.

WILLIAM LANE CRAIG

GOD ENTERED OUR WORLD IN JESUS CHRIST, whose life, teaching, and miracles point to his divine nature. And yet the ultimate proof of Jesus' divinity is his resurrection from the dead. Jesus predicted that he would rise, and after the crucifixion and resurrection, he appeared to the apostles and "gave many convincing proofs that he was alive."[1] If Jesus Christ did in fact come back from the dead, he must be the Son of God, just as he said he was. As I considered becoming a Christian during my college days, I was convinced by the overwhelming proof of the resurrection, and my confidence in the resurrection helped me decide to commit my life to Christ. I believe that you too will find the resurrection a deciding factor in your quest for faith.

The Foundation of Our Faith

The resurrection is crucial to the entire Christian message. It is "of first importance," according to the apostle Paul:

> For what I received I passed on to you as of first importance: that Christ...was raised on the third day according to the Scriptures, and that he appeared to Peter, and then to the Twelve...to more than five hundred of the brothers at the same time...to James, then to all the apostles, and... to me also (1 Corinthians 15:3-8).

Notice how Paul continues by responding to some who water down the reality and significance of the resurrection:

> And if Christ has not been raised, our preaching is useless and so is your faith. More than that, we are then found to be false witnesses about God...And if Christ has not been raised, your faith is futile; you are still in your sins. Then those also who have fallen asleep [died] in Christ are lost. If only for this life we have hope in Christ, we are to be pitied more than all men...If the dead are not raised, "Let us eat and drink, for tomorrow we die" (1 Corinthians 15:14-19,32).

Either the resurrection happened or it didn't, and either Jesus appeared after his death to a great number of people or he didn't. Christianity is a historical religion, based on real historical events. To remove the resurrection is to attack the very heart of the Christian message. Furthermore, if Christ was not raised...

> Preaching is useless.
>
> Christians are liars.
>
> Christian faith is useless.
>
> Sins are still unforgiven.
>
> The dead have no hope of salvation.

> Christians are the most pathetic creatures in the
> world.
> We might as well seek pleasure because life is so
> short.

Paul states these points emphatically, yet many claim that the Christian message and faith are still valuable even if Christ was not raised. They may insist, in a semblance of pseudospirituality, that even if there is no heaven, we should not live selfishly, but still remain Christians. This way of thinking stands in utter contrast—even opposition—to the biblical message of the resurrection. This wishy-washiness openly invites us to disprove the resurrection. But in reality, and according to the Bible, if the resurrection fails, the whole faith falls. And conversely, if we can accept the astounding miracle of the resurrection, we can certainly accept all the other miracles. The Christian faith is open to investigation—indeed, it begs you to examine it.

Corroborating Sources

Now that we understand that the claims of Jesus stand or fall on the resurrection, we should be eager to weigh the evidence for it. If you are not familiar with the story of the crucifixion and resurrection of Jesus, you will find it in Matthew 27:26–28:15; Mark 15:15–16:14; Luke 22:63-65; 23:26–24:12; and John 19:1–20:28. Select one of these accounts and become familiar with it.

Moreover, the details are documented in six independent biblical sources: Matthew's source (M), Mark, Luke's source (L), John, Acts (2:24; 3:15; 13:30, and many more texts) and 1 Corinthians 15:1-8. We also find references to the resurrection in 1 Clement (AD 96) and Polycarp (AD 110).

How old are these sources? In 1 Corinthians 15:3-11, Paul cites an earlier source for his faith in the resurrection, one he received from those who were in Christ before him. In Galatians 1:18, Paul indicates that his Jerusalem visit took place three years after his conversion, which itself occurred in AD 32 or 33. Thus the resurrection story is found at the earliest stratum of Christianity. It is not fictive, and to remove it would be to erase Christianity.

Fantasy Versus Reality

Two characteristics of the resurrection narrative stand out. First, although the basic details are the same in all accounts, they do not correspond in every detail. That is, minor discrepancies have not been ironed out, but allowed to stand. This testifies to the integrity of those who copied and compiled the New Testament. Second, no attempt is made to describe the resurrection itself. Compared to the elaborate accounts of the late second century and beyond, the Gospels are restrained. Consider the resurrection story from the Gospel of Peter (from about AD 180):

> Early in the morning of the Sabbath a crowd from Jerusalem and the surrounding countryside came in order to see the sealed tomb. Now in the night in which the Lord's Day dawned, while the soldiers kept guard in pairs in every watch, a loud voice rang out in heaven, and they saw the heavens opened and two men descending from there in great brightness and drawing near to the tomb. But that stone which had been placed at the door rolled by itself and withdrew to one side. The tomb opened and both of the young men entered. Then those soldiers, observing these things, awakened the centurion and the elders (for they themselves were on guard). And while they were relating what they had seen, again they saw three men coming out of the tomb—two of them supporting the one, and a cross followed them—and the heads of the two reached to heaven, but the head of the one being led by the hand extended above the heavens. And they heard a voice from heaven, saying: "Did you preach to those who slept?" And an answer was heard from the cross: "Yes."[2]

Now *that* is the stuff of legend! The accurate first-century accounts have been embellished, apparently to satisfy the curiosity of believers. But we are not interested in the apocryphal accounts; our aim is to examine the original resurrection story.

Jesus Died

Of course, the resurrection is a fiction if Jesus never died. And yet the historical record reveals that he was indeed executed, as 99 percent of all scholars agree. Even the skeptical scholar John Dominic Crossan admits, "That he was crucified is as sure as anything historical can ever be."[3] Jesus' execution is referred to in several extrabiblical sources, such as Josephus, Tacitus, Lucian, Talmud, and Mara Bar-Serapion.

Following is a diagram of the logical possibilities. It will be helpful to keep referring back to this diagram as you read about the evidence. We begin with the claim of the resurrection. Everyone agrees—the early Christians claimed that Jesus rose from the dead.

Then, regardless of whether Jesus was actually resurrected, the matter of the empty tomb remains. Either the tomb was occupied or it was vacant. Let's assume first that it was occupied, in which case there are two possibilities: (1) the first persons who proclaimed the resurrection went to the wrong tomb, or (2) all the appearances were hallucinations.

The Wrong Tomb

In 1907, Kirsopp Lake, a Harvard professor, invented the wrong-tomb theory. He thought that perhaps when the women went to prepare Jesus' body on Sunday at dawn, they accidentally went to the wrong tomb.[4] But is it really likely that they went to the wrong tomb? Or that none of the other disciples could remember the location of the new tomb, including Joseph of Arimathea, who owned the tomb and personally buried Jesus?[5] Sooner or later someone would have discovered the error and gone to the right tomb. Few have followed Lake in his speculation.

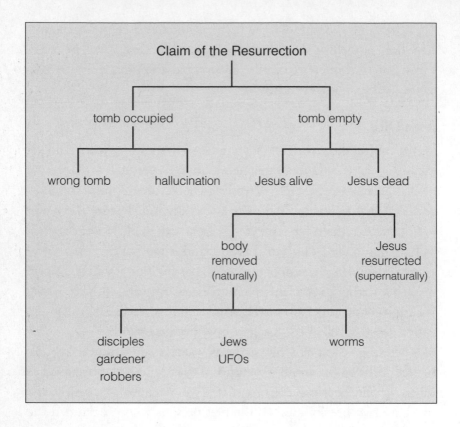

Hallucinations

One of my divinity school professors thought the claim of the resurrection was based on "holy hallucinations." This theory proposes that some overly excited followers were overcome with emotion and believed they saw a resurrected Jesus. But this theory has many problems: Why didn't Jesus' critics simply produce the body? And even if one or two of the disciples could conceivably have a hallucination, would *all* of them imagine they saw Jesus? Besides, visions of a dead person do not convince the bereaved that the person is alive. On the contrary, such subjective experiences confirm that the departed person is truly dead. Also, hallucinations occur when someone is hoping or expecting to see something (like a thirsty man in the desert imagining he sees an oasis). But the disciples were not expecting Jesus to be resurrected. If they had been, they would have been lined up at the tomb on Sunday morning because Jesus had predicted several times that he would rise from the dead on the third day.[6] They had heard Jesus say those words, but they never understood them, so they were not at the tomb, awaiting Jesus' return. They thought the crucifixion was the death of a dear friend, not the prelude to the resurrection. They expected no comeback.[7]

Another problem with this theory is Paul's reference in 1 Corinthians 15:6 to more than 500 eyewitnesses, most of whom were still alive—an odd claim to make if he didn't want these people to be independently questioned, to verify what they saw.

Yet the greatest flaw in the hallucination argument is the difficulty that we mentioned at first: the unsolved problem of the empty tomb. Where was the body? If everyone went to the tomb, why didn't the opponents of the faith simply produce Jesus' corpse? All of the attempts to explain away the resurrection operate under the same assumption: Jesus' body was missing.

Like the wrong tomb theory, the hallucination theory is a poor attempt to avoid the problem of the empty tomb and the missing body.

Swooning

The swoon theory proposes that Jesus never really died on the cross, but swooned and only appeared to die. After lying in the cool tomb for a few days, he revived and appeared to his disciples, and they thought he had risen from the dead. This theory has its proponents today, including Daniel Derrett and Barbara Thiering, who presume that Jesus lapsed into unconsciousness or a self-induced trance during the crucifixion. This hypothesis has several grave weaknesses:

- It assumes that Jesus deceived his disciples by allowing them to mistakenly believe he was raised. But would this be in line with Jesus' character? Was he really a deceiver?

- It assumes that Jesus survived 36 hours in the dark, cool tomb without food or water, wrapped up in linen and 75 pounds of preservative ointments.[8]

- It ignores the trauma that Jesus had suffered before being entombed: a sleepless night, clubbing, torture, flogging, the crowning with thorns, punching, weakness to the point that he stumbled under the weight of his own cross, crucifixion (nails being driven into his wrists and feet), and the thrust of a Roman soldier's spear into his heart.[9] Certainly Jesus died before he was laid in the tomb.

- It assumes that the Roman soldiers, experts in execution, were confused about whether Jesus was alive or dead. The executioners observed that the two thieves crucified along with Jesus were still alive, and they broke their legs to expedite their deaths, but they decided not to do this to Jesus because they were convinced he was already dead.[10]

- It assumes that Jesus, weakened by the crucifixion and then immobilized in linen wrapping, still had the strength to stand and walk on his pierced feet, roll the large stone away and overpower the Roman guards (with his pierced wrists), walk a considerable distance, and then manage to convince his doubting disciples that he had conquered death and risen from the dead.

The swoon theory refutes itself. Logic and the Scriptures alike tell us that Jesus was truly dead on the cross. The body was missing from the tomb that first Easter morning; this much is certain. So if we concede that Jesus died and his body was missing, where did the body go?

The Gardener

Some have suggested that the gardener moved Jesus' body. This hypothesis again raises the question of the motivation for removing the cadaver. It is true that Jesus' body was laid in a private tomb in a garden, but why would anyone move the body at such an early hour (dawn) on a Sunday morning? And how could a single gardener have overcome the Roman guards?[11] Breaking Pilate's seal on the tomb would have been a serious crime, an offense against the Roman state. And if the gardener did remove the body, why didn't he reveal its location once the resurrection was preached? Surely a friend of the Christians would have shown the body in order to spare them the persecution they were suffering, and a foe would have revealed its whereabouts to stop the rapidly growing Christian faith. Are we to believe that some unnamed gardener was patronizing the apostles, allowing them to believe and preach a patent falsehood, even when they began to be persecuted? The gardener can be declared innocent.

Thieves

Grave robbing was common in the ancient world. But even if we completely ignore the difficulty posed by the Roman guards, we must ask why grave robbers would take Jesus' body. Such thieves look for valuables, not corpses or bloodied grave clothes. Nothing of value was buried with Jesus. And who would steal a corpse weighing more than 200 pounds (counting the ointments and linens)? The suggestion that grave robbers stole the body of Jesus must also be dismissed.

The Jews

The Jews are the last ones on Earth we should suspect of removing and concealing the body, because they tried to stop the apostles from preaching about the resurrection (Acts 5:28,40). If they had Jesus' body, they could have put it on a cart, pulled it through the streets of Jerusalem, and shouted, "Yes, Jesus is risen indeed!" Jesus' body would have been the single most valuable evidence they could have used to stop the spread of the faith, so clearly they did not have it.[12] The possibilities are becoming fewer and fewer.

UFOs

The wildest alternative theory for the resurrection comes from people who have been stirred by the pens of science fiction writers. No evidence whatsoever implies that UFOs lifted Jesus' body from its resting place, and solutions like this are beyond the pale of verifiable data, so we will leave this suggestion where it belongs.

Worms

Coming up with a convincing solution for the disappearance of the corpse is becoming difficult. Did hungry worms eat it up (over a short weekend)? Abandoning these wild attempts to explain away the resurrection seems to be the sensible thing to do.

Deceitful Disciples

So far we have not considered the earliest explanation of the resurrection. The Jews immediately began to circulate a story that the guards were sleeping and the disciples stole Jesus' body from the tomb (Matthew 27:62-66; 28:11-15). Before we consider what happened to the body itself, we should notice that the Jews' explanation is a concession that the tomb was indeed empty.

(Incidentally, some critics have suggested that Christians inserted the presence of the guards into the story to show that the disciples could not have stolen the body. This too is a concession that the tomb was empty, for why would Christians invent the story of the guards if the Jews did not admit the tomb was empty? And of course, why would the Jews pretend the guards were asleep unless they conceded that the body was gone?)

To assess the theory that the disciples removed the corpse and then proclaimed that Jesus had risen from the dead, we must determine their motive. Why would they steal and lie, violating the clear teaching of their Master? Why would they suffer and die for a lie? From time to time a person of profound conviction will die for something he thinks is true (like Buddhist monks who set themselves on fire in protest of the Vietnam War or Shiite Muslims who believe that dying in the service of Allah guarantees a spot in paradise), but who would knowingly die for a lie? The apostles knew whether the tomb was empty—they all saw the tomb and the risen Christ firsthand. None recanted, even under intense pressure.[13] Consider these facts:

- Nearly all the original disciples were persecuted, beaten or flogged, and martyred.
- Paul and James (John's brother) were beheaded.
- Peter, Andrew (Peter's brother), and several others were crucified.

Besides, how would 11 timorous men (Judas had committed suicide) take on the Roman guard assigned to guard the tomb?[14] Furthermore, a deception could not account for the disciples' startling psychological transformation, in a matter of weeks, from timid and ineffective men to powerful preachers of Christ (compare John 20:19 and Acts 4:19-20).

Two more facts show that the disciples were not likely to have invented the resurrection. The first is the prominence of female testimony. Women were the first witnesses in all four Gospels. But women's words were inadmissible in a first-century Jewish court of law! If the Christians in that culture wanted to concoct a convincing story, they certainly wouldn't base it on the testimony of women. And second, the strict penalties against fraud (false testimony) in Jewish law weigh heavily against the charge of apostolic deception. We can safely conclude that the disciples could not have stolen the body.

Convinced Against Their Will

Now that we have rejected the alternate theories that attempt to explain away the resurrection, let us consider two more important issues. We have established that the disciples held to their story, even in the face of death. We should also note that some of the disciples were unlikely converts. Two deserve special mention. The Gospels portray James, one of Jesus' physical brothers, as a skeptic.[15] This is hardly surprising; after all, who would be inclined to believe that his older brother is the Son of God? Yet James joined the apostles after the resurrection and eventually served as a leader in the Jewish-Christian community. Around AD 62, James was martyred for his faith.[16] Hans Grass, a skeptic New Testament critic, admits that the conversion of James is one of surest proofs of the resurrection.

Another noteworthy convert is Saul of Tarsus, later known as the apostle Paul. He was not only a highly intelligent skeptic but also a sworn enemy of the church. He actively persecuted followers of Christ and did not hesitate to use deadly force to halt the spread of the faith.[17] Paul not only radically changed but also suffered repeatedly for his Christian convictions, eventually being executed during the reign of Nero.[18]

Historical Parallels

Some writers believe that nothing about Jesus or his resurrection is unique. They claim to have found numerous parallels from antiquity. The comparisons are so far-fetched that we will not waste too much space examining them. Many of the ancient myths are examples of *apotheosis*—a mortal becoming a god. Hercules built his own funeral pyre, immolated himself, and then rose to Mount Olympus. Aesculapius was killed by Zeus, who hurled a thunderbolt at him but later placed him as a star in the constellation Ophiuchus. Romulus (eighth century BC), son of Mars and cofounder of Rome, disappeared in battle and was mythologized as the god Quirinus. Other ancient myths involve dying and rising gods, such as the Semitic Tammuz and the Greek Adonis. The latter was killed by the tusks of a wild boar before being transported to the underworld. The classical accounts of Adonis do not mention any return to life.

Apotheosis is ascribed also to several historical figures. Empedocles (fifth century BC), the Greek philosopher who taught reincarnation, disappeared, and some of his disciples believed he was taken up to heaven. Julius Caesar and Augustus Caesar (first century BC) became gods and were venerated in emperor worship. Apollonius of Tyana, whom we met in chapter 8, was a first-century (AD) wonder-worker. When the aged Apollonius disappeared one day, his disciples erected shrines and claimed he had been caught up to heaven. He supposedly appeared in a vision to one of the Roman emperors in the late third century.

None of these parallels—and we have considered only a few— impresses. One last example, a favorite among critics, is that of the Egyptian god Osiris. This is the only pagan resurrection tale that clearly predates Christianity. Osiris was killed by his brother and later chopped into pieces. His sister-wife Isis found 13 of the 14 parts of his body, and Osiris came back as god of the underworld. But Osiris' story includes no bodily resurrection at all. Not much of a parallel!

In *The Quest of the Mythical Jesus,* radical New Testament scholar Robert Price alleges, "There was ample and early pre-Christian evidence for the dying and rising gods. The parallels were very close." And yet David Aune, specialist in comparative Near Eastern literature at Notre Dame, concludes, "No parallel to [the resurrection traditions] is found in Graeco-Roman biography." We must agree with Aune. None of these mythical accounts constitutes a true resurrection. Biblically speaking, a resurrection is more than simply a return to life. Being translated from the terrestrial plane to the celestial is not resurrection. It is the transformation of one's earthly body into a glorified heavenly body. On closer inspection, every alleged parallel turns out to be parallelomania!

He Is Risen!

Despite skeptics' clever attempts to explain away the facts, the traditional Christian explanation best supports the details of the narrative. Let's retrace our steps:

1. Jesus had to be either dead or alive when his body was placed in the tomb. He was certainly dead.
2. The tomb had to either be occupied or empty on the third day. All admitted it was vacant.
3. The body was either removed by others or resurrected by God himself. Others are unlikely to have taken the

> body away; the resurrection by God is the explanation
> that accounts for all the facts.

The chance that Jesus' corpse was resurrected by natural means is infinitesimally small, so the best explanation for the empty tomb is that Jesus rose from the dead. No naturalistic explanation accounts for all the data, including the appearances and the conversion of skeptics and enemies. A supernatural explanation is best: God raised Jesus from the dead. Jesus is who he (and his apostles) claimed he was. Jesus is the Messiah—the Son of God, both Lord and Christ.

In light of all the evidence, it takes more faith *not* to believe in the resurrection than to accept it as true. A supernatural resurrection is the only solution that makes sense of all the facts, including Jesus' repeated prediction that he would rise on the third day. The resurrection is also the best explanation for the radical transformation in the lives of the early disciples and so many Christians today. If the resurrection happened, we can draw three life-altering conclusions:

1. Jesus is exactly who he said he was. His resurrection confirms him as the Messiah (Romans 1:4).
2. We can be confident other biblical miracles occurred as well.
3. This historical event requires a personal response.

Paul boldly appealed to the resurrection when preaching to the freethinkers of Athens:

> In the past God overlooked such ignorance, but now he
> commands all people everywhere to repent. For he has set
> a day when he will judge the world with justice by the man
> he has appointed [Jesus]. He has given proof of this to all
> men by raising him from the dead (Acts 17:30-31).

Once we come to accept the truth of the resurrection, we are faced with a beautiful irony. The details of faith click into place as a logical consequence. Faith in the other miracles, indeed in the entire Bible, becomes a simple decision. Yet having come to faith, we must make the most difficult decision of all—whether to obey what we believe. The resurrection compels you and me to respond, just as it did the women who saw the empty tomb that misty morning 2000 years ago. It begs a choice, a commitment, a carrying of our own crosses so we too may rise anew.

Part 4

The Pursuit of God

So far we have examined reasonable evidence showing that God exists, that he has spoken to us in his Word, the Bible, and that Jesus Christ is who he claimed to be—the Son of God.

Yet many of us will still have a few psychological barriers to overcome before we can make an informed decision about God. First is the tremendous pressure we feel to adopt our postmodern society's religious pluralism. Might there be another way to God? Might people who practice other religions also believe implicitly in Christ? Second is the hurdle of doubt. Even when all the facts are laid out, we can always find further questions. Can we really be "sure of what we hope for and certain of what we do not see" (Hebrews 11:1)? And third is our natural resistance to commitment, which stops many of us at the brink of decision. How do we know we can safely entrust ourselves to God and to his Son, Jesus Christ?

In this final section of the book we will consider two pursuits that are currently in progress. For while we are contemplating and pursuing God, he has in fact been pursuing us all along—even before we had any conception of his existence.

One Way? The Bible and Other Religions

If all religions lead to God, how come most of them, having been given a thousand years at least, haven't yet arrived?

GORDON BAILEY

WE HAVE WEIGHED THE EVIDENCE for the existence of God. We have studied the reasons for accepting the truth of the Bible, the Word of God. We have examined the facts about Jesus of Nazareth, the Son of God. The case for Christianity is strong. When we allow God's Spirit to open our minds and quicken us, the voice of the ineluctable truth grips our hearts. At this point, some people begin seeking an escape route. Might there be another way to God?

To Kiev

I was about to board a flight from New York to Kiev, the capital city of Ukraine. The departure lounge was filling with passengers, at least 50 of whom were young men in black clothes and long beards. Some were reading prayer books, others chatting, all in high spirits.

These Hasidic Jews were heading to Kiev for Passover. I boarded and took my seat. No one was seated beside me, and I wondered if I was going to spend the next ten hours alone.

"Hi—I'm Chaim." The young man took the initiative, stretching out his hand as he took the seat beside me. He was from Brooklyn, and true to his name—the Hebrew word *chaim* means "life"—he was in good humor. We talked about life, faith, and his reason for going to Ukraine (to teach Jews how to celebrate the Seder). He and his friends, who were sitting all around us, had stayed up most of the night talking and praying about the trip. When I mentioned that I had spoken in a Manhattan synagogue not too long ago, Chaim said, "Wait a minute—I know you. I saw you on YouTube!" Sure enough, he had watched one of my debates with Shmuley Boteach.

I recognized Chaim too. Not that I had ever seen him before. The truth was, he reminded me of myself 30 years earlier, full of zest and eager to tell others. Might he be on the right track in his ardent Lubavitcher faith? Or to rephrase the question, don't all roads lead to God? Does it really matter which religion you follow, as long as you are zealous and devoted?

Do All Roads Lead to God?

Many people are asking these questions today. How could a loving God hold a difference in religion against anyone? After all, aren't we all worshipping the same God? In fact, a survey of 35,000 American adults shows that 70 percent believe there are many paths to God— all equally valid. Says Michael Lindsay of Rice University, "The survey shows religion in America is, indeed, 3000 miles wide and only 3 inches deep." Unfortunately, most people don't know why they believe what they believe, and they certainly do not understand the uniqueness of the Christian system. Subscribing to such beliefs, they dismiss Jesus' exclusive claim: "I am the way and the truth and the life; no one comes to the Father except through me" (John 14:6).[1]

I am deeply interested in world religions, so I have made it my business to study their scriptures and read their books. I have visited mosques in South Asia, synagogues in Europe and the United States, and Hindu, Buddhist, and Taoist temples the world over. I have dialogued with rabbis, monks, priests, imams, and other "holy men," sensing the religious impulse of fellow human beings looking for something beyond this life. In no way do I wish to trivialize their devotion or sincerity. But we aren't talking about sincerity—we're talking about truth.

As we shall see, various religions have divergent destinations. Moreover, the world's religious faiths are fundamentally different from the teaching of Christ. Choosing the right path does indeed matter. At first, such a statement may sound narrow or exclusive, but we should weigh the evidence before deciding.

Superficial Similarities

Contrary to public opinion, similarities among the world's religions are only superficial. All encourage five things:

> faith
>
> trust in a higher power
>
> obedience to that power
>
> group participation
>
> adherence to a code of behavior

All these elements applied to our Boy Scout troop. We were expected to be reverent and to attend a synagogue or house of worship. We obeyed the scoutmaster and our superiors, and we attended all the meetings, campouts, awards ceremonies, and so forth. The code of behavior was strict, and obedience was expected. And yet for all the good that Scouting has done for thousands of people, it is not a religion. These features could just as easily apply to the realm of politics:

> belief in the party line
>
> confidence in political power

promotion of legislation and civil obedience

attendance at rallies and congresses

commitment to the basic values of the party

Such qualities could also apply to participation in a sports league, Rotary club, or college degree program. Clearly, these superficial parallels are neither profound nor limited to religious beliefs. As we will see, the differences are much more significant.

I am working on this chapter from my hotel room in the United Arab Emirates. The *qibla* (indicating the direction of Mecca) is mounted on a table. Prayer rugs are available from reception on request. If I called on Allah, would I be praying to the Lord of the universe? No, for this is not the same God who is the Father of Jesus Christ.

Let's look at 12 of the most significant differences between the Christian faith and other world religions. These will show why "all roads lead to God" is a myth.

1. God

Christianity teaches that there is only one God, a personal heavenly Father beyond time and space, infinitely powerful and yet intimately concerned about our lives. He loves us and sent his Son, Jesus, to die for our sins. In a sense (and this is difficult to wrap our minds around), God himself died for our sins.[2] No other religion understands deity like this. In every other religion, man must reach up and out, hoping to find God. But in Christ, God has reached down to us. He has taken the initiative.

Other differences are also significant. Eastern religions like Hinduism identify God with the universe, so anything can be worshipped, and even humans are divine. Eastern religions usually accept many gods—Hinduism has more than 10,000. Many of these deities have human weaknesses: They are sexually starved, grotesquely fat and selfish, sadistic, or bloodthirsty. Indian and Chinese religions (Taoism and Buddhism) call for idol worship, which the Bible forbids.

The concept of God in Confucianism is vague. What counts is worshipping your ancestors. The Buddha actually refused to comment on the existence of God, and Buddhism was originally atheistic. In the Himalayas, I have seen prayer wheels spinning and prayer flags fluttering in the wind, attempts to secure a prosperous future for the believer. In Japan, adherents of Shinto attempt to persuade the *kami* (spirits) to answer prayers by writing them on pieces of paper and hanging them on prayer trees near the temple.

Islam's concept of God is more accurate: There is only one God (Allah), and he is majestic. But on the other hand, he is also distant from man, responsible for both good and evil, loving toward only the obedient (not sinners), and not the personal God of the Bible. In fact, Allah has predestined each person to go either to paradise or to hell, so fate is accepted as part of life. In Judaism the foundational concept of God is correct, but Jesus Christ is not accepted as the Son of David and Son of God, the deliverer predicted in the Old Testament (the Bible of Judaism). The full picture of God's love is missing.

The fact that many people use the word *God* does not mean they all believe in the same God, any more than sharing the name John means that everyone with that name is the same person. When I explain this point during lectures, I often ask, "Will John please stand up?" Usually, several men stand. Then I say, "You are all actually the same person—a human male with a head on a torso, a nose, ears, and so forth." The point is easily grasped: Superficial similarities do not prove identity.

Considering the differences, how can anyone say that we all believe in exactly the same God? Adherents of some religions would be quite offended if you told them that your God was the same one they believed in.[3] This first major difference deserves a lot of attention, for knowing God is what biblical faith is all about.

2. Sacrifice

Many religions offer animal or vegetable sacrifices to their gods or their ancestors. In Santeria, chickens are ritually killed. Until the

Romans destroyed the Jewish temple in AD 70, the Jews sacrificed bulls and goats. In parts of Africa, child sacrifice is still common. One reads about it in the newspaper weekly and sometimes daily. Human sacrifice was common before the advent of Christianity, though it has nearly been eliminated through the influence of the three monotheistic faiths—Judaism, Christianity, and Islam.

In paganism, man uses sacrifice to control the gods, who may reluctantly comply. Everything is backward. In Christianity, only the blood of Christ brings us close to God. More important, no further sacrifice effects atonement or merit of any kind.[4] This is a major divergence from the other faiths of the world.

The Major World Religions				
Religion	Origin	Founder	Date	Scriptures
Hinduism	India	—	1500 BC	Vedas, Upanishads, Bhagavad-Gita
Judaism	Middle East	Moses	1290 BC	Old Testament, Mishnah, Talmud
Zoroastrianism	Persia	Zoroaster	588 BC	Avesta
Buddhism	India	Buddha	536–483 BC	Tripitaka and others
Confucianism	China	Confucius	551–479 BC	Wu Ching, Ssu Shu (Analects)
Taoism	China	Lao Tse	600–500 BC	Tao Te Ching
Jainism	India	Mahavira	540–468 BC	Angas, Upangas
Christianity	Middle East	Jesus	6 BC–AD 30	Bible
Shinto	Japan	—	AD 550	Kojiki, Nihongi, Yengishiki
Islam	Arabia	Muhammad	AD 570–632	Qur'an, Hadith
Sikhism	India	Nanak	AD 1469–1538	Granth

3. History and Myth

In many faiths, mythical characters and legends are part of folklore and scripture. For example, Tibetan Buddhism has stories of holy men flying through the air, sitting still in cold caves for months at a time without eating, and even launching hailstorms with their fingertips. The ancient Greek religion taught that the world was carried on the back of the giant Atlas, and Indian mythology has the earth supported by four elephants on the back of a great serpent. Few Indians really believe this is true, but the myth continues to have religious meaning to Hindus.

When we come to Christianity, everything is different. Whether miracles actually happened matters. Whether a baby was born to a virgin in a particular country during a certain century is all-important. The idea is significant, but the idea without the fact behind it is useless. A man's resurrection from the dead is a central focus of the faith. In 1 Corinthians 15, the apostle Paul explained that if Jesus wasn't historically raised from the dead, the Christian faith is useless.

In 2 Peter 1:16, the apostle Peter insisted that the apostles, who first taught the message of Christ after his death and resurrection, knew the difference between truth and myth. His point is clear in every translation:

> "We have not followed cunningly devised fables" (KJV).
>
> "We did not follow cleverly devised tales" (NASB).
>
> "We have not depended on made-up legends" (GNT).
>
> "We were not making up clever stories" (NLT).
>
> "We did not follow cleverly contrived myths" (HCSB).

Fables, tales, legends, stories, myths—are these the stuff of Christianity? No, for it is a historical religion: Either certain crucial events happened or they didn't. Furthermore, the writers of the Bible knew the difference between history and myth and insisted that the distinction is vital. In contrast, other religions seldom insist on this distinction. Christians know the historical facts are important because if God, in Christ Jesus, didn't really visit our planet and pay the penalty for our sins, we are without any hope.

4. How God Speaks

Here again is an area in which the world's religions are deeply divided. Christianity, Judaism, and Islam urge that God speaks to man in Holy Scripture. Hinduism, Buddhism, Taoism, and Shinto play down the importance of scripture and instead emphasize looking within to discover truth. In other words, the Far Eastern religions hold to a subjective standard, the Middle Eastern and Western ones to a more objective standard.

In addition, in other religions, the teachings of the founder were originally more important than the founder himself. Muhammad, Buddha, and Confucius did not claim to be God but pointed to the truth as they understood it. This is not the case with Christianity. Jesus made himself the focus, not just his teachings. He said, "I am the way and the truth and the life. No one comes to the Father except through me."[5]

5. Commitment

Most religions lay down a law or set of rules and expect their followers to obey them. The commitment of the average member is usually expected to be lower than that of the holy person, whose devotion is a full-time obligation (a priest, rabbi, yogi, minister, monk, guru, and the like).[6] Christianity needs men and women to dedicate themselves to full-time service, but they are no more committed to God, in principle, than anyone else. The New Testament teaches that all members of the church should do the work of the church, not just the leaders. Every member prays, spreads the Word, learns the Bible, attends church, and employs the gifts the Spirit gives to empower believers for service. This high level of commitment is well beyond the expectations in most other religious groups.

Trying to get by with the minimum commitment leads to legalism, to being justified by adhering to a law. Religion becomes just a list of rules. If we can only be good enough, God will have to accept us. In the Qur'an, the holy book of Islam, Muhammad taught that by our own efforts we can earn Allah's mercy, earn salvation, and eventually earn paradise.[7] In fact, every religion is a legalistic, do-it-yourself approach to God—except Christianity, which teaches that we are saved only through the mercy of God. However, a true appreciation of this mercy should not cause us to be lazy, but to have an even stronger commitment. The real difference has to do with God's grace. Philip Yancey illustrates this truth with a story:

> During a British conference on comparative religion, experts from around the world debated what, if any, belief was unique to the Christian faith. They began eliminating the possibilities. Incarnation? Other religions have different versions of gods appearing in human form. Resurrection? Again, other religions have accounts of return from death. The debate went on for some time until C.S. Lewis wandered into the room. "What's the rumpus about?" he asked, and heard in reply that his colleagues were discussing Christianity's unique contribution among world religions. Lewis responded, "Oh, that's easy. It's grace."
>
> After some discussion, the conferees had to agree. The notion of God's love coming to us free of charge, no strings attached, seems to go against every instinct of humanity. The Buddhist eight-fold path, the Hindu doctrine of karma, the Jewish covenant, and Muslim code of law each of these offers a way to earn approval. Only Christianity dares to make God's love unconditional.[8]

The Bible teaches that commitment occurs naturally when grace is truly understood and appreciated.[9]

6. Scripture

With rare exceptions, in most religions, people don't read the sacred writings. That is left to the experts. This may be because the scriptures are difficult to understand. The result is that many members of other world religions are not familiar with their own scriptures. We should add that the Eastern religions (Buddhism, Shinto, Hinduism, and so on) place the least emphasis on studying scripture—which is for priests to do. Western religions focus more on scriptures but rarely resist the temptation to add to the text. Judaism adds massive commentary (Mishnah and Talmud), Islam adds tradition as important as the Qur'an itself (the Hadith), and Christendom added creeds, councils, statements of faith, and other authoritative writings.

Far from being readily comprehensible, Muslim, Hindu, and Buddhist scriptures contain enormous numbers of obscure passages, which even their top scholars cannot explain. This is to say nothing of the complicated laws and rituals. Eastern scriptures are so extensive that the average person could take several lifetimes to read the scriptures of his own religion. In Buddhism, the scriptures are hundreds of times longer than the Christian Bible. The Hindu creation story alone is hundreds of pages long, whereas the Bible puts the creation into just a few verses.

Biblical Christianity is unique in that nothing extra is added—under penalty of judgment.[10] It's the Bible plus nothing—except the personal responsibility of every follower to digest and spread the good news.

7. Outsiders

Most religions are little concerned with winning others to their position. Judaism focuses inward and rarely has converts. Hinduism, with its loose concept of truth, does not teach its followers to go and make disciples. Buddhism was a missionary religion a thousand years ago, but few Buddhists today consider outreach a priority. Even among fundamentalist Muslims, few spread the faith. (They firmly believe that they alone will be approved at the judgment day.[11]) Many Christian denominations, in the same way, avoid rocking the boat.[12] What Jesus modeled, on the other hand, is radically different from other religions. His followers are to actively make disciples of every nation.[13]

Critics of Christianity say it is exclusive. Actually, truth is exclusive of error and contradiction. Aside from that, the Christian faith is expansively inclusive. The ultimate vision is of multitudes of men and women from every nation, tribe, people, and language (Revelation 7:9). Are some of those who loudly proclaim that all roads lead to God actually just afraid to take a stand for truth?

8. Morality

Morality is another area in which we find tremendous differences among world religions. Most religions officially discourage drunkenness, bad language, gambling, premarital sex, and other actions, but they unofficially tolerate them because they are unable to give their members the determination or the power to live morally. This perspective and the Christian one are poles apart. Genuine Christians strive to live the moral life Jesus lived, so they have much more incentive to change and to offer each other help. Moreover, through the animating power of the Holy Spirit, Christians are able to overcome the flesh, building character and becoming more like the Lord.

The code of ethics in Jesus' Sermon on the Mount (Matthew 5–7) is second to none, with its emphasis on love for enemies, a pure heart, and a controlled mind. When questioned about which parts of the Old Testament were the most important, Jesus pointed to the commands to love God with all our hearts and to love our neighbors as ourselves.[14] Perhaps this is why Christianity has done so much to help the poor.

Other religions have lower standards of personal morality. The Qur'an authorizes holy wars (Jihad), polygamy, concubines, and wife-beating.[15] Hinduism has lusting gods and goddesses, to say nothing of a rigid caste system that seriously discriminates against the poor. The Hindu teaching that all suffering is the result of evil actions in previous lives and the Buddhist insistence that suffering is unreal have allowed millions to suffer alone. Shinto has no developed concept of morality at all, but speaks rather of duty. Christianity, however, demonstrates the highest standard of personal morality, for the goal is to be like Jesus.[16]

9. The Golden Rule

Jesus espoused the Golden Rule: "So in everything, do to others what you would have them do to you."[17] Other religions (Confucianism and Judaism) espouse the Negative Golden Rule, or the Silver Rule, which says, "Don't do to others what you wouldn't want them to do to you." Which is easier?

Christ taught that we should actively love our neighbors. Rather than wait for convenient opportunities to do good to others, we should create opportunities to help. Most persons try to mind their own business and not hurt anyone else, as though this were exemplary behavior. It is not exemplary at all. If that is all we do, Jesus would say we are unloving and selfish. Those whose eyes are open can always find opportunities to help meet others' physical, emotional, and spiritual needs.

10. Violence

A key distinction between the way of Christ and other faiths, seldom mentioned and sadly neglected, is the attitude toward violence. Nearly everyone seems to want peace, but war is accepted as a legitimate means for attaining it. At the risk of oversimplifying, violence is accepted in Confucianism, rejected in Jainism, virtually absent from modern Judaism, promoted in Islam and Sikhism, tolerated in Hinduism and (more rarely) Buddhism, but roundly condemned by Jesus.[18] Deplorably, in the fourth century, with the marriage of church and state, Christians engaged in acts of violence, including persecuting their enemies.[19]

11. Salvation

As we have already seen, salvation cannot be earned or deserved. It is God's gift to man. There is no way to work our way to God. But what is salvation? From what are we saved?

Most religions have some concept of salvation, but they disagree about what it is. In Islam it is freedom from hellfire. In Hinduism it is escape from the endless cycle of death and rebirth (reincarnation).

In Buddhism it is the realization that our self is only an illusion—we have no independent existence. Modern Judaism has little concept of salvation apart from a sort of salvation in this world (not the hereafter). In the Christian faith, however, salvation is freedom from sin and death. Only Christianity offers real hope: Jesus Christ dying on the cross in our place.

12. The Ultimate Goal

Do all religions lead to the same place? By now it should be plain that they do not. In Christianity the goal (heaven) is knowing God; in Islam, being rewarded by God in a paradise of wine, women, and song; in Hinduism, absorption into God and loss of personal identity; in Buddhism, loss of desire and the realization that there is no God and no you; in some other religions, discovering that you were God all along. How can we say that all religions have the same goal?

Moonlight and Sunlight

From my reading of the Qur'an, Bhagavad Gita, Upanishads, Sutras, Analects of Confucius, and other scriptures, I am convinced that every religion contains some truth, but no religion comes close to the Bible either in the amount of truth conveyed or in the purity of the teaching. The mixture of truth and falsehood is obvious. As David said, "And the words of the LORD are flawless, like silver refined in a furnace of clay, purified seven times."[20] If you're planning a very long lifetime, you may go ahead and systematically study all the scriptures of the world to find bits of truth. But you will save decades if you begin with the Bible.

The various world religions are like moonlight. Theirs is a reflected light, derived from the sun. Looking at God and the Scriptures that testify to Jesus Christ, on the other hand, is like looking at the sun itself. This is no reflected light, but the full incandescence of truth. Here is a summary of what we have seen about the Bible and other religions:

The differences far outweigh the similarities.

The Bible stands alone among the scriptures of the world.

All roads do not lead to God.

Oxford professor Alister McGrath provides this assessment:

The idea that all religions are the same, or that they all lead to the same God, is thus little more than an unsubstantiated assertion that requires refusal to acknowledge that there are genuine and significant differences among the religions. It is a kind of fundamentalism in its own right.[21]

As an ancient Jew once wrote about the Word of God, "Your word is a lamp to my feet and a light for my path."[22] Let's come into the light. There is a way to God—one way—but if we are going to find it, we'll need help from God's Word. To change the metaphor, other religious systems offer swimming instructions for a drowning person; Christ alone offers the life preserver.

There is no escape route from the truth. Though thousands of religions have been created, Jesus' claim stands: "I am the way and the truth and the life."

Double-Minded?
Dealing with Doubt

The beginning of wisdom is found in doubting;
by doubting we come to the question, and by
seeking we may come upon the truth.

PIERRE ABELARD

There are two ways to slide easily through life:
to believe everything or to doubt everything;
both ways save us from thinking.

ALFRED KORZYBSKI

EVEN IF YOU FIND THE EVIDENCE for God convincing, you may still have questions. There is always room to doubt. Theologians refer to God's modesty: He does not force us to believe. During our earthly lives, we are in control of our thoughts. If the spiritual world were visible, there would be little room to doubt. God's invisibility is a sort of guarantee that we are responding authentically. Faith is more than a response to evidence; it is a decision to believe.

Of course, faith, which involves willingness to accept the truth and trust the author of truth, develops *because* of the evidence, not in spite of it. When we see the proof, the time has come to respond accordingly. On the evening of the first Easter, Jesus approached "doubting Thomas" and said, "Reach here with your finger, and see My hands; and reach here your hand and put it into My side; and do not be unbelieving, but believing."[1] God understands our need for evidence.

Doubt, Good and Bad

Not all doubt is bad. It's like cholesterol—it comes in both good and bad varieties. The downside of doubt is that unbelief can flow from a wrong attitude toward truth, and when indulged it can lead us to some dark places. Persistent and deliberate doubt also distorts our thinking and eventually erodes faith. To be undecided is one thing; to prefer to be double-minded is quite another. Modest doubt may be the beacon of the wise (so said Shakespeare), but surely not immodest doubt or doubt that ignores the facts.[2]

The Bible has much to say about the unhelpful kind of doubt. It can be a consequence of refusal to submit to God's authority, a result of spiritual distraction, faithlessness in the face of otherwise potent prayer, or even a reflex to plain evidence when others are responding positively.[3] Thus doubt may have both intellectual and spiritual components.

However, doubt can serve positive purposes as well as negative ones. The upside is often discounted. Preachers may urge us to believe our beliefs and doubt our doubts, but is this healthy from a spiritual perspective? Believing everything and doubting nothing may seem like the simplest way to go, yet suppressing our questions and feelings leads to pretense. Intellectual dishonesty is not an admirable personal quality, nor is it encouraging to live with a sense of duplicity or hypocrisy. Better to ask the question. Questioning is actually conducive to conviction, for in fighting for our faith we engage both heart and mind. Moreover, when we authentically express doubt and seek for resolution, we strengthen our connectedness with others. We are more relatable and believable when we admit our struggles, and thus we connect with fellow seekers, including men and women of faith. Admitting our own struggles doesn't just provide an opportunity to strengthen our faith; it helps our relationships as well—and they in turn feed our faith. Honesty about our doubts, coupled with openness to real answers, creates a healthy cycle.

Sources of Doubt

Doubt has many causes:

- Witnessing the injustice in the world and the suffering of others can raise questions of faith, and if these concerns are left unaddressed, it becomes hard to believe. (See the discussion about suffering in chapter 1.)

- A lack of direction in life can cause angst and doubt, as can conflicting counsel or unexamined and conflicting principles. Clear thinking facilitates faith; confusion impairs spiritual vision.

- Yet another source of doubt is fatigue. When our physical or emotional reserves are low, it is easier to doubt than to believe. Enervated, so to speak, we lose our nerve.

- Seeing those we respect going through their own times of doubt or even quitting the faith also affects us. The fall of a leader easily fosters cynicism.

- Difficult passages in the Bible can dampen faith and zeal. We may give up too easily, falling prey to the facile explanations of skeptics. (See appendix C for help with the apparent contradictions in Scripture.)

- Perceived conflicts between faith and science affect many of us.

- Ironic as it may sound, trying too hard to believe can lead to doubt. When we overreach, committing ourselves to positions or interpretations not demanded by Scripture, we are setting ourselves up for disappointment.

We have already looked at most of these sources of doubt. Let's consider the last two.

Science

The evidence for the Big Bang constitutes cogent scientific testimony to the existence of a creator. We are confronted with a false choice when we are told, "Either there was a Big Bang *or* God created the universe." As we discussed in chapters 1 and 3, science is not the enemy of faith. Scientific knowledge is complementary to theological knowledge.

Some seek to create a supposedly biblical physics, mathematics, or biology. This is an inappropriate use of Scripture. Would we expect a biology textbook to contain the principles for building a healthy marriage? Not at all—though we would not be surprised to read that the biological purpose of marriage is to replicate genetic material with a minimum of copying errors. The Bible is not a science book, but a book primarily about our relationship with God but also our connections with other people (including family, friends, strangers, and the needy).

Another discovery of science is the enormity of the universe. In the 1800s, the Milky Way was thought to be the thickest part of the universe because of its great concentration of stars. In the 1900s, with the advent of more powerful telescopes, astronomers realized that our Milky Way is but one of perhaps a hundred billion galaxies![4] People often have one of two reactions to the stupendous enormity of the cosmos. The responses are poles apart, though each proceeds from a kind of awe.

One is the conclusion that we humans are as inconsequential as our planet, which is a satellite of a minor star in an insignificant galaxy. There is no God, no ultimate meaning. The flaw in this conclusion should be obvious. Are we really to believe that large things are more important than small ones? That large planets are necessarily more significant than moons and asteroids, elephants are more important than humans, and tall people are more important than short ones?

The opposite reaction combines awe with humility. Surely an intelligence is behind the cosmos—a being of such overwhelming wisdom and power that the only proper response is worship, not doubt.

Barking Up the Wrong Tree?

Like the Big Bang, evolution should not be a problem for Christians. Evolutionary theory attempts to explain *how* life came to be as it is, not why. The theory has no bearing whatsoever on the existence of the universe, only on how life has developed over time. Nor has the theory of evolution demonstrated that life was necessary—that is, that the conditions that permit it were destined to exist. Ultimately, Genesis is not a book about biology, and biological studies are not matters of salvation. True Christians differ widely in their views on the origins of life. Moreover, not many believers have taken the time to sift through the biological evidence. Nevertheless, opinions are strong.

In 2002, judges in Cobb County, Georgia (where my family resides), capitulated to political pressure and ordered stickers to be placed in science textbooks. They read, "Evolution is a theory, not a fact."[5] Yet by *theory* scientists do not mean that there is no evidence. In science a theory is a systematic explanation that makes sense of the facts, as in optical theory or gravitational theory. The word does not suggest a lack of data or imply that observations are pure guesswork. To defend one view of biology or another is not my purpose in this book. I simply want to demonstrate that we do not have to choose between God and evolution.

Polarization comes from both sides. A champion of atheism has written, "The fossil record screams out evolution, not creation."[6] Compare this to the assertions of a leading Scientific Creationist: "There is no evidence that the world is old," and "Satan himself is the originator of the concept of evolution," and "There are only two basic worldviews, creation or evolution."[7] But why is it necessary to choose one camp over the other? Could evolution not be part of God's plan, given that he normally works in processes?[8] Is there no common ground between faith in the Bible and the conclusions of science? Indeed there is.

While I was a student at Harvard Divinity School, the paleontologist and evolutionary biologist Stephen Jay Gould (1941–2002) worked 50 yards away at the Harvard Museum of Comparative Zoology. Though an atheist, he rejected the false division between faith and science: "Either half my colleagues are enormously stupid, or else the science of Darwinism is fully compatible with conventional religious beliefs—and equally compatible with atheism."

Gould was admitting that half his fellow academics, most of whom worked in the natural sciences, were believers. They joined the ranks of such giants as Dobzhansky, Gingerich, and Darwin himself, who was certainly not an atheist.[9] In his later years he described himself as either a theist or an agnostic, and he saw no necessary contradiction between evolution and theism.[10] Most of evolution's supporters in the nineteenth century were in fact churchmen. The polarization came once scientific jargon was hijacked to promote ideological ends. In truth, evolution should be a nonissue. Would that all Bible believers had the gracious spirit of Billy Graham:

> I believe that God did create the universe. I believe that God created man, and whether it came by an evolutionary process and at a certain point He took this person or being and made him a living soul or not, does not change the fact that God did create man...whichever way God did it makes no difference as to what man is and man's relationship to God.[11]

People who insist that seekers must choose between faith and science are presenting a false and unnecessary choice. The real issues, like the existence of God, the resurrection of Jesus Christ, judgment, and love are easily lost in the furor of court cases and private debates. When believers get sidetracked in discussions of evolution and other peripheral matters, they are barking up the wrong tree. False issues cause outsiders to doubt the Bible, which is actually silent on the matter.

Overreaching

The last source of doubt we will examine is yet another area where zealous believers create obstacles to faith. Some people strive so hard to believe that they commit to a premise with weak proof or even to an indefensible position. For instance, some people believe that no errors have crept into the Bible through the centuries—a difficult position to defend. But in chapter 7 we saw that minor copying errors in biblical manuscripts are not a problem because they do not prevent the message from being conveyed accurately.

Similarly, some people are convinced that Christians should not have to suffer illness—another unrealistic standard. The human body is indeed marvelous, but it's not perfect. Genetic errors and the wear and tear of life reveal its imperfections. Only if someone had been guaranteed the perfection of their body—a lifetime warranty, so to speak, for parts and service—should he or she be disappointed when things go wrong. God never promised a perfect body, just as he never promised a problem-free life.

Doubt and confusion also arise when we interpret illustrations beyond their limits. Christians understand God as the Father of Jesus Christ. Yet this is an analogical truth, not a biological one. The Son did not come into being as a result of sexual union between a Father and Mother. Understood on a literal level, the father-son analogy leads to the confusion exhibited in the Qur'an. Muhammad thought Christians taught that Jesus was the offspring of Allah and a consort. But the God of the Bible is not even sexual. In relation to us he is a Father, although maternal imagery is also used on occasion in Scripture.[12] Moreover, Christ is male in relationship to the church, compared to a groom with his bride. All Christians stand in a feminine relationship to Christ; we follow his headship as our husband and bear fruit for him through the implanted seed (the Word of God).[13] But we are not to conclude from these analogies that all Christians are females or that Jesus will rent a tux for a lavish wedding ceremony. This is not to say that the Bible's analogies are false, only that if we press them too far, we land in contradiction.

Genesis 1:27 contains another illustration that confuses many people: "So God created man in his own image." Yet God's image in humans has been tarnished, severely corrupted. Only in Christ, who is the image of the invisible God, is God's glorious image restored.[14] The image is not physical, but spiritual. But if we interpret "the image of God" literally, we end up with questions like these: What color is God's skin? Does he have a beard?[15] The image intended in Scripture is spiritual and includes such qualities as morality, self-determination, holiness, and virtue.

We are also overreaching when we create our own definitions. For example, when the Lord says in Genesis 1:26, "Let us make man," many Christians see the Trinity. After all, who could God the Father be talking to if not to the Son and the Holy Spirit? I am not saying that people are wrong to read the passage with Christian eyes and discern the Trinity. However, this conclusion is far from obvious in the text—which might refer to the angels, or a heavenly council, or might even be a royal plural (as when the queen of England might say, "We are not amused"). We should not be surprised if skeptics are slow to see the Trinity in such passages.

Preachers often tell us that the Hebrew word for *create* in Genesis refers to instantaneous *creatio ex nihilo,* and the word for *make* means to reshape something already existing. They do this in order to keep God as the Creator of the universe. Though it is true that cosmology and theology come together in Genesis 1, the linguistic insight is dubious. The same verb is used in Isaiah 43:1, where the Lord reminds Israel that he created them. Israel, of course, was not created in a day; the process took centuries. Dubious insights into ancient languages leave other people questioning the knowledge (or integrity) of the instructor.

Sometimes the translation of a Greek or Hebrew word or concept creates difficulties for modern readers. For example, the New Testament Greek word *teleios* is often translated *perfect,* which is correct but can be misleading.[16] Passages like Matthew 5:48 urge us, "Be perfect, therefore, as your heavenly Father is perfect." This perfection is maturity or completeness, not sinlessness—although God is certainly sinless. Some Christians easily become frustrated when day after day they fail to reach perfection. The opposite extreme is when people claim "sinless perfection"—that true believers no longer sin. As you can see from these examples, our interpretation of words has significant ramifications on our theology and faith.

Consider one more example of how overreaching can injure our faith. Biblical repentance is a change of heart and mind that leads to a change of life. The process is elegantly simple yet surprisingly profound. Some believers, after a period of maturing spiritually, realize how much they have grown in their appreciation of God's grace. If they approach the matter negatively, they conclude that they must not have understood the cross when they came to Christ initially. But we all grow in our gratitude over time. Tortured souls, however, may redefine repentance as brokenness, a state of total and mature surrender to God, and they begin to question their salvation.[17] They are overreaching. It is only a matter of time before spiritual struggles move them to doubt their conversion once again—and so the cycle continues.

The lesson these examples provide is simple: Don't make the Bible say what it does not say or force your faith to stretch beyond what God requires. When faced with a question or a doubt, don't panic or jump to unnecessary conclusions. Take the time to study, to think, to seek input. Find out if your issue is one God himself has ordered or if it was framed by men—well-meaning or otherwise—or even created by an oversensitive conscience.

Conclusion

The sacrifice of following Christ is high enough without adding false costs. Perhaps you have been plagued with doubt that you now realize was unnecessary because it was based on questionable interpretations, applications, or extensions of Scripture. Before you make a stand with your faith, be sure it is really one that the Bible demands.

God does not ask us to sacrifice our integrity or our intelligence, to check our brains at the door of the church, as some have charged. The greatest command, after all, is to "love the Lord your God with all your heart and with all your soul and with all your *mind*."[18] God gave us the ability to think, reason, and question. He asks for our minds but with our reason and logic intact. He wants our minds to be godly, not empty. He wants sincere loyalty, not blind devotion; he seeks sacrifice, not stupidity; he demands leaps, not lunacy.

Doubt, if accompanied by humility, patience, and persistence, can lead to a greater and sincerer faith. Confronting my doubts and pursuing answers to my questions has helped me grow in conviction since I first decided to follow Christ some 40 years ago. With an open mind, anyone can find truth in an age of doubt.

Biblical faith does not rule out intellectual struggle, as we see in the account of the desperate father imploring Jesus to heal his epileptic son. His prayer can be ours: "I do believe; help my unbelief" (Mark 9:24 NASB).

Taking the Plunge:
Making an Informed Decision

No man ever repented of being a
Christian on his death bed.

HANNAH MORE (1745–1833)

God has promised forgiveness to your repentance, but He
has not promised tomorrow to your procrastination.

AUGUSTINE (354–430)

WE HAVE SEEN THAT ACCEPTING THE MESSAGE of Christ is not a leap into the dark, but a step into the light. The evidence stacks high on the Christian side. I have presented substantial, logical evidence that supports three all-important, life-changing facts:

- God is real. His existence is a reasonable conclusion of many lines of evidence.

- The Bible is the Word of God. It conveys God's message to mankind.

- Jesus is the Son of God. In Christ, God has come to our world.

I hope this book will bring you faith if you have had none, strengthen your faith if you doubt, and give you courage and conviction if you have kept your faith to yourself. You have seen the evidence and weighed the arguments on both sides. If you are lingering in indecision, I urge you to consider the words of the prophet Elijah in 1 Kings 18:21: "How long will you waver between two opinions? If the LORD is God, follow him." Take the time to review the facts and then make a decision to believe.

But don't stop there! The leap of faith is more than an intellectual assent. True, saving faith includes obedience, as James wrote:

> What good is it, my brothers, if a man claims to have faith but has no deeds? Can such faith save him?...Faith by itself, if it is not accompanied by action, is dead...You believe that there is one God. Good! Even the demons believe that— and shudder (James 2:14-19).

Now that you know the truth, are you going to act in integrity? This is your decision—the most important one you will ever make. As Jesus said, "Now that you know these things, you will be blessed if you do them" (John 13:17). On the other side of the coin, he also said, "If you were blind, you would not be guilty of sin; but now that you claim you can see, your guilt remains" (John 9:41). What about you? What will you do with Jesus?

The True Seeker

Throughout our study, we have examined compelling evidence for God and the Bible. Are we to imagine that seeking God is merely an intellectual pursuit, like a crossword puzzle, Sudoku, or 1000-piece jigsaw puzzle? Do we figure it out and then move on to something else? Not at all, for in our pursuit of God we come to realize that dynamic forces are in play and that he has been pursuing us all along. From Genesis to Revelation, the Bible consistently describes God as the one taking the initiative and Jesus Christ as the one who came "to seek and save the lost."[1] What kind of God are we deciding to believe in? How does the Bible describe him? Let's review.

A Forgiving Father

God is portrayed as a loving Father. Although he knows our hearts and their inclinations, he is the Father of the prodigal, longing for us to reciprocate his love and preparing our way back to him. He is ready to forgive and more patient than we can imagine.[2]

A God for All Nations

God has worked among the Jewish people for generations, beginning with their founding fathers, Abraham, Isaac, and Jacob, and culminating with their most famous descendant, Jesus Christ. Yet the plan was never to bless just one nation. Throughout both Testaments we see a plan of universal scope. This is no ethnic God![3]

Transcendent yet Immanent

When Paul addressed the intellectuals of his day in Athens, he underscored two truths. The infinite God cannot be put into a box or reduced to a formula. He is transcendent. At the same time, he is not far from us; he is the element in which we live. He is immanent. And he longs for us to reach out to him.[4]

The Cross

Nowhere does God come closer to us than in the cross, where deity suffers for humanity. The wounded one has conquered sin and death, and through his death we may be born anew. Equally marvelous is the revelation that if we have been truly transformed through Christ but then wandered, he is ready to receive us again.[5] If you are not familiar with the story, set aside time to learn about the cross. Read the account in one of the four Gospels. Perhaps you might begin with the arrest of Jesus and then study the message that launched the church in Acts 2.[6]

What conclusion does the evidence point to? Why should we believe in the God of the Bible? It would not be far off the mark to say he believes in us.

Priorities

I got a chuckle reading the newspaper the other day. In Germany, an 80-year-old woman was robbed of her handbag. Like the woman, the thief, a man of 41, was on a bicycle. What did she do? She pursued him. As a result of her determination, in time the police joined the chase. The woman wanted her handbag back—and she got it. We too want some things back, items of inestimable value: innocence, truth, life, and a relationship with our Creator.

I once had the opportunity to meet the president of India. The meeting I had attended of the *Hind Kusht Nivaran Sangh* (a national leprosy relief foundation) had concluded, and hundreds of people swarmed in the lecture hall, hoping to rub elbows with the moguls of the political world. I spied the president in the crowd. Turning sideways, I maneuvered my feet into position and then my body. With a turn to the left and a twist to the right, I slid my feet toward my goal, carefully keeping them on the ground lest I step on anyone. Repeatedly smiling, saying "Pardon me," and zigzagging my way through the throng, soon I was not far from the president. I spoke loudly and clearly over the ambient chatter, the crowd parted slightly, and I slipped through the opening. The president, glancing up, noticed me (probably partly because of my height and light skin). I extended my hand, and we connected.

Why did I make the effort? Because it seemed important. If we will take such steps to meet a flawed, mortal, fellow human, how enterprising, zealous, and determined should we be to know the infinitely holy God?

God has sought us; now it is our turn to seek him. We must respond in faith, making an informed decision. Simply agreeing with the evidence is not enough. God expects us to repent (change) and entrust our lives to him. We must reorder our priorities.

Jesus promised that if we seek, we will find. Our search must not be idle; we are to seek first his kingdom (his sovereign rule in our lives). Few are willing to pay the price, though the reward is beyond all comparison.[7]

But I Need More Time!

If you are not acclimatized to the spiritual world, the gospel can be a lot to take in. When I visited the Himalayas, I learned a lesson: Move too quickly, and light-headedness takes over. The body needs time to adjust to the altitude. If you are new to faith, you may spend some time feeling as if you're hyperventilating, but eventually belief will begin to feel normal. God understands that some of us need time to grow. That's why Jesus has not yet returned to claim his own: "The Lord is not slow in keeping his promise, as some understand slowness. He is patient with you, not wanting anyone to perish, but everyone to come to repentance."[8]

Some people ask for more time not because they are overwhelmed, but because they don't want to change. Their excuses are merely ploys—delay tactics—and God is not fooled. It is always easier to talk, endlessly seeking, than to find and commit.[9]

We need a game plan, a strategy. Procrastination is not a strategy. The decision to become a Christian is too important for either idleness or haste. We must weigh the evidence, but then we must make an informed decision as soon as possible.

We hold two truths in tension. Our situation is critical; tomorrow is not promised. And yet we need time to process, and some people need more time than others. One person comes to terms with the gospel in a day, and another needs a month. I have shared the good news with several people who have taken a decade or two to make their decision. Pondering the implications of biblical truth can be helpful, but if you delay the inevitable, the sprout of faith in your heart might wither. Take the time you need to cultivate your faith but with a sense of urgency, knowing that "you are a mist that appears for a little while and then vanishes" (James 4:14). As the saying goes, "Take your time, but hurry."

Where to Go from Here

How can we ensure that our faith grows while our quest continues? What practical steps can we take?

Are You New to Faith?

- *Reading.* To begin with, keep reading. Read to learn, read
  with an open heart and mind, and read to let God change
  your life. To get started, refer to appendix A.

- *Friends.* You need someone who can help you understand
  the Scriptures. Even the noble and intelligent Ethiopian
  solicited help from Philip. Find a committed Christian
  who can teach you more about the Bible, someone you
  can trust to challenge you and empower you to give your
  best to God.

- *Prayer.* Pray for God to purify your heart so you can see
  his truth clearly. A truly spiritual life is based on daily
  study and prayer, which require forming new habits in
  your daily routine.

- *Practice.* In John 8:31-32, Jesus said, "If you hold to my teaching, you are really my disciples. Then you will know the truth,
  and the truth will set you free." Sometimes, as they say, the
  proof is in the pudding. If you get hung up in your head,
  try out some of the principles of the Bible and see how they
  work in the real world. In John 7:17, Jesus said, "If anyone
  chooses to do God's will, he will find out whether my teaching comes from God or whether I speak on my own."

- *Church.* This word literally means "assembly," and involvement in an assembly of believers is vital to your spiritual
  well-being. The church is the body of Christ, and our survival as disciples and members of that body depends upon
  our active involvement.

- *Conversion.* As you continue to study, you will see exactly
  what is involved in your decision. Finding out what God

requires is easy—just read the book of Acts. There you will find many accounts of men and women becoming Christians. You will see what God has to say about faith, repentance, and baptism.[10]

Are You a "Doubting Thomas" (Wrestling with Your Faith)?

- Honestly and clearly write out your questions and doubts. Talk about them with a person who can help you sort through them, and come up with a plan for researching and studying these issues. Laziness and inertia are some of the enemy's favorite weapons against faith.

- Write down the convictions you already have and why you believe them. Remind yourself of what you believe (and why) whenever you are tempted to vacillate.

- "Stop your doubting, and believe!" (John 20:27 GNT). The Christian walk is an adventure through an ever-changing landscape. Have the maturity to realize that your faith will be tested and forced to grow throughout your Christian walk. Some things you may never fully understand—the Bible acknowledges that God and some of his ways will always be mysterious—but you can surely know enough to put your faith and trust in God and in Christ.[11] Don't let doubt paralyze you for the rest of your life. There comes a time to make a decision. Most of your questions (perhaps all of them) can be answered reasonably, and once your biggest questions are satisfied, the time has come to move forward in peace and confidence.

Is Your Faith Strong?

- Continue to grow, to feed your faith with books like this one. The bibliography can help.

- Explore new areas of biblical education.

- Find someone with whom you can share your convictions—
  a young believer, a Christian with weaker faith, or a person
  who has not yet heard the truth.

A Shock to the System

I was with a friend in Finland, a beautiful country of forest and lakes. Our cabin stood in dense woods with a sauna nearby. The air in the sauna was overpowering—nearly 200 degrees Fahrenheit (93 degrees centigrade). And yet it was nothing compared to what came next. We dashed out of the sauna and plunged into an ice-cold lake. Jolted to reality, I was breathless. Despite the shock, the experience was deeply refreshing.

Coming to Christ can be that way. Yes, it is an encouraging, sensible step, the beginning of a fabulous journey with an indescribably wonderful destination. Repentance is refreshing; we undergo a new birth. If inertia, pride, or fear do not paralyze us, we take the plunge. We are beginning to live for God by the Word of God and through the Son of God. At last, we find rest for our souls. It's like coming home, coming to our senses—but it can be a shock all the same.

The day before I came to Christ, I was at a Christian retreat that included a class on the evidence for fulfilled prophecy and the resurrection of Christ. Suddenly something clicked. *This is phenomenal!* I thought. *If I could learn this material and share it, I could help people know the truth. I could make a difference in the world!* My notes were interspersed with the names of friends I would want to talk to. I wasn't yet a follower of Jesus Christ, but for the first time in my life I was becoming convinced about matters of faith. My heart was pumping—hard. Courage was growing, and I knew I couldn't turn back. I was ready to take the plunge.

Even as I was born again, a passion to study and share the evidence for God and the Bible was taking root and coming to life in my heart. This is a significant part of my ministry to this day. The world is dying of hunger for the truth found in the Bible. I can attest to this fact, as I have had the opportunity to present the Christian message in more than 100 nations.

Jesus said, "Blessed are those who have not seen and yet have believed."[12] We are among the blessed, who believe because of the evidence and testimony of reliable witnesses.

In an age of doubt, why believe in God? Because all of creation testifies to his presence. Why believe in the Bible? Because it offers true and reasonable answers to the fundamental questions about our universe, our planet, our civilization, and ourselves. Why commit to Christ? Because in him we meet the God who loves us and by whose light we are able to see reality.

"For Christ's love compels us" (2 Corinthians 5:14).

Appendixes

Appendix A:
Bible Study Strategies

A Man Without a Plan

NOT UNTIL AGE 16 did I meet someone who read the Bible, followed it, and talked about it. I was intrigued, to say the least. By 17 I was reading 10 or 20 minutes a day, usually when waiting to pick up my father at the train station. If his commuter was delayed, I read entire chapters of Scripture; if it was on time, only a few verses. The first time I read the Scriptures for myself, I had no method. When I had nearly finished the whole Bible, I took a notebook, skimmed through my Revised Standard Version, and wrote out many "nice verses" on such themes as light, freedom, and goodness. I was looking for inspiration, but my approach was not balanced. Omitted from my notebook were all the challenging verses, like Luke 9:23 and John 12:24. To be honest, I had great difficulty finding my way around. Unlike the Ethiopian government official, I had no one to guide me.[1]

My approach drastically changed with my conversion to Christ. I read books that helped me go deeper, paid attention to church classes, memorized Scripture, and shared what I was learning with anyone who would listen. Most important, I developed a daily routine and commitment to Bible study that has stayed with me.

Four Levels

I learned that having a plan enables us to get more out of the Scriptures. In this appendix we will identify four levels of Bible study, using the analogy that God's Word is like the ocean—vast, deep, and life-sustaining.

When I was a little boy in Florida, I was afraid of the water. I had a few swimming lessons but was always fearful of drowning. I much preferred to walk on the beach, looking for shells and interesting flotsam, though walking into the waves was also fun. Required equipment: none. *Level 1.*

Later, in the murky lakes of northern New Jersey, I learned to swim. My confidence grew, and in the Scouts I earned the swimming and lifesaving merit badges. Required equipment: swimsuit. *Level 2.*

Fifteen years later, I used a snorkel. En route to Australia, my wife and I stopped in Hawaii. The breathtaking underwater views, even close to shore, were as mesmerizing as they were unexpected. Even with such simple gear, the clarity of vision and the bright colors of the undersea creatures were delightful. Required equipment: snorkel, mask, and fins. *Level 3.*

Ten years after that, I took a scuba course. In places like Thailand, Puerto Rico, and Guam, I have donned the air tank and been submerged in the sea. Scuba is different from snorkeling, as the magnificence of sea life is all around you, not just below you. Scuba is also more hazardous, and as you look up at the surface of the water, perhaps 40 or 80 feet overhead, you are reminded of your mortality. But the experience is worth the risk! I have navigated submarine canyons, swum with turtles, beheld an enormous Portuguese man o' war, held an octopus in my hands, maneuvered around wreckage from World War II battles, and wondered what was beneath me in the dark blue abyss. Required equipment: mask, tank, buoyancy vest, regulator, depth gauge, and more. *Level 4.*

Shore

Like beachgoers, most Bible readers stay on the shore, content to be amused by whatever is easily visible (shells, driftwood, and perhaps dolphins frolicking). They hunt for interesting verses with little regard for context.

Why do so many stay at level 1? Perhaps because even reading the Bible randomly has its payoffs. Every page contains good stuff, even if the sense of the whole is lacking. Besides, going deeper can get lonely. Fewer people are willing to go there, and the crowd brings a sense of security. Also, most churches promulgate a shallow theology. For example, preachers often foster attitudes like these:

- "The Bible interprets itself." This wrongheaded axiom sometimes appears in other avatars, like "The Spirit will show you what a passage means," or "If you are a true Christian, you won't go wrong."

- "Deeper study is unnecessary. It leads to few positive results and often to spiritual disaster." Associated ideas include the notion that one need read no other book besides the Bible and the still-common opinion that there is only one authorized translation—be it the King James Version or the New International Version.

- "If a certain interpretation of a passage works (that is, if it leads to good results), it is probably correct." Such pragmatism, so deeply rooted in our culture, is a potent disincentive to deeper study.

The shore may be a great place for a beginner, but in time it will become old. Searching for lone verses is not the best strategy. At some point, we need to swim.

Swimming

Going from level 1 to level 2—taking to the water—requires a small investment of time and discipline, but it's certainly within the capacity of even a moderately educated person. Rather than reading isolated passages, a swimmer reads paragraphs and develops a feel for context. Our natural tendency is to read atomistically—moving verse by verse and focusing on minute portions of a text rather than studying it as a whole. But each verse is part of a flow of thought, a developing argument, a logical sequence, a greater whole. We should be asking ourselves questions like these:

> What is the point of this paragraph?
>
> Who is speaking or writing, and to whom?
>
> What is the occasion for the message?
>
> How does this relate to us? Does it include a biblical principle?

Every passage has a context—a setting in which a truth of God's Word is somehow revealed, clarified, illustrated, or applied. Beware of the isolated verse taken out of context, especially if it is being pressed into service to prove a dubious point. Remember, as many others have said, "A proof text out of context is a pretext."

For example, 1 Corinthians 1:10 urges us to be of one mind, to be completely united in thought. Taken by itself, the passage might seem to encourage us to hold the same opinions, with no allowance for variation. And yet that is not the meaning of the text. The disunity referred to is clarified in the rest of the chapter: following personalities rather than following God. That (correct) interpretation allows for considerably broader possibilities than the narrow view that all Christians have the same opinions. Or consider 1 Corinthians 11:1. Paul urges his readers to imitate him. Is this an undefined order to imitate him in every way? No. Even the isolated verse itself qualifies the imitation: "as I follow Christ." Paul did not ask us to imitate him in his marital state, to change our name to *Paul,* or to spend more time in prison. Nor did he ask us to imitate his weaknesses. The context is a discussion of voluntarily surrendering Christian liberties for the sake of Christian love. Paul reminds us that Christ gave up certain freedoms, as should Paul and his readers. Again, a grave error of misinterpretation is avoided by simply reading around the passage to determine the context.

Next, as we move farther from shore, we need to develop the discipline to complete what we have started. Make a habit of reading each book of the Bible all the way through. When you begin reading the Bible, do not feel compelled to start with Genesis and read every book of the Bible in order. But when you choose a particular book to read, read that one book all the way through before you choose another. This will help you remember what is in each book and appreciate each author's unique offering and the larger point of that part of the multivolume library of the Bible. Further, if you have never done so, finish reading the entire Bible. This builds self-confidence and credibility with others. If this is your first time through, you may want to keep track of where you have been. Find a system that works for you. If you read three or four chapters a day, you can read the entire Bible in a year. I know many Christians who have read the whole Bible 10, 20, 30, or 40 times through simply by consistent daily reading—year in, year out. This has been my own practice since I began to follow Jesus Christ.

One last suggestion if you are at level 2: Keep one foot in each Testament. If we were to give equal time to every book or chapter of the Bible, we would be spending three quarters of our time in the Old Testament. That is fine if you study, say, four chapters a day, three from the Old Testament and one from the New. But unless we carefully balance our study, we can lose sight of Christ. He is, after all, the ultimate goal to which every book in both Testaments points. My advice is to do some reading in the Old Testament and in the New Testament every day. And remember the old adage: "The Old Testament is the New Testament concealed; the New Testament is the Old Testament revealed."

Snorkeling

Despite the spectacular vistas and breathtaking inspiration, few bother to don facemask, snorkel, and fins. The mask clarifies and magnifies our underwater optical field. The snorkel enables us to breathe while keeping our faces in the water and enjoying an uninterrupted view. The fins enable us to move more efficiently through the water. The equipment is easy to use.

However, many have not overcome their fear of the water (level 1), or if they do enjoy a swim (level 2), they prefer to keep their heads above the surface. In level 3, Bible students have moved well beyond developing personal discipline, deepening their feel for context, and grasping the big picture of the biblical story. Like snorkelers, they have learned to use basic equipment. No longer do they read solitary verses or even chapters. When they study the Scriptures, they study an entire book of the Bible. They understand how each book is constructed, and its themes, arguments, and literary genres. Study at level 3 is even more exhilarating than at level 2. What are the tools of the trade? Here are a few.

- *A good Bible version.* Be careful about paraphrases and loose translations, such as The Message, The Living Bible, and The New Living Translation. Lean on the more literal versions, like the New American Standard Bible and the New King James Version. Take advantage of the newer, readable, and reasonably accurate versions, like the Holman Christian Standard Bible, the New English Translation, the New International Version, Today's New International Version, and the English Standard Version. Study Bibles are available in each of these versions, chock full of tables, maps, cross-references, synopses, and other data. A study Bible is a wise investment.

- *A second version.* The original Greek and Hebrew manuscripts (which we no longer have) were perfect, but because of the nature of languages, no translation can perfectly replicate the original. You can learn a lot about the idiosyncrasies of translation simply by opening up more than one Bible at a time. This is vital if you are preparing lessons for teaching or preaching.

- *A concordance.* This reference book lists every appearance of a word in the whole Bible and is very useful for word studies, thematic studies, and easy location of passages. Many Bibles include them, and software programs make word searches fast and simple.

- *An Old Testament survey* and a *New Testament survey.* These books will introduce you to the background of the Bible; present the basic history and geography behind the various books; explore issues of authorship, dating, and provenance; and identify the literary genres.

- *How to Read the Bible for All Its Worth* by Gordon Fee and Douglas Stuart. This is a compact and readable introduction to the various literary genres of the Bible, including narrative, epistle, law, prophecy, apocalyptic, and gospel. Also get a copy of their companion volume, *How to Read the Bible Book by Book.*[2]

- *Web sites.* Ample online resources are available.[3]

- *Commentaries.* As you explore the text, turn to commentaries as the last step rather than the first. Still, they can be very helpful. Series generally have many authors, so you may want to create your own collection by author rather than investing in one huge series.

- *Other resources.* Take advantage of Bible dictionaries, topical Bibles, Bible handbooks, and Bible software.

These basic tools will equip you to navigate Scripture with relative facility.

The biblical story takes place in space and time, so geography and history are vital for understanding the background of biblical times.

This is just as true for the New Testament as for the Old. To bring biblical places to life, maps are essential. Even better, if you ever have the opportunity to visit these locations, how much you will gain! Many times I have prayed in Gethsemane, walked in Capernaum, and sloshed through Hezekiah's Tunnel. I have spoken in the theater in Ephesus, scaled the Areopagus, clambered over the ruins of Corinth, crawled into pyramids, preached in Philippi, ascended Mount Nebo, sweated in the Desert of Sinai, and even swum in the Dead Sea.

In addition to geography, a serious Bible student will learn the basic flow of biblical history. This includes the sequence of the historical stages, ideally with their dates.

primeval era	Assyrian exile
patriarchal age	Babylonian exile
slavery in Egypt	Persian period
Exodus and desert wanderings	Greek period
conquest	Hasmonean period
united kingdom	Roman period
divided kingdom	

Together, a little bit of history and geography go a long way to orient you to the world of the Bible.

The overwhelming majority of Bible readers stay at level 1 while some move on to level 2. Both groups lack this orientation we have discussed in level 3. Let me be bluntly straightforward. Much of the Bible, perhaps most of it, is hard to understand. I am not saying that the message or the major themes are obscure. But considering the large portion of the Scriptures that are poetry (a third of the Bible) or that assume familiarity with ancient locations and events, the average reader does not fully grasp most of the Bible and easily becomes bored or confused. If this sounds ungracious of me, or if you doubt the veracity of my observation, just take a look at the average person's Bible.

You will see that the most worn (the most read) parts are in the New Testament, Psalms, and Proverbs. But most of the historical, poetic, and prophetic books remain untouched. This is lamentable. *All* of the Bible is interesting and applicable if we have equipped ourselves—if we have truly made the transition from level 2 to level 3.

Back to our swimming analogy: The great benefit of snorkeling is the improved underwater vision. Similarly, Psalm 119:18 records this prayer: "Open my eyes that I may see wonderful things in your law." The modest investment in equipment is well worth the expense.

Scuba

Only a few study the Scriptures at level 4. Scuba gear is not cheap, even to rent. In the same way, the freedom of moving freely through the pages of the Bible comes with a price. When diving, breathing underwater has its risks. At greater depth, divers are exposed to greater pressure and can succumb to nitrogen narcosis and other hazards. Yet the freedom to approach a matter from multiple angles—from above, alongside, or beneath—truly affords a three-dimensional perspective.

What is the sophisticated equipment of the biblical scholar? Though many affect proficiency in the original languages (Hebrew, Aramaic, and Greek), linguistic facility should not be feigned. It takes years of study at the university level, sustained by regular practice.[4] Theological courses are essential. A serious approach is demanded by the depth and seriousness of the subject matter. This attitude is all the more vital for one who teaches others.

Profound

If you are a Bible student, at which level do you function? What would it take to move to the next level? And if you are new to the Scriptures, are you willing to invest in a strategy? Do not be lured by fraudulent and facile claims. Shortcuts are never helpful in this terrain.

Of course, given the immensity of the domain of biblical studies, there is no room for pride. Even if we lived to be 200 with full possession of our faculties, we could only scratch the surface. This should not be surprising. The average ocean depth is 12,430 feet, or 2.35 miles (3790 meters), with some regions as deep as 35,840 feet, or 6.78 miles (10,924 meters).[5] *Profound* is scarcely the apposite term to describe the Bible, for the correct word should also denote reverence and humility. God's Word is utterly and unfathomably profound, for "who has known the mind of the Lord?"[6]

Appendix B:
The Trinity

No Simple Doctrine

THIS APPENDIX CONTAINS INFORMATION about the doctrine of the Trinity. I accept this doctrine, though during the course of my theological studies, I did not embrace it immediately. Maybe it's my high-church upbringing or my instinctive distrust of the abstractions of medieval theology, but something about the doctrine of the Trinity felt contrived—it's just too neat, too simple. (Or maybe it's too deep for my shallow mind!) Yet I know I must not shirk my authorial duty; moreover, it's good to push oneself. I like what C.S. Lewis said:

> If Christianity was something we were making up, of course we would make it easier. But it is not. We cannot compete, in simplicity, with people who are inventing religions. How could we? We are dealing with Fact. Of course anyone can be simple if he has no facts to bother about.[1]

We are indeed concerned with the facts, with sifting truth and error. The truth is, the Trinity is not the sort of doctrine that inventors of religions would concoct—which is one reason it may have the ring of truth to it. The doctrine of the Trinity, in my opinion, gives as good an explanation of the nature of the godhead as anything man has come up with—even though, as many have pointed out, the term appears nowhere in the Bible.

What Is the Trinity?

The *Oxford English Dictionary* defines *trinity* this way: "Being three; group of three. From Latin *trinitas,* 'triad.'" Surely, the persons of the Trinity are not distinct beings like the Three Musketeers, the Three Stooges, the Three Tenors, or the Three Little Pigs. On the other hand, we aren't simply dealing with one person in three roles, like a person who functions as mother, wife, and professional. The first error to be avoided is tritheism, or three separate gods; the second is modalism, in which God morphs from one form to another according to the need of the hour.

What do theologians mean when they discuss the *persons* of the Trinity? In modern English, *three persons* strongly implies a triad of gods. But the theological term *person* is from the Latin *persona,* which means "mask, part, or character," as in the characters of a play.[2] This of course does not mean that God is somehow pretending, like an actor.

In brief, the Holy Trinity is the three in one.

Biblical Basis

The New Testament often mentions the Father, Son, and Spirit together (2 Corinthians 13:14; Matthew 28:19; John 14:17-23).[3] They are three in personality but one in nature or essence. Father, Son, and Spirit are each God (in essence), but none can be identified with the other.

Again, we must guard ourselves against false understandings of the Trinity, or we will drift into either the errors of unitarianism (which roundly rejects the Trinity) or tritheism. (The Qur'an mistakes belief in the Trinity for tritheism when it condemns "those who say Allah is three."[4])

In short, all three persons are divine. Obviously, our heavenly Father is God.[5] In addition, many verses state that Christ is divine (2 Peter 1:1; Titus 2:13; John 1:1,14) or demonstrate his deity, as when he forgives sins (Mark 2) and claims as his own the very name of God (John 8:58). But how can Christ have two natures simultaneously? An illustration may help. Orange juice is 100 percent wet and 100 percent citrus. It isn't somehow half wet and half citrus—it's wholly both at the same time. In the same way, Jesus is human and God.[6]

Finally, the Scriptures clearly indicate that the Spirit, the third person of the Trinity, or the "Spirit of God," is divine. Let's consider the *Oxford English Dictionary* definition of the Spirit: "The active essence or essential power of the Deity, conceived as a creative, animating or inspiring influence." Now this may be an accurate definition, but it doesn't show how the Spirit draws us closer to God. We must sense and appreciate that God, through his Spirit, is living within us (John 14).[7] The Spirit in nature is God; all members of the Trinity are equally divine.[8]

The Doctrine of the Trinity in Church History

The early ecumenical councils strove to define and describe the relationships between the members of the godhead (these include Nicea in 325, Constantinople in 381, Ephesus in 431, Chalcedon in 451, and others). For generations, theologians in the early Christian era hammered out the doctrine of the Trinity, investigating the intricacies of the Spirit. Even in the Middle Ages, interest in the Trinity was strong. Thomas Aquinas produced "The Blessed Trinity," the most thorough treatise of his age on the topic.[9]

Some circles, especially in the nineteenth century, witnessed a reaction against trinitarian language. The original version of the famous hymn "Holy, Holy, Holy" mentions "God in three persons, blessed Trinity!" And yet some publishers, overreacting against traditional doctrines, changed these words to "God over all and blessed eternally." Was this alteration really necessary? Are not the Father, Son, and Spirit all divine?

Analogies Good and Bad

Yes, the Father, Son, and Spirit are all God, but we cannot correctly say that the Father is the Son or that Spirit and Son are interchangeable. We therefore need to select our analogies carefully lest we inadvertently support false doctrine while trying to refute it.

The analogy I most often use to explain the Trinity is this: H_2O can be solid ice, liquid water, or gaseous steam. But ice is not a gas or liquid, and water is not steam. Yet even this analogy has its short-coming. It implies the false doctrine of modalism, that God appears in one form now, another at another time.[10] I have heard worse analogies: time includes past, present, and future; an egg includes a shell, the white, and the yolk.

Opponents of the Trinity ask how one plus one plus one can equal one. But the mathematics is all wrong. Better to consider that one times one times one equals one. Moving from simple arithmetic to geometry, a triangle may better illustrate the truth about the relations among the persons of the Trinity.

Consider this more academic explanation: "A better illustration based in human nature would be...the relation between our mind, its ideas and the expression of these ideas in words. There is obviously a unity among all three of these without there being an identity. In this sense, they illustrate the trinity."[11]

No single analogy captures the divine mystery, but the various pictures will be more or less helpful for various people.

Trinity and Our Walk with God

Now that we have considered the doctrine of the Trinity, let me suggest some ways in which thinking about the Trinity illumines our walk with the Lord.

1. The doctrine of the Trinity brings us great assurance. Metaphorically speaking, the Father is God above us, the Son is God beside us, and the Spirit is God within us.

2. The doctrine of the Trinity helps us to see that God is love. How could God be eternal love without someone to love outside of ("before") creation? Augustine commented that love always existed among the members of the Trinity. C.S. Lewis and Francis Schaeffer discussed and elevated this theme in the twentieth century. The three-in-one God is a divine family who has always shared perfect love.

3. Respect for the Trinity deepens our humility because it reminds us of God's transcendence. As Isaiah says, his ways are not our ways, and his ways and wisdom are unfathomably distant from our own.[12]

Summary

If the whole concept seems complicated, don't fret. Theologians have struggled for centuries to put the divine mystery into words, so you're not likely to manage it in half an hour! Let's wrap up by reiterating what the doctrine of the Trinity does *not* mean:

- There are three gods, or tritheism. (Rather, there is one God.)

- God morphs from one person into another, or modalism. (Instead, the persons of the Trinity always remain distinct.)

- We are to pray to Jesus or pray to the Spirit. (In John 16:23-26, Jesus explains that we are to pray to the Father in Jesus' name, although occasionally in the New Testament prayer is also addressed to the Lord Jesus.[13])

- This appendix is the last word on the subject. (God cannot be put in a box.)

But we do know this about the Trinity:

- It is a biblical concept. Though the word itself never appears in the Bible, the concept is valid. (Even the word *Bible* does not occur in the Bible, yet it is a completely functional and useful term.)

- God's nature is a mystery, so we will always have to strive to our utmost to embrace and accept the nature of God in our lives.

- We need to dig deeper into the Word of God if we are going to go higher in our walk with him.

Holy, Holy, Holy!

Despite my initial apprehension about the use of the term *Trinity*, my study has led me to accept this time-honored doctrine. Returning to the reactionary corrections made to the old hymn, I do not mean to dispute the alternate words, for he is certainly "God over all and blessed eternally." Yet to distance ourselves from the original wording of this majestic hymn is wholly unnecessary. Its final verse spoke the truth perfectly well:

> Holy, holy, holy! Lord God Almighty!
> All thy works shall praise thy name in earth,
>   and sky, and sea;
> Holy, holy, holy! Merciful and mighty!
> God in three persons, blessed Trinity!

Appendix C:
Apparent Contradictions in the Bible

I STEPPED INTO A DORMITORY ELEVATOR and nodded to the two students waiting inside. Unconcerned by my presence, they carried on their debate. One said to the other, his voice ringing with confidence, "The Bible is full of contradictions."

My ears perked up. I could not resist jumping in. "Name one."

The student was stopped cold; he gaped at me wordlessly, apparently unable to think of a single contradiction. (Or perhaps he was just stunned by my impertinence!)

Many people parrot similar statements, but few can give a specific example when pressed. Most people, having never studied the Bible for themselves, will have nothing to say. Their information is only secondhand and provides them with an easy excuse for not reading or obeying the Bible.

Of course, some people have genuine doubts, and answers are available for people with legitimate questions and the desire to investigate. I'm certainly not implying that every part of the Bible is easy to understand. The Bible is a compilation of books that is thousands of years old, written in three ancient languages, and widely separated in culture from our own, so it is bound to present difficulties.[1] Even so, most alleged contradictions clear up after a second reading or with further study. And some people claim to see inconsistencies where none exist. In a moment we will take a look at varieties of false contradictions.

Through my Web site I receive thousands of Bible questions each year, some of which concern apparent difficulties. In my replies, I try to be heuristic and not just an answer man. Coaching others in their approach to perceived inconsistencies equips them to think for themselves. This chapter provides a sampling of the sorts of questions that come my way and how I field them. Let's first investigate an array of false contradictions and then propose several principles to keep in mind when difficulties arise.

False Contradictions

Chronology

The Bible incorporates several chronological schemes that are different from our own. People often ask about the chronology of Jesus' resurrection. Was he to rise "on the third day" or "after three days"?[2] The two phrases are used interchangeably. Ancient counting was typically inclusive, but our modern system is exclusive. The distinction first confronted me when I began to translate Latin letters. I read, "the fifth day after the first of the month," which sounds like the sixth day of the month. But no—it is the fifth. In ancient thought, the third day after Friday is Sunday.[3] For another biblical example, compare Esther 4:16 and 5:1.

The time of Jesus' execution is another problem for some people. Matthew 27:45 differs from John 19:14. In Matthew's account of the crucifixion, by the sixth hour, Jesus had been on the cross for some time, whereas in the Gospel of John, he is still before Pilate on the Stone Pavement. Was Matthew confused, or was John? And how could their stories differ so much if they were both in Jerusalem when their Master was executed?[4] This does not seem to be the kind of minor chronological misunderstanding we have discussed above.

Neither writer was confused; they were simply following different time-keeping systems. Matthew, whose Gospel is the most Jewish of the four, was following the Jewish system of timekeeping. The sixth hour is actually midday, and Jesus died at the ninth hour, or three p.m. John, on the other hand, who was writing for a non-Jewish audience, was following the Roman method, which is like our own. By John's reckoning the sixth hour was six a.m. After Pontius Pilate decided to have Jesus executed, the soldiers still had plenty of time to abuse him for a while before the crucifixion.[5] This apparent contradiction would be difficult to resolve without the missing historical information, which most Bibles do not supply.

Ancient writers did not take the same approach to chronology we do. For example, in Matthew, Mark, and Luke, Jesus cleanses the temple and overturns the moneychangers' tables at the end of his public ministry. John, however, moved it to the beginning of Jesus' ministry, grouping it with other material related to the contrast between the old and the new.[6] Such thematic grouping of material is common in ancient histories.

Jesus' temptations are recorded in Matthew 4 in the order 1, 2, 3. Luke 4, however, lists them in the order 1, 3, 2. This is hardly a contradiction, for the details of the two temptation accounts are virtually identical.

On the whole, Bible writers were at least as careful about chronology as their contemporaries.[7]

Poetry and Prose

Much of the Bible is poetry—about a third! Literalizing poetry is highly problematic. If we read Psalm 50:10 woodenly, we would have to accept that the Lord has title to the livestock on only 1000 hills. To the ancient mind, 1000 is simply an enormous number—it might as well be the largest possible number. Psalm 58:3, if taken literally, would mean that unbelievers actually begin lying before they are born! The language is hyperbolic. Certainly ancient readers knew the difference, and we modern readers should too.

Sometimes a straightforward historical account is retold poetically. We read of the Exodus from Egypt in Exodus 14, and then comes the more dramatic and colorful poetic version (the Song of Moses) in the next chapter. This is allowable and even expected in poetry. Similarly, Judges 5 (the Song of Deborah) retells the straight narrative of the preceding chapter. Many of the details do not match up. Why? Because they do not need to. The rules of expression are more flexible in poetry.

The Old and New Testaments

We see major differences between the Old and New Covenants (Testaments). For example, under the Torah, the people of God sacrificed animals.[8] Not so under the New Covenant; Jesus himself is "the lamb of God."[9] The change itself was predicted in Jeremiah 31:31-34 and other passages. Under the old law, polygamy was tolerated (though never commended), divorce was easier, oaths were taken, war was permitted, and of course, Sabbath days and years were central. Under the New Covenant, much has changed. Matthew 5:21-48 emphasizes this in striking terms. Yet an update, or covenantal modification, is not a contradiction. This brings us to the next category, which is closely related.

Progressive Revelation

Just as the Old Testament law is reinterpreted in the New Testament, numerous biblical doctrines that appear embryonically in the Hebrew Scriptures are well developed by the time of the Greek New Testament. The doctrine of Satan was partially worked out in the Old Testament but completed in the New. The person and role of the Messiah become clearer in the later books of the Old Testament and is revealed and explained in the New. God's presence is first manifested in Eden and then progresses to the tabernacle, the temple, the church, the heavens, and finally the new creation.

To explain what is meant by *progressive revelation*, consider the field of education. My first-grade teacher never told us about long division because the concept is beyond most six-year-olds. My algebra teacher did not explain trigonometry either. Was this deception? Of course not. Each stage builds on the previous level. I eventually took three years of calculus and worked for the math department at Duke University. But even then my professors knew more than they told. A good teacher does not get too far ahead of the students.[10] In the same way, God gradually revealed his will in the pages of Scripture.

Approximate Numbers

The Bible often uses round numbers and other approximations, especially where large quantities are involved. For example, in Matthew 14:21 we read of the feeding of "about five thousand men." This is clearly a round number, and in keeping with biblical counting and censuses, only adult males are reckoned. The same is the case in Acts 2:41 and 4:4, where only men are included in the count of church members, and numbers are rounded to the nearest thousand.

Copying numbers in ancient manuscripts was difficult. Numbers were represented by letters of the alphabet and were not easy to read. As a result, the numbers in some manuscripts were incorrectly copied. But of course, these minor manuscript discrepancies do not controvert any biblical doctrines.

Paraphrases

Speeches in the Bible are usually condensed and paraphrased. Biblical writers did not feel a need to report the exact words when they recorded a conversation. In fact, everything Jesus said that is recorded in the Bible can be read aloud in just a couple of hours. Surely Jesus spoke for more than two hours during his three-year ministry. If Matthew, Mark, Luke, and John recorded everything he said, the Gospels alone would be tens of thousands of pages long!

Consider Peter's Pentecost sermon in Acts 2:14-36. I can read it aloud in English in two minutes and ten seconds. Are we to believe that the apostle's inaugural message lasted only two minutes? Of course not. Besides, Luke himself tells us that Peter spoke "many other words" (Acts 2:40). Furthermore, Peter was speaking Aramaic, not the Greek Luke used to write Acts or the English we read.

Critics contend that Luke put words into Peter's mouth. However, if you have ever been in a heated discussion and told the other person that he was putting words into your mouth, you were accusing the person of misrepresenting you. We do not, however, object when others paraphrase, reword, or summarize us, provided they accurately preserve the intent behind our words. Paraphrasing is not misrepresentation, so biblical dialogue is yet another class of false contradiction.

Historical Attestation

For years, critics derided the Bible because of its frequent references to the Hittites.[11] (Remember Uriah the Hittite? He was the husband of Bathsheba, with whom King David committed adultery.) For centuries, we had no archaeological evidence that the Hittites ever existed. The only record was the Bible—that is, until 1906, when archaeologists unearthed massive amounts of archaeological evidence for the existence of the powerful Hittite nation (1600–717 BC). In 1983, when I lived in London, I attended a lecture on the Hittites at the Institute of Archaeology. This was no mythical people; they truly existed. Today the University of Pennsylvania offers a masters degree in Hittite language, and the University of Chicago offers a PhD in Hittite studies.

In the same way, the stories of Genesis were once regarded as pure legend by some historians until excavations at the beginning of the twentieth century and again in the 1970s yielded valuable archaeological insights. The names, places, and customs referred to in the biblical patriarchal narratives are corroborated by literary and archaeological evidence unearthed from sites representing the ancient Near East of the late third and early second millennia BC.

In 1993, an Aramaic inscription naming King David was discovered at Tel Dan in northern Israel.[12] The discovery confounded the minimalists—skeptics who claim that such characters as Moses, David, and Solomon never existed. Hundreds of discoveries have been made confirming the record of the Bible, and hundreds of other sites have yet to be explored. The message of the Bible has not been proven wrong by archaeology up to this point, so when considering a disputed passage, drawing any hasty conclusions would seem unwise. The old dictum is apropos: Absence of evidence is not evidence of absence.

Sometimes biblical accounts lack historical attestation because an extrabiblical source suppressed the evidence. Ancient regimes did not often publish embarrassing or self-incriminating information. One such embarrassing event is described in 2 Kings 19:35. While Assyria's King Sennacherib was besieging Jerusalem (701 BC), his army suffered catastrophic loss at the hand of the Lord. The official Assyrian records, however, do not mention the defeat. Are skeptics right—is this really a contradiction? Drawing attention to the debacle would have been out of character for the Assyrians. Sennacherib portrayed this part of his campaign in the most positive light possible. His boastful words were carved in cuneiform in the Taylor Prism (before 681 BC):

> As for Hezekiah, the Judean who did not submit to my yoke, I surrounded and conquered 46 of his strong-walled towns and innumerable small settlements around them by means of earth ramps and siege engines and attack by infantry men…He himself I shut up in Jerusalem, his royal city, like a bird in a cage.

The Assyrian monarch tacitly admits that his purposes were frustrated; he failed to breach the walls of Jerusalem. This is a patent example of political spin. Interestingly, the garbled account of the Greek historian Herodotus (484–425 BC) also refers to this incident. As Sennacherib prepared to challenge Egypt (the destination of a military campaign that took him through Israel), Herodotus tells us that the god "sent field mice to eat Assyrian bowstrings, quivers, shield handles." A tempting harmonization emerges. Herodotus mentions rodents, the angel of death that struck the Assyrians implies a plague,[13] and Sennacherib hints that he left off the siege, so all three accounts could possibly capture different facets of what happened that terrible night.

Finally, sometimes an ancient source flatly contradicts a biblical one. This is the case with the Jewish historian Josephus, who places the revolutionary Theudas before the revolutionary Judas the Galilean.[14] But why should the benefit of the doubt be extended to Josephus? Some scholars favor Josephus when he is in conflict with the Scriptures even though Luke is a meticulous writer. A more perplexing problem is that Luke apparently disagrees with Josephus and the epigraphical evidence in the dating of the Quirinian census.[15] This event took place in AD 6, when Jesus was easily nine or ten years old. Several solutions are possible; here are two. First, Tertullian (c. AD 200) places the census during the rule of Saturninus, not Quirinius; perhaps an early manuscript of Luke referred to the former governor instead of the latter. Second, Luke 2:2 is translated "the first census," but it might possibly be translated "the census before." If the second translation is correct, it solves the problem nicely. Considering Luke's customary accuracy, he deserves the benefit of the doubt.

Adaptation

Gospel writers selected from an enormous pool of written sources, reminiscences, stylized stories, and oral traditions, choosing what fit best with their individual theological purposes.[16] Christians believe that this took place under the guidance of the Holy Spirit. Second, the writers arranged these materials—sometimes chronologically, and sometimes in clusters according to theme—in order to best develop the spiritual themes that would be of most benefit to their readers.[17] As we have already discussed, chronology was more flexible in antiquity, and such arranging enhanced the accounts. Third, the Gospel writers adapted the material they drew from. This is less intuitive for modern readers, but the principle is not hard to grasp once it has been explained.

The roofs of houses in Galilee were commonly sodden. That explains how the friends of the paralytic were able to dig through the roof (Mark 2:4). When Luke tells the story for a broader Gentile audience, he has the men removing tiles (Luke 5:19). Roofs in Galilee did not normally feature tiles, but Luke's Gentile readership would expect tiles on roofs. Luke adapts the story to make it more relatable to his intended audience. This is only a problem if we make it one. Here's another example: Matthew sometimes doubles things in his Gospel. Whereas Mark, which is the older document, has a single demoniac and only one blind man, Matthew has two of each.[18]

When the writers adapt the material, they don't affect any doctrine except the modern doctrine that the biblical writers are not permitted the freedom to shape their sources in order to underscore the theological points they made.

Minor Variations Among Ancient Manuscripts

Jesus found the demon-possessed man (Mark 5:1-2) in the region of the Gerasenes—or was it the Gadarenes? Or the Gergesenes? An ancient scribe's geographical confusion would be understandable. (Similarly, people today might confuse Newark and New York, or New York City and New York State.) At any rate, scholars are not sure which reading is original. But does it really matter? No surviving manuscript is an exact copy of the original New Testament and Old Testament writings, although many ancient manuscripts are extremely close copies. The alternative readings listed in the footnotes of your Bible are not contradictions. They are simply instances in which translators were unsure of the correct reading. The principle is this: Inspiration applies to the original text, not to copies. Most Bible believers do not hold that modern translations are perfect; only the original *autographs* (as scholars call them) are held to be pristine. However, most differences are so minor that listing them would be pointless. No Christian doctrine is affected.

Differences in Modern Versions

No modern translation of the Hebrew and Greek text is perfect, though some versions are more accurate than others. For example, the word translated *disciples* in Acts 11:26 is rendered *believers* in the paraphrased Living Bible. There is, of course, no contradiction in the original text.

Even skilled translators can make errors. In the NIV, Psalm 100:3 reads, "It is he who made us, and we are his." Earlier English versions read, "It is he who made us, and not we ourselves." Here's why: In the older translations, the Hebrew word for *his* was mistaken for the word *not* because of a common spelling variant.

Some degree of translational variation is bound to occur because Hebrew, the principal language of the Bible, is not as precise as such modern languages as Russian, English, or German. And though the Greek of the New Testament is more precise than Hebrew, words or phrases can often be translated in more than one way. If you are unfamiliar with the facts and the nature of these ancient languages, you may find what appear to be contradictions when you compare Bible versions.

Scientific Precision

The Bible is not a science textbook. It speaks of sunrise and sunset (as we continue to do), yet we know that the earth moves and not the sun. The terms *sunrise* and *sunset* are phenomenological—that is, they describe phenomena as they appear rather than as they truly are.

Another example occurs in the kosher laws of the Torah, where bats are included with the birds.[19] Of course, the ancients knew a bat is different from a bird (it has no feathers, for starters), but in a phenomenological description, bats and birds are naturally grouped together. Both are flying animals. The kosher code also says rabbits chew the cud, whereas in fact they practice refection.[20] To the observer, however, this action appears similar to that of the cow or the camel. Again, biblical descriptions are phenomenological.

Can you imagine Genesis 1 ("In the beginning God created...") if it were rewritten scientifically? We might read, "At the alpha point of space-time, the Supreme Being so ordered the cosmos that conditions favorable for the eventual synthesis of deoxyribonucleic acid would come to exist within a mere 11 billion years." Ancient readers would have been baffled; most modern ones would be too.

The Bible does not bother to correct the ancient cosmology shared by its original audience: The firmament is a firm, hemispherical cover above the earth; the earth is flat and is orbited by the sun.[21] This is what theologians call accommodative language. That is, the Lord accommodated himself to our level. The ancient languages and the science of the day served as vehicles for divine truth and didn't need to be modified. The point was not to correct current notions of cosmology, geography, or medicine, but to show that God is the Lord of the cosmos, the Creator of the earth, and the true physician of the soul.

Sadly, and to her shame, the church has often failed to take account of the Bible's accommodative language. Historically she has fought several unnecessary battles, taking her stand on Scriptures that were never intended to teach science. The early Greeks knew of the sphericity of the earth as early as the third century BC, but most Christians did not concede the point until nearly 1000 years later.[22] The church also defended the geocentric model against the heliocentric theory until sometime in the seventeenth century.[23] Even today battles rage in the area of biology (specifically evolution).

Galileo Galilei (1564–1642) put it well: "The Holy Spirit intended to teach us in the Bible how to go to heaven, not how the heavens go." At any rate, lack of scientific understanding is not a true contradiction.[24]

Errant Notions of Inspiration

The words of Satan appear in Scripture, as do those of Job's "miserable comforters," whose theology the Lord himself eventually rebukes.[25] Are these passages infallible? And what do we make of the imprecatory prayers, such as appear in some of the Psalms?[26] If the words are inspired, should we too wish ill on our enemies? When biblical writers quote pagans—as Paul does in his Areopagus speech in Acts 17—are their sources inspired? Are we to take the figurative passages literally (rivers clapping their hands, stones crying out, stars falling to the earth)?[27] We need to think clearly about the distinction between the medium and the message. The message is inspired; the medium is merely a vehicle for truth.

Second Timothy 3:16-17 states that all Scripture is both inspired and useful. But in what way? Many Christians confine themselves to a doctrine of inspiration that makes no allowance for such questions. To them, *inspired* is synonymous with *true,* and every word is pregnant with doctrine. That is why the matter of the inspiration of Satan's words causes them to stumble. They may say, "The Bible has the answers"— which, in my view, it does—but they mean that it somehow addresses every area of knowledge, human and divine. Every verse has a profound meaning, and nothing is incidental. But this turns out to be a restrictive, flat theology; it presses the Scriptures into unnatural service, making them a textbook of science, medicine, or philosophy.

Some go even further and use the Bible as a kind of sanctified Ouija board, flipping through its pages randomly in search of patterns, codes, or clues as to God's will for their lives. Surely this is a misguided approach. God's Word is more textured than this; it is not a talisman. Simple faith is a wonderful thing, but simplemindedness is not. Our view of inspiration must hold up under scrutiny and address such questions.

God's Word to us comes in two forms: the person of Jesus Christ and the book of Scripture. The earthly Jesus was perfect morally, and his powers of observation and knowledge were above those of his peers, not only in degree but also in their supernatural quality. Here's something that may set your head (or your theology!) spinning: Was the earthly Jesus necessarily omniscient? Did he know everything about bacteria, or the geological formation of Antarctica? During his earthly ministry, could he have answered our questions about the Permian and Cretaceous extinctions? Even he admits ignorance on at least one occasion.[28]

If Jesus in human form did not have full knowledge about the cosmos, why assume the Bible is accurate in every incidental detail? Must we subscribe to the geocentric model of the solar system simply because it was the likely view of the apostles and the early Christians? If Jesus was unaware of the existence of Australia, should it vanish from our mental image of the earth?

Could the Bible share in certain limitations? Surely when 2 Timothy 3:16-17 affirms the usefulness of the Scriptures for teaching, it is referring to theology (how to know God and how to live a godly life). It does not directly pertain to astrophysics, chemistry, or zoology!

Can we pinpoint the nature of inspiration? How about this: The Bible is "reliable in all that it genuinely affirms, and authoritative for guidance in doctrine and behavior."[29] The biblical books are inspired and teach "firmly, faithfully and without error the truth which God wanted put into the sacred writings for the sake of our salvation."[30]

Back to the matter of the devil's words. He is quoted in Scripture so we can learn something. *Inspiration* does not mean a statement is inspirational (motivating), nor does it necessarily mean it is true. *Inspiration* refers to the function of revelation—to its ability to guide, shape, and direct our lives Godward. If we appreciate the biblical doctrine of inspiration, resisting the temptation to import our own presuppositions—even about Scripture—we will avoid a host of false contradictions.

Solutions to Apparent Contradictions

Let's take a look at a few specific apparent contradictions. Each example can teach us a valuable lesson.

Two Sides of a Coin

Romans 3:28 is thought by some to disagree with James 2:24. Paul claims that we are made right with God "by faith apart from observing the law," while James says, "You see that a person is justified by what he does and not by faith alone." Who is right, Paul or James?

This apparent contradiction was so disturbing to sixteenth-century

Protestant reformer Martin Luther that he decided to insert the word *alone* after faith in his personal translation of Romans 3:28. He even separated the epistle of James and three other New Testament books from the Bible, relegating them to an appendix. But the solution is not hard to understand: True faith always expresses itself in deeds, or as James says, "Faith without deeds is dead."[31] Faith without deeds is not true faith. Neither Paul nor James is confused—what both of them wrote is inspired by God.

In this supposed contradiction we see that the two views are really two sides of a coin, and they fit together nicely. Often a seeming contradiction resolves itself when we take the time to be reasonable and think it through.

Beware of Your Assumptions

We have already warned of the dangers of attempting to use the Bible as a science book. The premise that it was written for our scientific betterment is unsubstantiated. Similarly, readers bring many other questionable assumptions to the text.

A few weeks ago I received an e-mail from Germany. The writer wanted to know how a solar eclipse could cause the darkness at Jesus' crucifixion when in fact Passover takes place when the moon is full.[32] But the Bible nowhere mentions an eclipse; this is a later speculation that is astronomically impossible.[33] Of course, this is not a contradiction. The idea that the darkness was caused by an eclipse has been read into the text.

What about the Mosaic authorship of the Pentateuch (the first five books of the Bible)? In Deuteronomy 34 we read of the death of Moses—which is remarkable if Moses wrote all of Deuteronomy. How could Moses have accomplished this feat? He didn't, any more than Jesus took notes on his own birth or crucifixion. We must be aware of (or wary of) our presuppositions. But if Moses was not the author of the Pentateuch, or if he is to be credited with only partial authorship, then the contradiction vanishes.

When visiting a church in my college days, I remember entering a Sunday school classroom and reading 4004 BC above the blackboard—as the date of creation! Contrary to popular belief, the Bible never states when the earth was created; 4004 BC was an uninspired guess by an otherwise intelligent archbishop four centuries ago, but many people have actually taught his calculation as the biblical date of creation.[34] Beginning in the early 1700s, the notes in many King James Bibles included this date, leading readers to believe that the piece of commentary itself was inspired.

Do you want some more examples?

- The Bible never says that three wise men brought gifts to the infant Jesus. It only mentions three different gifts.[35]

- *Hades,* the New Testament Greek word for the underworld (*Sheol* in the Old Testament) is incorrectly rendered *hell* in some Bibles (including the King James Version and the New International Version), leading to some rather interesting views about what happens immediately after death.

- Ancient genealogies did not need to be complete. It was acceptable to stylize them or to skip generations. They could even include "descendants" of no direct biological connection, such as adopted children. When we read the genealogies, we tend to see them through modern eyes, with modern preconceptions. This is bound to lead to problems.

A Little Imagination

How can we resolve the two accounts of the death of Judas? In Matthew's account he hanged himself, but Luke (who wrote Acts) said Judas fell, his body burst open, and his intestines spilled out.[36] Who's right? (By this time you're probably cautious about choosing sides.) Perhaps someone (other than Judas) threw Judas' body into the field. Maybe Judas had been dead for some time, or maybe he fell when he was cut down from the tree from which he hanged himself.

Or perhaps not—who cares? The precise solution is irrelevant. There is no necessary contradiction, and it doesn't take a lot of imagination to think of a solution.

Look Before You Leap!

Another surface-level contradiction occurs in the account of Jesus' healing of the centurion's servant. In Matthew the centurion personally asks Jesus to heal his servant, whereas in Luke we read that he sent some elders of the Jews to put the question to Jesus.[37] Which is right?

They are both right. The centurion authorized the elders to go on his behalf; he did not have to be there himself. In the same way, someone might say, "You brought my car to the station last week, didn't you?" Would I be a deceiver if I said, "That's right," even though I actually had my wife take in the car? Isn't this an acceptable way of putting things? Yes.

Even if we admit that we have three different forms of the same story (if we include John 4:46-54), the theological points made by the accounts are the same. Most readers have no problem with such variations.

We also jump to conclusions by assuming a biblical passage contains the entire truth on a subject. The majority of the Proverbs are generalizations about life; they do not tell us everything we might like to know. Proverbs 16:3 tells us that if we commit our plans to the Lord, they will succeed. And yet the principle must be read in the light of other biblical passages that encourage us to take God's will into account. We do not always get our way just because we have asked nicely (in the name of the Lord). Proverbs 22:6 highlights the correlation between godly instruction and how our children turn out. Once again, this is a generalization, not an ironclad promise. Certainly a few excellent parents have rebellious children, just as some children grow up to be outstanding persons despite their own atrocious upbringing. One more example: Proverbs 26:4 directly contradicts the verse that follows it. Each verse presents a single facet of the truth. (In this case, the phrase *according to* has a different meaning in verse 4 than it does in verse 5.)

Hasty reading creates difficulties where there are none. Before we write off a problem as a contradiction, we would do well to search diligently for a solution. We can be overly narrow in our interpretations, and we must be careful that we have the full picture before jumping to conclusions—or convulsions. Often a parallel passage in another part of the Bible helps to resolve the apparent contradiction. Here the old adage is appropriate: Look before you leap!

Conclusion

No historians, theologians, or archaeologists are likely to make a discovery that will cause the walls of Christian faith to come tumbling down. Critics have tried for 2000 years, but the bulwarks of Christianity stand as solid as ever. In short, apparent contradictions generally...

> are caused by our preconceptions and
>
> evaporate on close inspection or ·
>
> are so minor as to have no impact on Christian life
> or doctrine.

The Bible does have some difficult passages, but none disproves or discredits the fundamental message. Moreover, verses can be difficult to understand without being contradictory. After all, people do not reject the Bible because it contradicts itself, but because it contradicts them. Our natural human striving for autonomy prevents us from humbly accepting the truth (James 1:21). Finally, we should never let the few parts we can't understand keep us from obeying the many parts we can!

Bibliography

Helpful Books on Apologetics

Abbot, Edwin A. *Flatland.* Oxford: Blackwell, 1875.

Anderson, J.N.D. *Evidence for the Resurrection.* Downers Grove: InterVarsity, 1984.

Barrett, C.K. *The New Testament Background: Selected Documents.* New York: Harper & Row, 1961.

Barrett, Eric C. and David Fisher, eds. *Scientists Who Believe: 21 Tell Their Own Stories.* Chicago: Moody Press, 1984.

Bauckham, Richard. *Jesus and the Eyewitness: The Gospels as Eyewitness Tesimony.* Grand Rapids: Eerdmans, 2006.

_____. *Jesus and the God of Israel: God Crucified and Other Studies of the New Testament's Christology of Divine Identity.* Grand Rapids: Eerdmans, 2009.

Beaver, R.P. *Eerdmans' Handbook to the World's Religions.* Grand Rapids: Eerdmans, 1982.

Berry, R.J., ed. *Real Science, Real Faith: Sixteen Leading British Scientists Discuss Their Science and Their Personal Faith.* Eastbourne: Monarch, 1991.

Bock, Derrell L. and Daniel B. Wallace. *Dethroning Jesus: Exposing Popular Culture's Quest to Unseat the Biblical Christ.* Nashville: Thomas Nelson, 2007

Bowman, Robert and J. Ed Komoszewski. *Putting Jesus in His Place: The Case for the Deity of Christ.* Grand Rapids: Kregel Publications, 2007.

Bradley, David G. *A Guide to the World's Religions.* Englewood Cliffs, NJ: Prentice-Hall, 1963.

Bruce, F.F. *Jesus and Christian Origins Outside the New Testament.* London: Hodder & Stoughton, 1974.

_____. *New Testament Documents: Are They Reliable?* Downers Grove: InterVarsity, 1984.

Charlesworth, James H. *The Historical Jesus: An Essential Guide.* Nashville: Abingdon Press, 2008.

Colling, Richard G. *Random Designer: Created from Chaos to Connect with the Creator.* Bourbonnais, IL: Browning Press, 2004.

Collins, C. John. *The God of Miracles: An Exegetical Examination of God's Action in the World.* Wheaton: Crossway Books, 2000.

Collins, Francis S. *The Language of God: A Scientist Presents Evidence for Belief.* New York: Free Press, 2006.

Comfort, Philip Wesley, ed. *The Origin of the Bible.* Wheaton: Tyndale, 1992.

Craig, William Lane. *On Guard: Defending Your Faith with Reason and Precision.* Colorado Springs: David C. Cook, 2010.

_____. *Reasonable Faith: Christian Truth and Apologetics,* third edition. Wheaton: Crossway Books, 2008.

Craig, William, and Quentin Smith. *Theism, Atheism, and Big Bang Cosmology.* Oxford: Clarendon Press, 1993.

Denton, Michael J. *Evolution: A Theory in Crisis.* Bethesda: Adler & Adler, 1985.

_____. *Nature's Destiny: How the Laws of Biology Reveal Purpose in the Universe.* New York: The Free Press, 1998.

D'Souza, Dinesh. *What's So Great About Christianity?* Washington DC: Regnery, 2007.

Eddy, Paul Rhodes and Gregory A. Boyd. *The Jesus Legend: A Case for the Historical Reliability of the Synoptic Jesus Tradition.* Grand Rapids: Baker Academic, 2007.

Evans, Craig A. *Fabricating Jesus: How Modern Scholars Distort the Gospels.* Downers Grove: InterVarsity, 2006.

Falk, Darrel R. *Coming to Peace with Science: Bridging the Worlds Between Faith and Biology.* Downers Grove: InterVarsity, 2004.

Finegan, Jack. *The Archeology of the New Testament: The Life of Jesus and the Beginning of the Early Church.* Princeton: Princeton University Press, 1992.

Glover, Gordon J. *Beyond the Firmament: Understanding Science and the Theology of Creation.* Chesapeake: Watertree Press, 2007.

Goldsmith, Martin. *What About Other Faiths?* London: Hodder & Stoughton, 1999.

Habermas, Gary R. and Michael R. Licona. *The Case for the Resurrection of Jesus.* Grand Rapids: Kregel, 2004.

Hayward, Alan. *Creation and Evolution: Rethinking the Evidence from Science and the Bible.* Minneapolis: Bethany, 1995.

Hurtado, Larry W. *How on Earth Did Jesus Become God? Historical Questions About Earliest Devotion to Jesus*. Grand Rapids: Eerdmans, 2005.

_____. *Lord Jesus Christ: Devotion to Jesus in Earliest Christianity*. Grand Rapids: Eerdmans, 2003.

Jacoby, Douglas. *Jesus and Islam*. Spring: Illumination Publishers International, 2009.

Johnson, Paul. *Intellectuals*. New York: Harper & Row, 1988.

Kaiser Jr., Walter C. *The Old Testament Documents: Are They Reliable and Relevant?* Downers Grove: InterVarsity, 2001.

Keller, Timothy. *The Reason for God: Belief in an Age of Skepticism*. London: Dutton, 2008.

Kennedy, D. James and Jerry Newcombe. *What If Jesus Had Never Been Born?* Nashville: Thomas Nelson, 1994.

Komoszewsky, J. Ed, M. James Sawyer, and Daniel B. Wallace. *Reinventing Jesus: How Contemporary Skeptics Miss the Real Jesus and Mislead Popular Culture*. Grand Rapids: Kregel Publications, 2006.

Koster, John P. *The Atheist Syndrome*. Brentwood: Wolgemuth & Hyatt, 1989.

Kreeft, Peter and Ronald K. Tacelli. *Handbook of Christian Apologetics: Hundreds of Answers to Crucial Questions*. Downers Grove: InterVarsity, 1994.

Lamoureux, Denis O. *Evolutionary Creation: A Christian Approach to Evolution*. Eugene: WIPF & Stock, 2008.

Lewis, C.S. *Mere Christianity: A Revised and Enlarged Edition*. New York: Simon & Schuster, 1997.

_____. *Miracles: How God Intervenes in Nature and Human Affairs*. New York: Touchstone Books, 1996.

_____. *The Problem of Pain: The Intellectual Problem Raised by Human Suffering, Examined with Sympathy and Realism*. New York: Touchstone Books, 1996.

Licona, Michael R. *The Resurrection of Jesus: A New Historiographical Approach*. Downers Grove: InterVarsity Academic, 2010.

Lightfoot, Neil R. *How We Got the Bible*. Grand Rapids: Baker, 1988.

McCallum, Dennis. *The Death of Truth*. Minneapolis: Bethany, 1996.

McDermott, Gerald R. *Can Evangelicals Learn from World Religions? Jesus Revelation, and Religious Traditions*. Downers Grove: InterVarsity, 2000.

McGrath, Alister. *Intellectuals Don't Need God and Other Modern Myths: Building Bridges to Faith Through Apologetics*. Grand Rapids: Zondervan, 1993.

McGrath, Alister, and Joanna Collicutt McGrath. *The Dawkins Delusion: Atheist Fundamentalism and the Denial of the Divine*. Downers Grove: InterVarsity, 2007.

McGuiggan, Jim. *If God Came: An Approach to Christian Evidences*. Lubbock: Montex, 1980.

Miller, Kenneth R. *Finding Darwin's God: A Scientist's Search for Common Ground Between God and Evolution.* New York: Harper Perennial, 1999.

Morison, Frank. *Who Moved the Stone?* Grand Rapids: Zondervan, 1987.

Murray, Michael J., ed. *Reason for the Hope Within.* Grand Rapids: Eerdmans, 1999.

Neufeld, Thomas R. Yoder. *Recovering Jesus: The Witness of the New Testament.* Grand Rapids: Brazos Press, 2007.

Numbers, Ronald L. *The Creationists: The Evolution of Scientific Creationism.* Berkeley: University of California Press, 1992.

Olson, Roger E. *Questions to All Your Answers: The Journey from Folk Religion to Examined Faith.* Grand Rapids: Zondervan, 2007.

Philips, J.B., *Your God Is Too Small.* New York: Macmillan, 1997.

Polkinghorne, John and Nicholas Beale. *Questions of Truth: Fifty-one Responses to Questions About God, Science, and Belief.* Louisville: Westminster John Knox Press, 2006.

Price, Randall. *The Stones Cry Out: What Archaeology Reveals About the Truth of the Bible.* Eugene: Harvest House, 1997.

Roberts, Mark D. *Can We Trust the Gospels? Investigating the Reliability of Matthew, Mark, Luke, and John.* Wheaton: Crossway Books, 2007.

Satterthwaite, Philip E., Richard S. Hess, and Gordon J. Wenham, eds., *The Lord's Anointed: Interpretation of Old Testament Messianic Texts.* Grand Rapids: Baker, 1995.

Sheler, Jeffery L. *Is the Bible True?: How Modern Debates and Discoveries Affirm the Essence of the Scriptures.* Grand Rapids: Zondervan, 1999.

Sire, James W. *The Universe Next Door: A Basic World View Catalog,* third edition. Downers Grove: InterVarsity, 1997.

Sparks, Kenton L. *God's Word in Human Words: An Evangelical Appropriation of Critical Bible Scholarship.* Grand Rapids: Baker Academic, 2008.

Stott, John R.W. *Basic Christianity.* Grand Rapids: Eerdmans, 1986.

Story, Dan. *Defending Your Faith: How to Answer the Tough Questions.* Nashville: Thomas Nelson, 1992.

Strobel, Lee. *The Case for a Creator: A Journalist Investigates Scientific Evidence That Points Toward God.* Grand Rapids: Zondervan, 2004.

_____. *The Case for Christ.* Grand Rapids: Zondervan, 1998.

_____. *The Case for Faith.* Grand Rapids: Zondervan, 2000.

_____. *The Case for the Real Jesus: A Journalist Investigates Current Attacks on the Identity of Christ.* Grand Rapids: Zondervan, 2007.

Ward, Keith. *God, Chance and Necessity.* Boston: Element, 1996.

Warfield, Benjamin B. *Counterfeit Miracles.* New York: Charles Scribner's Sons, 1918.

Winter, David. *But This I Can Believe.* London: Hodder & Stoughton, 1980.

Wise, Michael, Martin Abegg Jr., and Edward Cook. *The Dead Sea Scrolls, A New Translation.* San Francisco: Harper, 1996.

Wright, N.T. *Evil and the Justice of God.* Downers Grove: InterVarstity Press, 2006.

_____. *The Resurrection of the Son of God.* Minneapolis: Fortress Press, 2003.

_____. *Simply Christian: Why Christianity Makes Sense.* New York: HarperCollins, 2006.

_____. *Who Was Jesus?* Grand Rapids: Eerdmans, 1993.

Yancey, Philip. *The Jesus I Never Knew.* Grand Rapids: Zondervan, 1995.

_____. *Reaching for the Invisible God: What Can We Expect to Find?* Grand Rapids: Zondervan, 2000.

Young, Davis A. *The Biblical Flood: A Case Study of the Church's Response to the Extrabiblical Evidence.* Grand Rapids: Eerdmans, 1995.

Young, Dvais A., and Ralph F. Stearly. *The Bible, Rocks and Time: Geological Evidence for the Age of Earth.* Downers Grove: InterVarsity, 2008.

Young, John. *The Case Against Christ.* London: Trafalgar Square, 1994.

Zacharias, Ravi. *A Shattered Visage: The Real Face of Atheism.* Grand Rapids: Baker Books, 1990.

_____. *Can Man Live Without God?* Dallas: Word, 1994.

_____. *Deliver Us from Evil: Restoring the Soul in a Disintegrating Culture.* Dallas: Word, 1996.

_____. *Jesus Among Other Gods: The Absolute Claim of the Christian Message.* Nashville: Word, 2000.

Helpful Web Sites for Christian Evidences

Alister E. McGrath—users.ox.ac.uk/~mcgrath

American Scientific Affiliation—www.asa3.0rg

Ben Witherington—www.benwitherington.com, benwitherington.blogspot.com

Beyond the Firmament (Gordon Glover)—www.blog.beyondthefirmament.com/welcome/Bible.org

Bible Gateway—www.biblegateway.com

Bible Contradictions—www.kingdavid8.com/Contradictions/Home.html

The BioLogos Foundation (Francis Collins)—www.biologos.org

Brainbank Other Reference–Religion—www.cftech.com/BrainBank/OtherReference/Religion/ ReligionIndex.html

Christian Classics Ethereal Library—www.ccel.org

Christian Research Institute—www.equip.org

Craig Evans—www.craigaevans.com

Dean Overman—www.deanoverman.com

Denis Lamoureux—www.ualberta.ca/~dlamoure/index.htm

Does God Exist?—www.DoesGodExist.org

Dr. Gary R. Habermas—www.garyhabermas.com

The Faraday Institute for Science and Religion—www.st-edmunds.cam.ac.uk/faraday/index.php

Evidence for Christianity—www.evidenceforChristianity.org

International Teaching Ministry of Douglas Jacoby—www.douglasjacoby.com, jacobypremium.com

Interpreting Ancient Manuscripts—www.stg.brown.edu/projects/mss/overview.html

John Polkinghorne—www.polkinghorne.net

Larry Hurtado–Devotion to Jesus Course Web site—www.wesleyministrynetwork.com/DJ/Texts.html

N.T. Wright—www.ntwrightpage.com

Offline Resources—www.megabaud.fi/~osmosa/index.htm

Outside the Box Blog: Cliff Martin—cliff-martin.blogspot.com

Putting Jesus in His Place—www.deityofchrist.com

Random Designer (Richard Colling)—www.randomdesigner.com

Ravi Zacharias International Ministries—www.rzim.org

Reasonable Faith (William Lane Craig)—www.reasonablefaith.org

Reasons to Believe—www.reasons.org/index.shtml

Religion/Religions/Religious Studies—www.clas.ufl.edu/users/gthursby/rel/

Religious and Sacred Texts—webpages.marshall.edu/~wiley6/rast.htmlx

Religium/Religion Index—www.teleport.com/~arden/religium.htm

Resource Pages for Biblical Studies—www.hivolda.no/asf/kkf/rel-stud.html

Risen Jesus (Mike Licona)—www.risenjesus.com

Science and Theology: Exploring the Nexus—sites.google.com/a/drvinson.net/science

Society of Christian Philosophers—www.societyofchristianphilosophers.com/membership/

Stand to Reason—www.str.org

Theological Texts—www.mcgill.pvt.k12.al.us/jerryd/cm/thltxt.htm

A Time to Tear Down, a Time to Build Up (Peter Enns)—peterennsonline.com

UCCF: The Christian Unions—www.bethinking.org

The Veritas Forum—www.veritas.org

Walking Thru the Bible—fly.hiwaay.net/~wgann/walk.htm#nt

Notes

Introduction: In Search of Something

1. Atheists (from the Greek *a-*, not, and *theos*, God) believe God does not exist. Agnostics (from *a-*, not, and *gnostos*, known or knowable) either don't know if God exists or assert that if he does exist, he is unknowable. Deists (from the Latin *deus*, God) affirm his existence but not his present involvement. He set the cosmos in motion and then basically left. Finally, theists normally affirm a personal God who is involved in the world.

2. Mark Twain, *Following the Equator* (Hartford: American, 1897), 132.

3. Sam Harris, *The End of Faith: Religion, Terror, and the Future of Reason* (New York: Norton, 2004), 65.

4. See Hebrews 11:1 and 2 Corinthians 5:7.

5. Matthew 7:13-14.

Chapter 1: Clearing Away the Debris

1. Richard Dawkins, *The God Delusion* (Boston: Houghton Mifflin, 2006); Daniel C. Dennett, *Breaking the Spell: Religion as a Natural Phenomenon* (New York: Penguin Books, 2006); Sam Harris, *The End of Faith;* Christopher Hitchens, *God Is Not Great: How Religion Poisons Everything* (New York: Twelve, 2007).

2. Hitchens, *God Is Not Great*, 282.

3. Gherman Titov, "Titov plans second fair visit," *Seattle Daily Times*, May 7, 1962, p.2.

4. The reasoning below does not refer to God's holiness, which prevents our seeing him in the full intensity of his attributes (Exodus 33:20; Habakkuk 1:13; John 1:18). Instead, it refers to his metaphysical (as opposed to physical) reality.

5. John 4:24.

6. Jeremiah 23:24; 1 Kings 8:27.

7. It could be countered that God is an energy field, but if that's true, he is still physical, and he has not so far been detected.

8. Psalm 19:1,7.

9. Francis Bacon, *Advancement of Learning,* book 1, 1605.

10. See Romans 8:28.

11. The technical word for the problem of divine justice in the face of evil is *theodicy,* from the Greek *theos* (God) and *dike* (justice).

12. Of course, eternity is outside of time as we know it, but the analogy is helpful nonetheless.

13. From the transcript of the radio broadcast "Scientists Study Children Who Feel No Pain," *Science in the News,* Voice of America, February 2007. For another example, leprosy (Hansen's disease) eradicates sensation in body extremities. Injured over and over, these parts easily succumb to infection and may even fall off.

14. Psalm 139:14.

15. Romans 5:3-4.

16. Source unknown.

17. Colossians 2:4.

18. See Genesis 1:1; Isaiah 40:21; 43:13; 46:10; Romans 1:20; 1 Timothy 1:17; Revelation 1:8; 21:6; 22:13.

19. See 1 Corinthians 14:33.

20. See Proverbs 26:5.

21. Of course disagreement need not be unpleasant. In the opinion of Durant, "Intolerance is the natural concomitant of strong faith; tolerance grows only when faith loses certainty; certainty is murderous" (Will Durant, *The Age of Faith* [Norwalk: Easton Press, 1992], 784). Yet this is far from obvious. Faith can enhance patience, even as many saintly men and women have led lives of exceptional kindness and tolerance. Certainly this was not because they harbored secret doubts. Rather, true faith makes us better people, and Christian faith makes us more like Christ, who combined kindness and conviction in his demeanor and interactions with all people.

22. See, for example, 1 Corinthians 15:19.

23. Acts 24:25.

24. See Job 12:10.

Chapter 2: Why Atheism Fails

1. I am not suggesting that it is the duty of government to mandate religion, but then

neither do I believe it is appropriate for government to restrict it, as is the case in most of the world's nations, the United States included. The founding fathers of the United States were not against religion. Rather, they stood opposed to coercion in religion—they were against ideological control.

2. Ten examples must suffice: Armenia, the Australian Aborigines, Bosnia, the (Belgian) Congo, Darfur, Ethiopia, Kurdistan, the Native Americans, Rwanda, the Soviet Union. This list does not include Hitler's Holocaust. It must also be conceded that purges, pogroms, and ethnic cleansing have been committed in the name of religion. But what is the conclusion? That all religion is evil, as Hitchens asserts? Not at all. Atrocities are nearly always rationalized, and if a religious pretext can be found, so much the better (or so say the persecutors).

3. Plato, *Republic,* 338c.

4. Niccolò Machiavelli, *The Chief Works and Others,* A. Gilbert. trans., 3 vols. (Durham: Duke University Press), 1965; and *The Prince,* Q. Skinner and R. Price, eds. (Cambridge: Cambridge University Press, 1988).

5. Cited in Regis Nicoll, "One Nation Under God," Christianity.com. www.christianity.com/1392017/print.

6. Nor am I saying that atheists are fools, as some preachers insist, based on Psalm 14 and 53 ("The fool says in his heart, 'There is no God'"). The error here is not so much to espouse atheism as to *live* as though there were no God—whether one is religious or not.

7. Ecclesiastes 12:13.

8. Of course, *meaning* itself has two meanings, one metaphysical and the other semantic. The two are closely related.

9. Theism does not rise or fall with evolution. That is, God may have prepared the human race to think and act morally through the course of evolution. But without a God, there would be no morality in the first place.

10. Charles Darwin, letter to Joseph Hooker, July 12, 1870.

11. Charles Darwin, *The Autobiography of Charles Darwin,* ed. Nora Barlow (New York: Harcourt Brace and Company, 1958), 87. The sentences cited were written in 1871.

12. Alister E. McGrath, *Intellectuals Don't Need God and Other Modern Myths: Building Bridges to Faith Through Apologetics* (Grand Rapids: Zondervan, 1993), 135.

13. Ephesians 2:12, speaking of the alienation of the Gentiles before they were included among the people of God, reads, "Remember that at that time you were separate from Christ, excluded from citizenship in Israel and foreigners to the covenants of the promise, without hope and without God in the world."

Chapter 3: Is Anyone at Home?

1. Carl Sagan, *Cosmos* (New York: Random, 1985), 1.

2. Refining the Kalām argument of medieval Islamic scholars, and combining it with Big Bang theory, William Lane Craig has forcefully presented the cosmological argument. See William Lane Craig and Quentin Smith, *Theism, Atheism, and Big Bang Cosmology* (Oxford: Clarendon Press, 1993).

3. Robert Jastrow, *God and the Astronomers* (Toronto: George McLeod, 1992), 104-5. Einstein was initially so adamantly opposed to the Big Bang that he fudged his equations in his theory of general relativity, adding a "cosmological constant" to preserve the temporal infinity of the cosmos. He later admitted that this was the biggest mistake of his career.

4. A minority view, championed by Fred Hoyle, was the steady state theory, which affirmed that the universe is continuously creating itself. This of course contradicts the first law of thermodynamics—that matter and energy may be interconverted but not created or destroyed. The view is not entertained by most serious physicists.

5. Besides, an actual—as opposed to mathematical—infinite is impossible. If the world began at a moment in the infinite past, then the present would still not have arrived!

6. So Michael Shermer: "Maybe our universe is just one of those things that happened for no reason at all." *How We Believe: The Search for God in an Age of Science* (New York: Henry Holt, 2000), 109.

7. 1 John 4:8,16.

8. Alfred Lord Tennyson, *In Memoriam A.H.H.,* canto 56, 1850.

9. Robert Jastrow, *God and the Astronomers,* 107.

10. As *telos* is the Greek word for *end,* teleology is the study of purpose, especially purpose in design.

11. For Paley's original analogy, see en.wikipedia.org/wiki/Watchmaker_analogy.

12. Of course an analogy is only an analogy; it proves nothing. In fact, one weakness of the watch argument is that the ground beneath it, with the proliferation of biological activity, is far more complex than the watch itself.

13. Creationism is the belief that the cosmos owes its existence to a Creator, and ought not to be confused with "scientific creationism," the view that the universe is only a few thousand years old and that biology, physics, and geology are therefore bogus.

14. Peter Singer, *Writings on an Ethical Life* (New York: Harper Collins, 2000), 53, 193.

15. Richard Taylor, *Ethics, Faith, and Reason* (Englewood Cliffs: Prentice Hall, 1985), 84, 90. Cited in William Lane Craig, *Reasonable Faith,* third edition (Wheaton: Crossway Books, 2008).

16. The "provisional ethics" of Michael Shermer in his *The Science of Good and Evil* (New York: Henry Holt, 2004) is only a variation on moral relativism. He wants to have it both ways.

17. I am a regular reader of Shermer's column "The Skeptic" in *Scientific American* and

appreciate the contributions of thinking men and women, whether atheist, theist, or agnostic. In fact, after our debate on evolution at the University of Florida, Michael Shermer and I went out for a burger.

18. See Deuteronomy 13:1-3; 1 Thessalonians 5:21-22; Acts 17:11-12.

19. Flew was not referring to the ID (intelligent design) movement, but to the apparent intelligence and design in the cosmos. In his famous *New York Times* interview, Flew was hardly a senile and fearful man, turning to God in a moment of mental and corporal debility.

Chapter 4: God

1. James Redfield, *The Celestine Prophecy* (New York: Warner Books, 1993); Shirley MacLaine, *The Camino: A Journey of the Spirit* (New York: Simon & Schuster, 2000) and *Going Within* (New York: Bantam, 1990); Rhonda Byrne, *The Secret* (Hillsboro: Atria Books / Beyond Words, 2006); Eckhart Tolle, *A New Earth* (New York: Penguin, 2005). Shirley MacLaine's Web site even has Nature's Gem Energy Collars for your dog!

2. Dan Brown, *Angels and Demons* (London: Transworld, 2000), 585.

3. For now, we will have to be content to let the theologians and philosophers work out how   or whether   God experiences time.

4. Genesis 1:27.

5. Colossians 2:9.

Chapter 5: The Bible

1. Paul's argument in Romans 1, which itself is based on Wisdom of Solomon 13, is not that nature tells us all we need to know about the Deity, but rather that it points to his omnipotence and transcendence.

2. Romans 10:17.

3. I have heard many near-death accounts, often involving out-of-body experiences. My Swedish teacher underwent one of these experiences. This interesting subject is beyond the scope of this book.

4. Mortimer Pretzeltwist, *Theology Made Easy* (Aberystwyth: Abstruse Press, 1959), 222. (Just kidding!)

5. See, for example, Luke 3:1-2.

6. Regarding the Old Testament, the copious finds include the Gilgamesh Epic and the Epic of Atrahasis; the Amarna letters; the House of David inscription from Tel Dan; the reliefs from Sargon's palace; the reliefs from Nimrud; ancient Near Eastern ziggurats (some 30 in all); the Black Obelisk of Shalmaneser III; excavations at Ebla, Mari, Nuzi, Ur, Çatalhöyük, Hazor, Laish, Jerusalem, and many other cities; Hezekiah's Tunnel; the Taylor prism; the Nabonidus tablets; the Cyrus Cylinder; and of

course the Dead Sea Scrolls. This list is far from complete, but to explain even these remarkable finds would require another volume in itself.

New Testament and early Christian discoveries include the excavations at Caesarea Maritima, Caesarea Philippi, Capernaum, Bethsaida, Beth Shean (Scythopolis), Ephesus, Pergamum, Rome, and Jerusalem, to name only a few; the Caiaphas ossuary; the Gallio inscription; the Erastus pavement; the skeletal remains of a crucified man; first-century tombs; the synagogue at Capernaum; the Soreg Inscription; the Pilate Stone; the Pool of Siloam; the Alexamenos Graffito; and references to Jesus and primitive church in Josephus, Suetonius, Tacitus, Thallus, Pliny the Younger, the Talmud, Lucian, and other writings. These are some of my favorites, and the list is in no way complete. The bibliography can lead you to more information.

7. Other examples include the remains of Noah's ark, the skeletal remains of giants, the Ark of the Covenant (though the Ethiopians claim to have it in their possession), the remains of Pharaoh's drowned army, the tomb of Adam and Eve, alleged Bible codes, remnants of the cross, and the Shroud of Turin. Literary frauds include Nicolas Notovitch's *Unknown Life of Jesus Christ* (1887); the *Aquarian Gospel of Jesus the Christ,* supposedly channeled by Levi Dowling (1908); the late medieval Islamic forgery *The Gospel of Barnabas;* and the *Secret Gospel of Mark,* a modern forgery.

8. For more on this, see Gordon Fee and Douglas Stuart's superb volume, *How to Read the Bible for All Its Worth.*

9. See, for example, John 8:46-49.

10. John 17:17.

11. John 8:31-32.

12. John 7:17.

13. 1 Thessalonians 2:13.

Chapter 6: Dialogue with a Critic

1. See also Robert M. Price, *The Incredible Shrinking Son of Man: How Reliable Is the Gospel Tradition?* (New York: Prometheus Books, 2003) and also his article "The Quest of the Mythical Jesus" at www.centerforinquiry.net/jesusproject/articles/the_quest_of_the_mythical_jesus.

2. See 2 Timothy 2:14,23-26.

3. We could take the argument a step further. Skeptics also offer a neurobiological critique of religion. As humans are pattern-seeking creatures, they remind us, the ability to see patterns, even "design," aided in the survival of the species (so Dennett, Dawkins, Shermer). The theistic counter, as you might have guessed, is that God allowed neural networks to evolve that were able to identify patterns and design. For every atheist criticism, we can expect a sound theistic response.

4. The integrity of the Old Testament text as received is approximately 97 percent, and that of the New Testament is nearly 99.5 percent. The weighted average, considering

that more than 75 percent of the Bible is the Old Testament, is approximately 98 percent. In other words, the text has suffered a low level of deterioration or corruption. And as we will see in chapter 7, these variants did not alter the biblical message or any significant point of doctrine.

Chapter 7: Before Xerox

1. If you are interested, I recommend two years of Greek at the university level. Enrolling in a college-level class is the simplest way to master the language and benefit from a disciplined and structured approach. Either a course in classical (Attic) Greek or one in New Testament (Koine) Greek will do.

2. You can view it for yourself at www.codexsinaiticus.org/en/manuscript.aspx.

3. It is well worth a visit to their Web site, www.lib.umich.edu/pap.

4. One of the most memorable things I found was in a tenth-century Greek manuscript. It was a sketch of a doleful man in a robe, along with the words: "I, Clement, the worthless monk, have copied this"!

5. Other cities, home to lesser manuscripts, include Athens, Beuron, Birmingham, Bucharest, Chicago, Copenhagen, Damascus, Escorial, Frankfurt, Geneva, Gotha, Grottaferrata, Jerusalem, Leiden, Lesbos, Maywood, Meteora, Naples, Patmos, and Zurich. And there are thousands more Greek manuscripts.

6. Suras 5, 6, 37, and 40.

7. But this is simply not true! The Qur'an evolved and has been changed, and evidence of that fact has been found in Yemen, where thousands of manuscripts of earlier versions of the Qur'an have been found and photographed. (See "What Is the Koran?" in *Atlantic Monthly,* January 1999, which disproves the Muslim assertion that the Qur'an has not changed since it was dictated to Muhammad by Allah.) Moreover, several different versions of the Qur'an are in use today. For more on the Qur'an, please see my *Jesus and Islam* (Spring: Illumination Publishers International, 2009).

8. My wife introduced me to the Kando brothers, their father having by then passed away. Though one of the sons has died since our first meeting, the others still operate the Kando Store in Bethlehem.

9. Fragments have been identified from all books of the Old Testament except Esther. With so many fragments, it is possible that this book too is represented. There are 19 copies of Isaiah, 25 of Deuteronomy, and 30 of Psalms—which happened also to be the three most-cited books of the Old Testament in the New Testament. There are also numerous commentaries on the Scriptures, such as the explanation of the sacrifice of Isaac (Genesis 22), which is interpreted messianically.

10. These include the Aleppo Codex and the Leningrad Codex, dated to AD 900 and 1005, respectively.

11. Oxford University Press has published the Dead Sea Scrolls in *Discoveries in the Judean Desert* (Oxford: Oxford University Press, 2001). Volume 33 may currently be the most

useless book ever produced—but could still turn out to be useful. It contains 380 pages of 3000 fragments nobody can identify, some containing only one word or part of a word. Most are smaller than a fingernail. It *is* useful, though, because from time to time people claim that some of the Scrolls have been hidden or concealed in the Vatican and that they disprove Christianity. Such a statement is ridiculous. The publishing of such a seemingly useless book shows exactly how thorough the publication of the Scrolls has been. Cost: $252.

12. Here are a few books for those who care to dig deeper: Michael Wise, Martin Abegg Jr., and Edward Cook, *The Dead Sea Scrolls: A New Translation* (San Francisco: HarperCollins, 1996); Hershel Shanks, *Understanding the Dead Sea Scrolls* (New York: Random House, 1992); and *Discoveries in the Judean Desert,* 41 volumes, multiple editors (Oxford: Oxford University Press). For those who would like to follow the ongoing discussion, you may wish to consider subscribing to the journal *Biblical Archaeological Review.* If you would prefer a more compact, one-shot overview of the subject, try the Logos CD-ROM *The Dead Sea Scrolls Revealed* (Pixel Multimedia and Aaron Witkin Associates, 1994).

13. Isaiah 40:8; 1 Peter 1:25.

14. See John 13:34-35 and Romans 10:17.

15. James 1:22-25.

Chapter 8: The Luminous Figure

1. Matthew 14:2; John 7:20; 8:48,52; 10:20.

2. John Dominic Crossan, *The Historical Jesus: The Life of a Mediterranean Jewish Peasant* (New York: Harper Collins, 1992).

3. Robert Price, *The Incredible Shrinking Son of Man: How Reliable Is the Gospel Tradition?* (New York: Prometheus Books, 2003), 354.

4. Dan Brown, *The Da Vinci Code* (New York: Doubleday, 2003).

5. Bart D. Ehrman, *Misquoting Jesus: The Story Behind Who Changed the Bible and Why* (New York: HarperCollins, 2005), 10-11. According to Barbara Thiering, in AD 7, Jesus went to Egypt and was influenced by Buddhism. He was crucified in 33, along with Judas Iscariot and Simon Magus(!), but he recovered, having been drugged and presumed dead. Soon he married Mary Magdalene (and later Lydia) and a few years afterward returned to public ministry. How did Thiering arrive at her conclusions? By carefully reading the Dead Sea Scrolls and the New Testament, which she alleges are cryptic and require decoding! No serious scholar gives these zany notions any credence. Barbara Thiering, *Jesus the Man: Decoding the Real Story of Jesus and Mary Magdalene* (New York: Simon & Schuster, 2006).

6. Matthew 5:22; 19:28; Mark 2:7; 12:35-37; 14:62; Luke 22:29-30. Also, in Mark 10:18, Jesus may draw attention to his divinity, and in Mark 14:58, he claims to be one who builds the temple—yet another divine prerogative. (See Exodus 15:17; Jubilees 1; 1 Enoch 90; 11Q Temp.).

7. C.S. Lewis, an Oxford and Cambridge scholar who became a believer after considering the evidence, insisted, "A man who was merely a man and said the sort of things Jesus said would not be a great moral teacher. He would either be a lunatic...or else he would be the Devil of hell...Either he was, and is, the Son of God: or else a madman or something worse" (*Evidence That Demands a Verdict* [Nashville: Thomas Nelson, 1992], 103-10). (*Mere Christianity*, [New York: Simon & Schuster, 1997] 56). Josh McDowell further popularized this approach in his "Lord, Liar, or Lunatic?" Since the 1980s I have included the important fourth possibility: legend.

8. "Why I Am Not a Christian," March 6, 1927.

9. These are the non-Christian sources: Celsus, Josephus, Lucian, Mara Bar-Serapion, Phlegon, Pliny the Younger, Suetonius, Tacitus, and Thallus.

10. Philostratus (AD 170–247) wrote about Apollonius around AD 220 and was paid to do so by Julia Domna, mother of Caracalla, who had donated funds to build a temple dedicated to Apollonius.

11. Ancient sources for the Cynics include Seneca, Epictetus, and Cicero.

12. Josephus, *Antiquities,* 14.22.

13. 1 Corinthians 1:23.

14. John 10:41.

15. Matthew 27:63; John 7:12,47.

16. Acts 20:35.

17. Deuteronomy 18:15-18; Psalm 110:1,4; Isaiah 11:1; 52:13–53:12; Ezekiel 34:15-24; Daniel 7:13-14; Zechariah 9:9; 12:10; Malachi 3:1-3; 4:1-6. The Messiah is also prophesied in several extracanonical sources, such as 1 Enoch 37-71 and 4 Ezra 7,13.

18. See Psalm 27:1; John 8:12; 1 John 1:5.

19. Luke 6:46; 17:7-10.

Chapter 9: That's Impossible!

1. *Oxford English Dictionary.*

2. For example, see John 11:47; Acts 14:3.

3. For more on God's work through the Spirit, see my book *The Spirit: The Work of the Holy Spirit in the Lives of Disciples* (Spring: Illumination Publishers International, 2005).

4. Matthew 11:3-5.

5. Michael Wise, Martin Abegg Jr., and Edward Cook, *The Dead Sea Scrolls: A New Translation* (San Francisco: Harper Collins, 1996), 421.

6. Psalm 107:29; Mark 4:39; John 11:43-44; Isaiah 42:5.

7. Pseudo-Matthew; Acts of Thomas; Infancy Gospel of Thomas; Acts of Peter; Acts of Paul.

8. John 20:30-31.

9. Of course it is possible that Jonah's appearance stunned the Assyrians, but this is not mentioned in the text.

10. 1 Kings 10:1-13; Jonah 3.

11. Luke 16:19-31; see also Luke 20:17,27-40; John 7:17.

12. Matthew 12:40; 1 Corinthians 15:12-19.

Chapter 10: Many Convincing Proofs

1. Acts 1:3.

2. Craig A. Evans, *Fabricating Jesus: How Modern Scholars Distort the Gospels* (Downers Grove: InterVarsity, 2006), 81-82. The excerpt is Evans' own translation.

3. John Dominic Crossan, *Jesus: A Revolutionary Biography* (New York: HarperCollins, 1994), 145.

4. Matthew 28:1.

5. Matthew 27:57-60; John 19:38-42.

6. Matthew 16:21; 20:19; and others.

7. Luke 18:33-34; John 20:19,24-25.

8. John 19:39.

9. John 19:34.

10. John 19:32-33.

11. Matthew 27:66.

12. Some say the corpse would not be recognizable after the 50 days between Easter and Pentecost; decomposition would have made identification problematic. But even if the body was in an advanced state of decomposition, we would expect Christ's wounds to be visible. Besides, *any* cadaver paraded through the streets would tend to discredit the Christian cause, throwing the burden of proof back onto the apostles. ("Prove this isn't Jesus' body!") That never happened, so we know the body was gone.

13. In contrast, consider the Latter-day Saints (Mormons). Most of the "witnesses" to the golden plates of Joseph Smith later recanted. Yet after the resurrection, none of the apostles recanted.

14. And would the guard really sleep on the watch? See Acts 12:19; 16:27.

15. Matthew 13:55-57; Mark 3:20-21; John 7:3-5. James was the second-born of Mary's five sons.

16. James' martyrdom is recorded by Josephus (*Antiquities* 20.197-203) as well as by Hegesippus and Clement of Alexandria.

17. Acts 8:1-3; 9:1-2,13-14; 26:9-11,14-15; Galatians 1:13,23.

18. Acts 9:23; 2 Corinthians 11:23-33; 2 Timothy 3:10-12; 1 Clement 5:2-7.

Chapter 11: One Way?

1. Eric Gorski, "Many Paths to God," *South Bend Tribune,* June 24, 2008, page A3.

2. Acts 20:28.

3. To better appreciate how naive is the view that all gods are the same, see Michael Jordan, *Encyclopedia of Gods: Over 2,500 Deities of the World* (New York: Facts on File, 1993). .

4. Hebrews 7:27; 9:28.

5. John 14:6.

6. This mind-set has even infiltrated the church. A Christian publication suggests that the ideal or "target" percentage of church members involved in the small groups of the church is 60 to 70 percent, that 50 percent should be expected to be engaged in specific ministry efforts either in the church or in the community, and that 25 percent should receive training in sharing their faith (Reggie McNeal, "Healthy Numbers," in *Leadership: A Practical Journal for Church Leaders,* vol. XX, no. 1, winter 1999).

7. Suras 40:9; 39:61; 7:43.

8. Cited with permission from Philip Yancey, *What's So Amazing About Grace?* (Grand Rapids: Zondervan, 1997), 45. Yancey credits Calvin College professor Scott Hoezee for this story (*The Riddle of Grace: Applying God's Grace to the Christian Life* [Grand Rapids: Eerdmans, 1996]). Hoezee told me he heard it from Peter Kreeft, professor of philosophy at Boston College and the King's College. When I contacted Kreeft, he said that he had heard or read this account but did not remember where. He added, "My version said 'the forgiveness of sins' rather than 'grace,' but that would not be quite correct since Judaism has this too." Sleuth work has its limits. Apocryphal or genuine? For students of Lewis, the story certainly rings true.

9. 1 Corinthians 15:9-10; Titus 2:11-14.

10. Deuteronomy 4.2, Proverbs 30.6, 1 Corinthians 4:6; Revelation 22:18-19.

11. Radical Islamists divide the planet into *Dar al-Islam* (the House of Islam) and *Dar al-Harb* (the House of War). *Dar al-Islam* is territory where Muslim governments are in control, ruling by Islamic law. Non-Muslims are permitted to live there by the gracious permission of their Muslim rulers. *Dar al-Harb* (the rest of the planet) is yet to be dominated and is accordingly the House of War. A de facto (and perpetual) state of *jihad* exists. This holy war may be interrupted by truces (when appropriate). As a matter of practical necessity, Islamic regimes cannot afford to sustain continuous warfare against their non-Muslim neighbors. Yet the ultimate goal is clear: global domination. One day all the world will be in the House of Islam. Of course, not all Muslims share this vision, but the minority who do wield considerable influence. For more on this, please see my book *Jesus and Islam* (Spring: Illumination Publishers International, 2009).

12. "All should heal themselves from the obsession of converting others." Source: "Conversion: Assessing the Reality," Vatican Pontifical Council for Interreligious Dialogue and the World Council of Churches Office on Interreligious Relations and Dialogue, 2006.

13. Matthew 28:19-20.

14. Matthew 22:37-40.

15. Qur'an, Suras 4; 24; 8.

16. 1 John 2:6.

17. Matthew 7:12.

18. Matthew 5:43-48.

19. The consistent position of the early church may be found in the Ante-Nicene Fathers' writings. Christians serving in the army, apparently converted after enlistment, were not permitted to kill, take oaths, or offer sacrifices to idols. Even in the late 200s, Christians were considered of more service to the realm by praying than by fighting. They were nearly universally pacifist. Attitudes changed once emperor and state aligned with the Christians (311). Soon, Christians were forbidden to resign from the army. Just War theory followed, formulated by Ambrose (340–397) and Augustine (354–430). For more, please hear my dialogue with Rabbis Shmuley Boteach and Elie Abadie on *Judaism, Christianity, and Peace* (November 11, 2008).

20. Psalm 12:6.

21. Alister E. McGrath, *Intellectuals Don't Need God* (Grand Rapids: Zondervan, 1993), 115.

22. Psalm 119:105.

Chapter 12: Double-Minded?

1. John 20:27 (NASB). Less literal though still on the right track, the NIV reads, "Put your finger here; see my hands. Reach out your hand and put it into my side. Stop doubting and believe."

2. "Modest doubt is call'd / The beacon of the wise, the tent that searches / To the bottom of the worst." William Shakespeare, *Troilus and Cressida,* ed. Daniel Seltzer et al. (New York: New American Library, 2002), 2.2.15-17.

3. Deuteronomy 28:65-66; Matthew 14:29-30; James 1:6; Matthew 28:16-17; Luke 24:38.

4. *Galaxy* comes from the Greek word for *milk, gala.*

5. The decision was reversed and the stickers removed in 2005.

6. Michael Shermer, *How We Believe: The Search for God in an Age of Science* (New York: Henry Holt, 2000), 113.

7. Henry M. Morris (1918–2006) was a leading advocate of Scientific Creationism.

8. Examples include gestation, forestation, photosynthesis, and volcanism.

9. Theodosius Dobzhansky, a geneticist and twentieth-century architect of evolutionary thinking, said, "I am a creationist and an evolutionist. Evolution is God's…method of creation." Harvard professor of astronomy Owen Gingerich, also author of *God's Universe* (Cambridge: Harvard University Press, 2006), wrote, "A common-sense and satisfying interpretation of our world suggests the designing hand of a superintelligence," and also, "The universe has been created with intention and purpose…This belief does not interfere with the scientific enterprise."

10. Consider this passage in *Autobiography of Charles Darwin,* ed. Nora Barlow (New York: Harcourt Brace and Company, 1958), 92-94:

> Another source of conviction in the existence of God, connected with the reason and not with the feelings, impresses me as having much more weight. This follows from the extreme difficulty or rather impossibility of conceiving this immense and wonderful universe, including man with his capacity of looking far backwards and far into futurity, as the result of blind chance or necessity. When thus reflecting I feel compelled to look to a First Cause having an intelligent mind in some degree analogous to that of man; and I deserve to be called a theist…This conclusion was strong in my mind about the time, as far as I can remember, when I wrote *The Origin of Species*; and it is since that time that it has very gradually with many fluctuations become weaker. But then arises the doubt—can the mind of man, which has, as I fully believe, been developed from a mind as low as that possessed by the lowest animal, be trusted when it draws such grand conclusions?…The mystery of the beginning of all things is insoluble by us; and I for one must be content to remain an agnostic.

Notice that Darwin expresses epistemological doubt, just as we discussed in chapter 2. If purely random forces, and not intelligence, lie behind the creation, and thus the formation of the human brain, why should anyone trust his own cognition? Consider also this passage from Darwin's private letter to John Fordyce (May 7, 1879):

> It seems to me absurd to doubt that a man may be an ardent theist and an evolutionist. You are right about Kingsley. Asa Gray, the eminent botanist, is another case in point. What my own views may be is a question of no consequence to anyone except myself. But as you ask, I may state that my judgment often fluctuates. Moreover whether a man deserves to be called a theist depends on the definition of the term: which is much too large a subject for a note. In my most extreme fluctuations I have never been an atheist in the sense of denying the existence of a God. I think that generally (and more and more so as I grow older) but not always, that an agnostic would be the most correct description of my state of mind.

The Duke of Argyll recalled a conversation he had with Darwin in 1882, the last year of Darwin's life:

I said to Dr. Darwin, with reference to some of his own remarkable works on the "Fertilization of Orchids" and upon "The Earthworms," and various other observations he made of the wonderful contrivances for certain purposes in nature. I said it was impossible to look at these without seeing that they were the effect and the expression of mind. I shall never forget Mr. Darwin's answer. He looked at me very hard and said, "Well, that often comes over me with overwhelming force; but at other times," and he shook his head vaguely, adding, "it seems to go away" (*Good Words*, April 1885, 244; see also the *Stanford Encyclopedia of Philosophy* online at plato.stanford.edu/entries/teleological-arguments/notes.html).

11. David Frost, *Billy Graham: Personal Thoughts of a Public Man* (Colorado Springs: Cook Communications, 1997), 72-74.

12. Deuteronomy 32:11-12; Isaiah 42:14; 49:15; 66:13; Hosea 13:8; see also Matthew 23:37; Luke 13:34.

13. Luke 8:11; Ephesians 5:22-33; 1 Peter 1:23.

14. Genesis 1:26; 1 Corinthians 11:7; 2 Corinthians 3:18; 4:4.

15. In Scripture, Deity is often described through *anthropomorphism*. That is, we read that he has eyes, arms, a memory, and so on. Such descriptions are for our sake only. For example, in Genesis 3, God is portrayed as a gardener, walking in Eden and asking Adam where he is—as though the omniscient one relied on information from one of his creatures! God is also depicted as feeling in human ways (regret, sadness, surprise). The technical term for this is *anthropopathism*.

16. See also Colossians 1:28. That we all begin in a state of relative spiritual immaturity is implied in passages like 1 Corinthians 3.

17. Regarding brokenness, see Psalm 34:18.

18. Matthew 22:34-39.

Chapter 13: Taking the Plunge

1. Luke 19:10 NET. I have found more than 80 passages in the New Testament that stress that the purpose of Jesus' coming to Earth was to save others.

2. Genesis 6:5; 8:21; 2 Samuel 14:14; Psalms 103; 131; Luke 15:11-32; Romans 2:4; 2 Peter 3:9.

3. See, for example, Genesis 12:3; Psalm 100; Isaiah 49:6; Zechariah 8:23; Matthew 28:19; Colossians 1:6; Revelation 7:9.

4. Acts 17:18-34.

5. John 3:3-7; Romans 6:3-7; Titus 3:5; James 5:19-20; Revelation 3:20; 5:6.

6. Start with these verses and keep reading in each section: Matthew 27:46; Mark 14:32; Luke 23:47; John 18:1; Acts 2:14.

7. Matthew 6:33; 7:7,13; 13:44-46.

8. 2 Peter 3:9.

9. Acts 26:24-29.

10. Also see Psalm 5:3; 119; Matthew 5:8; Acts 2:37-41; 8:30-31; 1 Corinthians 12:12-27; Colossians 1:18; Hebrews 3:12-14; 10:23-25.

11. Isaiah 55:8-9.

12. John 20:29.

Appendix A: Bible Study Strategies

1. Acts 8:31.

2. Gordon Fee and Douglas Stuart, *How to Read the Bible for All Its Worth,* third ed. (Grand Rapids: Zondervan, 1993); *How to Read the Bible Book by Book* (Grand Rapids: Zondervan, 2002).

3. For 52 tips for improved Bible study, see my articles at www.douglasjacoby.com/view_ article.php?ID=5304 and www.douglasjacoby.com/view_article.php?ID=5779.

4. Although Hebrew is grammatically the simpler of the two languages by far, it is difficult for most people because of its alphabet (technically, its syllabary) and because of its right-to-left orientation. Greek, though more familiar in its orthography and orientation, is a far more inflected language, with hundreds of forms for each verb in addition to the noun declensions.

5. See www.encarta.msn.com/media_461547746/The_World's_Oceans_and_Seas.html.

6. Romans 11:34.

Appendix B: The Trinity

1. C.S. Lewis, *Mere Christianity* (New York: Macmillan, 1943), 145.

2. If you are a theatergoer or thespian, think about the term *dramatis personae.*

3. Several religions have trinities. Hinduism has Shiva, Vishnu, and Brahma. The Druids had Taranis, Esus, and Teutates. The ancient Egyptians also had their trinity. Yet, unlike the biblical Trinity, these trinities are triads of gods, not one triune god.

4. See Sura 5:73. Islamic accusations denied that God, Jesus, and Mary were gods. This reflects the exalted position of Mary in the seventh century AD.

5. For further reading on the nature and divinity of God, see Edwin A. Abbot, *Flatland* (Oxford: Blackwell, 1875); J.I. Packer, *Knowing God* (Downers Grove: InterVarsity, 1975); Francis A. Schaeffer, *He Is There and He Is Not Silent* (Wheaton: Tyndale, 1972); and *The God Who Is There* (Downers Grove: InterVarsity, 1968).

6. For further reading on the nature and divinity of the Son of God, see William Barclay, *The Mind of Jesus* (New York: Harper & Row, 1961); Charles Edward Jefferson, *Jesus— the Same* (Billerica: DPI, 1997); *Jesus with the People,* ed. Jones & Jones (Woburn: DPI, 1996); and Philip Yancey, *The Jesus I Never Knew* (Grand Rapids: Zondervan, 1995).

7. We will not join the feminist dialogue about the gender of God, whom the Bible consistently describes as *he*. Interestingly, I have never heard a feminist lobby for a pronoun change for Satan—the devil is always a *he!*

8. For further reading on the nature and divinity of the Spirit, see Frederick Dale Bruner, *A Theology of the Holy Spirit* (London: Hodder & Stoughton, 1970); and John R.W. Stott, *Baptism and Fullness* (London: InterVarsity, 1975).

9. Thomas Aquinas (1225–1274), *Summa Theologica*.

10. Worse, that the Father is "harder" than the Son, the Spirit more ethereal than both, and so forth.

11. Norman L. Geisler and Abdul Saleeb, *Answering Islam* (Grand Rapids: Baker, 1993), 269.

12. Isaiah 55:8-9; see also Romans 11:33-36.

13. Acts 7:59, for example.

Appendix C: Apparent Contradictions in the Bible

1. The entire New Testament was written in Greek, but 99 percent of the Old Testament was written in Hebrew and the remaining 1 percent in the sister language of Aramaic (Ezra 4:8–6:18; Jeremiah 10:11; Daniel 2:4–7:28, and two words in Genesis 31:47).

2. Regarding "the third day," see Matthew 16:21; 17:23; 20:19; Luke 9:22; 18:33; 24:7,46. Regarding "after three days," see Matthew 27:63; Mark 8:31; 9:31; 10:34.

3. One little detail remains: the nights and days. We would consider *three days and three nights* to be 72 hours or so because nights and days are both mentioned. And yet to the Hebrews, a day (usually) equals a night and a day regardless of whether it is a full 24 hours. Thus *three days* is equivalent to three nights and three days. Never mind that it could equally well (as in this case) signify one night, a day, another night, and part of the following morning—scarcely 36 hours!

4. The point does not hinge on traditional apostolic authorship.

5. Matthew 27:27-31.

6. Commentators quibble as to whether the cleansing took place once, twice, or even four times (to account for all differences in detail among the four versions!). This seems to miss the point. The evangelists arranged the material in order to suit their theological purposes. All versions are equally true.

7. See especially Luke 2:1-2; 3:1-2.

8. See Leviticus 1, for example.

9. John 1:29; 1 Corinthians 5:7.

10. See Mark 4:33.

11. *Hittite* and *Hittites* appear more than 50 times in the NIV.

12. Avraham Biran, "An Aramaic Stele Fragment from Tel Dan," *The Israel Exploration*

Journal 43 (1993), 90. I once had the honor of meeting the gentle scholar when he was in his nineties.

13. 2 Samuel 24:15-17.

14. *Antiquities* 20:97; Acts 5:36-37.

15. *Antiquities* 20.5.2; Luke 2:1-2.

16. See John 20:30; 21:25; Luke 1:1-4.

17. For example, if I return from a speaking tour and tell my friends about it, I am not obligated to proceed in strict chronological order. I might first mention a few of the cities I visited, then the various cuisines I sampled, then some of the more interesting persons I spent time with, and so on.

18. Compare Mark 5:1-2 (Luke 8:26-27) with Matthew 8:28 and Mark 10:46 with Matthew 20:29-30.

19. Leviticus 11:13-19; Deuteronomy 14:11-18.

20. Leviticus 11:6.

21. The Hebrew *raqia'* (Genesis 1:6, for example) means an extended surface, particularly the metallic dome that covers the disk (circle) of the earth. See Isaiah 11:12; Revelation 7:1; 20:8 regarding the flat earth and James 1:11 regarding the sun orbiting the earth.

22. Eratosthenes measured the circumference of the earth with 99 percent accuracy. Muslims of the ninth century made similar calculations with 96 percent accuracy.

23. The thirteenth and fourteenth century Arab astronomers may well have preceded Copernicus in their heliocentric model.

24. Lack of scientific precision is characteristic of the Bible's poetry as well—and of poetry today. Poetry typically uses words and concepts to evoke images and emotions. Consider Psalm 18:8-10. Physically, the heavens cannot be parted, the wind has no wings, and smoke and fire would destroy anyone's nostrils! This colorful language is contradicting nothing; it is poetry. More specifically, Psalm 18 is an example of apocalyptic language. This common biblical genre is exemplified by parts of Isaiah, Ezekiel, Zechariah, Revelation, and the mini-apocalypse of Mark 13 (also Matthew 24 and Luke 21).

25. Job 16:2; 42:8.

26. Psalms 35; 109; and 137, for example.

27. Psalm 98:8; Luke 19:40; Revelation 6:13.

28. Matthew 24:36; Mark 13:32.

29. See the Lausanne Covenant at www.religioustolerance.org/evan_cove1.htm.

30. Vatican II.

31. James 2:26.

32. Matthew 27:45; Mark 15:33; Luke 23:44.

33. In the early 200s, Christian historian Sextus Julius Africanus wrote that the darkness was caused by an eclipse. This errant notion is often regurgitated in evangelism.

34. Archbishop James Ussher (1581–1656) was Professor of Theological Controversies at Trinity College, Dublin. The date of creation, according to his calculations, was October 23, 4004 BC.

35. Matthew 2:11.

36. Matthew 27:5 and Acts 1:18.

37. Matthew 8:5 and Luke 7:3.

More Great Apologetics Books
from Harvest House Publishers

THE GOD QUESTION
J.P. Moreland

A leading evangelical thinker offers this brand-new way of addressing life's most important questions: Does God exist, and can we know him? J.P. Moreland abandons traditional didactic apologetics and invites skeptics and dissatisfied believers to trade their emptiness and anxiety for the abundant life Jesus offers.

WHY THE BIBLE MATTERS
Mike Erre

Mike Erre, teaching pastor of a large, culturally relevant church in Southern California, offers intelligent answers to questions emerging generations are asking about the Bible. He upholds the Bible's authority in creative, engaging, and intellectually satisfying ways. Erre's contagious enthusiasm and deep respect for the Scriptures match his first-rate scholarship.

EVIDENCE FOR FAITH 101
Bruce Bickel and Stan Jantz

Bruce and Stan present Christian apologetics without clichés as they tackle vital questions people of all ages and beliefs are asking. Readers are invited to examine evidence—from history, the lives of people changed by faith, and from our world—as they form and understand their convictions about God.

UNDERSTANDING INTELLIGENT DESIGN
William A. Dembski and Sean McDowell

Are you confused by the Intelligent Design (ID) dialogue because of educational bias and one-sided attacks? This guide explains the central theories of information and irreducible complexity, provides the basis for ID's scientific validity, demonstrates that both ID and evolutionary theories have religious and philosophical underpinnings, and explains the cultural controversy and implications—and what you can do about them.